CGP

GCSE OCR
Music

There's a lot to get your ears around in OCR GCSE Music, and the new Grade 9-1 courses are tougher than ever. Luckily, help is at hand...

This brilliant CGP book explains everything you'll need to do well in your coursework and exams. Musical knowledge, listening practice, compositions — you name it.

What's more, each section has plenty of warm-up questions and exam-style practice. And to help you finish the course on a high note, we've even included a realistic practice exam at the end!

Complete
Revision & Practice
Everything you need to pass the exams!

Contents

Section Seven — Rhythms of the World

Section Eight — Film Music

Section Nine — Conventions of Pop

Published by CGP

Editors: Caley Simpson, Ben Train, Ruth Wilbourne

Contributors: Catherine Baird, John Deane, Elena Delaney, Rob Hall, Angela Major, Peter Maries, Mel McIntyre, Sam Norman, James Reevell.

With thanks to Rebecca Lawton, Sam Norman and Karen Wells for the proofreading.
With thanks to Jan Greenway, Laura Jakubowski and Holly Poynton for the copyright research.

Audio CD edited and mastered by Neil Hastings.

For copyright reasons, this book can only be sold in the UK.

ISBN: 978 1 78294 616 8

Clipart from Corel®

Printed by Elanders Ltd, Newcastle upon Tyne.

Based on the classic CGP style created by Richard Parsons.

What You Have To Do For GCSE Music

Music GCSE doesn't cover every single aspect of music — if it did it would take forever.
Instead you focus on five main 'Areas of Study' (AoS for short).

You Learn About **Five Areas of Study**

AoS1 — MY MUSIC
You study your own instrument, with a focus on performance and composing. This could be a musical instrument that you play, your voice (singing, beatboxing or rapping), sequencing (creating music on a computer) or DJ-ing. The background knowledge you'll need is covered in Sections 2-5.

AoS2 — THE CONCERTO THROUGH TIME (covered in Section 6)
You study how the concerto (a composition for soloist(s) and orchestra) developed over the period from 1650 to 1910.

AoS3 — RHYTHMS OF THE WORLD (covered in Section 7)
This covers music from the following locations: India and the Punjab region, the Eastern Mediterranean and the Middle East, Africa, and Central and South America.

AoS4 — FILM MUSIC (covered in Section 8)
You study music composed for films, and classical music used within films. You also study music composed for video games.

AoS5 — CONVENTIONS OF POP (covered in Section 9)
This covers pop music from the 1950s onwards. It focuses on Rock 'n' Roll in the '50s and '60s, Rock Anthems in the '70s and '80s, Pop Ballads in the '70s, '80s and '90s, and Solo Artists from the '90s onwards.

They Test You With **Coursework...**

The coursework is split into two modules called the 'Integrated Portfolio' and the 'Practical Component'. You do some performing (see p.3) and some composing (see p.4-6) for each module.

INTEGRATED PORTFOLIO

worth 30% of the total marks

- **PERFORMANCE 1** — you do a performance on your own instrument (see AoS1 above). It should be a solo performance, or a performance with a group where you play a key role.
- **COMPOSITION 1** — you compose a piece of music in a style of your choice.

PRACTICAL COMPONENT

worth 30% of the total marks

- **PERFORMANCE 2** — this is an ensemble performance. It should be a performance involving two or more people, in which you play a significant role.
- **COMPOSITION 2** — this is based on a brief set by the exam board. There'll be briefs for each Area of Study and you can choose which one you do.

...and a **Listening Exam**

worth 40% of the total marks

At the end of Year 11 you do a Listening and Appraising exam. You listen to extracts of music from Areas of Study 2-5 and answer questions that ask you to analyse the features of the music you hear.

Err, Miss... is it too late to change to Physics?

Welcome to the wonderful world of GCSE Music. Breathe in the cool clear air. Listen to the birds. Relax.

Performing

Pick your pieces carefully and practise till your fingers bleed and the neighbours beg for mercy.

You Have To Do Two Performances

The combined time of both performances must be at least four minutes, and your ensemble performance (Practical Component module) must last at least 1 minute. Each performance can be made up of more than one piece, but if you don't follow the time rules you won't get any marks.

PERFORMANCE 1 (Integrated Portfolio Module)

You play one (or more) piece(s) of your own choice. It can be a solo (with a live or recorded accompaniment if you like). It can also be a group performance in which you play a significant part. The piece(s) shouldn't be your own composition, but can involve improvisation if appropriate (e.g. if you are rapping, beatboxing or DJ-ing). Your performance could also involve a sequenced recording created using a computer, but you need to have some active input during the performance — you can't simply play back a piece you've already sequenced.

PERFORMANCE 2 (Practical Component Module)

This must be an ensemble performance. For a traditional performance, there must be at least two of you performing, and for most of the piece your part shouldn't be doubled by another part. Improvisation can be used. You could also sequence a piece for at least two instruments, but you can't just play a piece you've already made — you have to play an active role (like in Performance 1).

For both performances, you have to hand in a score of your piece. For an improvisation you'll need to provide evidence of the inspiration behind your performance, such as a note or chord pattern, or a recording by a professional musician. Recordings must be made of your performances.

You Get Marks for the Quality of Your Playing...

In each performance, you need to show off your 'musicality'. The marks are given for these key areas:

1) **TECHNICAL CONTROL AND FLUENCY**: You'll be marked on your accuracy, so learn the notes and play them in time and in tune. Things like breathing control (on a wind instrument), diction (if you're singing) and coordination (e.g. on a piano or string instrument) will also be assessed. Your performance needs to be fluent, so keep going — lots of stopping and starting or slowing down for tricky bits will lose you marks. Don't worry about the odd slip, but start off well prepared. If you create a sequenced recording, your ability with the computer software will be assessed.

2) **EXPRESSION AND INTERPRETATION**: Your performance needs to be expressive — to make the audience feel something. Pay attention to stuff like dynamics, tempo, mood, articulation and phrasing. It's all about how well you communicate — i.e. how you interpret the music.

When you're playing in an ensemble, there are other things that you'll get marks for. Play in time and in tune with the other players. Really listen to the other parts, so you know when you should be part of the background and when you should make your part stand out — the ensemble should be balanced.

...and Marks for the Difficulty of the Piece

1) It's obvious really — a very simple piece will get fewer marks for difficulty than a complicated piece. But there's no point trying to play something that you're not capable of and then messing it up...

2) Choose your pieces carefully — ideally they should be the hardest level that you can play well. Pick something too easy and you'll throw away difficulty marks — but pick something too hard and you won't be able to play your best so you'll lose marks that way. Ask your music teachers for advice.

3) If you choose an easy piece, you won't be able to get top marks for the areas described above. If you play more than one piece, you'll get difficulty marks for the easiest piece.

Composing

When you write your GCSE pieces you can't just write whatever you like. Well, you can for one of them — but for the other, you have to follow a set brief. Read on to find out more...

You Have to Write **Two Pieces** for **Coursework**

1) Your two compositions must have a total combined time of at least three minutes (you won't get any marks if they're less than three minutes).

2) You can compose for any combination of instruments or voices (unless the set brief tells you otherwise).

3) The composition you write as part of the 'Integrated Portfolio' module can be in any style you like. You'll need to use your musical knowledge to come up with an idea and develop it.

4) The other piece — the one for the 'Practical Component' module — has to follow a set brief. The exam board will provide a brief for each area of study (AoS2-AoS5) — you choose which area of study you'd like to work in. The brief will outline the style you should compose in, and the audience or location that the piece is for. The exam board will also provide eight 'stimuli' — some will be more suitable for your chosen area of study than others. You pick one of them as a starting point for your composition. The eight stimuli will have the following forms:

- a **rhythm pattern** (there'll be two to choose from)
- a **note pattern** (two choices here too)
- a **chord sequence**
- four lines of **poetry**
- a **short story**
- an **image**

5) You'll be given the set brief halfway through your GCSE course — by which point, you should have studied all the different areas in detail. You'll be able to use what you've learnt to create your own composition in a style you've seen and heard.

6) Your compositions will need to be performed and recorded. You can perform them yourself, or someone can play them for you. You can also use sequencing, or software such as Sibelius®.

7) You'll need to submit a written version too — there's more information about this on p.6.

You'll be **Marked** on Lots of **Different Points**

Each composition is worth 30 marks. The mark you get will depend on:

- the quality of the musical ideas that you come up with,
- how successfully you develop those ideas,
- how you demonstrate your understanding of the style you're composing in,
- whether your composition has a clear and sensible structure,
- the way you use elements such as tonality, rhythm, melody, harmony, texture, tempo, dynamics and articulation,
- your understanding of the instrument(s) you compose for,
- how imaginatively you respond to the brief (in your set brief composition).

There's lots of advice on each of these points over the next couple of pages.

Set briefs aren't a special type of underwear...

The music you study for AoS2-AoS5 is more than just exam fodder — you need it for your compositions too. So it's doubly important that you get listening and learning about it (it's covered in Sections 6-9).

Composing

Well, the <u>good news</u> is... you're not being asked to come up with anything very long. Just make sure your compositions have a combined length of <u>more than 3 minutes</u> — no one's expecting an opera.

To get **Top Marks** Think About...

DEVELOPING YOUR MUSICAL IDEAS

Don't just use a good idea once and then forget about it. <u>Build up</u> and <u>develop</u> the good bits — e.g. by changing the <u>rhythm</u> from short notes to long notes or the <u>key</u> from major to minor. See Sections 3-4 for loads more <u>techniques</u> and <u>devices</u> for developing your ideas.

MAKING THE STYLE CONVINCING

Listen to <u>lots</u> of music from the style you're composing in. Make your piece sound like 'the real thing' by using <u>similar musical ideas</u> — e.g. a classical Indian piece would have a drone, a repeated rhythm pattern, and use a raga scale.

THE POTENTIAL AND LIMITS OF YOUR RESOURCES

Once you've chosen the instruments, think about <u>all</u> the ways they can make <u>interesting</u> and <u>contrasting</u> sounds — e.g. <u>pizzicato</u> bits for strings. But also remember the <u>limitations</u> — e.g. clarinet players need time to <u>breathe</u>. Think about the <u>highest</u> and <u>lowest</u> notes your chosen instruments can play — there's no point composing a brilliant piece if <u>no one can play it</u>.

One of your pieces will have to meet the set brief, so there'll be extra things you have to bear in mind for that.

STRUCTURE

Organise your music with a <u>clear</u>, <u>definite structure</u> (there's lots of information on different structures throughout this book). Even if your composition doesn't follow a <u>traditional form</u>, you'll need to make sure it doesn't just <u>ramble on aimlessly</u>.

When You're Composing, Make Plans **Before** You Start

1) Making a <u>musical plan</u> helps to <u>organise</u> your ideas — it's a bit like writing an essay plan.

2) Music's got to be organised, or it just sounds like a load of <u>random notes</u>. The <u>most basic</u> bit of organisation is the timing (<u>beats in a bar</u>). The next biggest chunk is the <u>phrasing</u>.

3) The <u>overall shape</u> is called the <u>structure</u> or <u>form</u>. The structure could be the <u>verses</u> and <u>chorus</u> in a pop song, or the <u>movements</u> of a symphony. Composers usually <u>decide</u> on the <u>structure</u> of a piece of music <u>before</u> they get into the detail.

4) It's OK to <u>design your own</u> musical plan, but a lot of people use '<u>tried and tested</u>' structures like the ones described throughout this book — because they know they'll work.

5) 'Tried and tested' structures are like <u>templates</u>. The <u>general organisation</u> of your ideas is decided for you — you just need to add the <u>details</u>.

6) For the piece that follows the <u>set brief</u>, it's probably a <u>good idea</u> to use a 'tried and tested' structure as your composition will need to be in a particular <u>style</u> or <u>form</u>.

7) Your plan should include ways to <u>vary</u> the different <u>sections</u> — have a look on the next page for some ideas.

Clarinet players need time to breathe? Amateurs...

So the main thing to take away from this page is 'be organised'. I'm not expecting you to be organised in all aspects of your life, just in your compositions — and planning really helps.

Composing

There are lots of things you need to think about when composing. This is not a complete list (just a few general ideas), but it'll give you a few things to bear in mind.

Most Music Uses Repetition Repetition Repetition...

1) <u>Repetition</u> means using a <u>musical idea</u> — a chunk of tune — <u>more than once</u>.

2) Repeating bits is a really good way of giving music <u>shape</u>. A recognisable tune works like a <u>landmark</u> — the audience recognises that tune <u>later</u> in the piece. That's how <u>choruses</u> work.

3) If you're planning <u>your own</u> piece of music, try repeating the best part of the tune.

4) You can even repeat <u>whole sections</u> — in <u>rondo form</u> (see p.94), one section is repeated lots of times.

5) In your <u>set brief</u> composition, if you choose a <u>rhythm</u>, <u>note pattern</u> or <u>chord sequence</u> as a stimulus then it could be a good idea to <u>return</u> to that throughout the piece.

...and Contrast

Repetition is really important — but <u>constant repetition</u> is <u>boring</u>. Good compositions balance repetition with <u>contrast</u>. The aim is to do something <u>different</u> from the repeated bits to add <u>variety</u>. Here are some ways you can <u>vary</u> your compositions:

PITCH AND TONALITY

You can create contrast by changing the <u>organisation of pitch</u> — e.g. changing the melody from a <u>high register</u> to a <u>low register</u>, and swapping between <u>conjunct</u> and <u>disjunct</u> tunes (see p.54). You can also change the tonality (key) by <u>modulating</u> between <u>major</u> and <u>minor keys</u>.

TEMPO AND RHYTHM

Changing <u>speed</u> from <u>fast</u> to <u>slow</u> (or vice versa) is a good way of creating contrast. You can also change the rhythms — try a mix of <u>dotted</u> and <u>straight rhythms</u>, or <u>long</u> and <u>short notes</u>. You can change the <u>articulation</u> too — try <u>legato</u>, <u>staccato</u>, <u>slurs</u> and <u>accents</u> to vary your piece.

DYNAMICS

Changes in <u>dynamics</u> (<u>loud</u> to <u>soft</u> and vice versa, and <u>crescendos</u> and <u>diminuendos</u>) will instantly create contrast.

TEXTURE

Changing between a thin, <u>monophonic</u> texture and a thicker <u>homophonic</u> or <u>polyphonic</u> texture (see p.45) will create contrast.

Decide How To Hand In Your Work

For each piece, you have to submit a <u>recording</u> and a <u>written version</u> — there are a few different <u>options</u> for the <u>written</u> part. Your <u>teacher</u> will be able to advise you which to choose — it'll depend on the <u>type</u> of composition you've produced. The options are:

1) a <u>score</u> — this is the best option for a <u>classical</u> piece.

2) a <u>lead sheet</u> — this is often used for songs. It specifies the <u>melody</u>, <u>lyrics</u> and accompanying <u>chords</u>, but the harmony <u>isn't</u> written out in full. You might choose this option if you've written a <u>song</u> with an <u>improvised</u> accompaniment.

3) a <u>written account</u> — this is probably the best option for <u>sequenced</u> compositions (you should submit <u>screen shots</u> too if you've used sequencing).

Give as much <u>information</u> as possible. <u>Dynamics</u>, <u>tempo</u>, <u>expression</u> and <u>articulation</u> will all improve your mark. There should be <u>enough detail</u> for someone else to be able to <u>recreate</u> your piece.

I'm going to submit my work by telepathy...

Composing is a great chance to write your own stuff rather than listening to and playing other people's work. Who knows, 200 years from now some lucky GCSE students might be studying *your* pieces...

Listening and Appraising

At the end of the course, you have the joy of a listening exam. All 1 hour and 30 minutes of it.

The Listening and Appraising Exam Tests Areas of Study 2-5

1) The Listening and Appraising Exam is worth 80 marks in total (40% of your total mark). You listen to music from a CD and answer written questions about it. You're given 2 minutes at the start to read through all the questions.

2) You're given extracts to listen to — each one has its own set of questions. You'll be told what area of study the piece is from and how many times it'll be played. Some of the extracts will be from the suggested repertoire in your course specification, but other pieces will be used too. You're given writing time after each playing of an extract.

3) There are a few different types of question:

Some Questions are Multiple Choice

Don't mess these up by rushing — read all the options carefully.

If you're stuck — guess the answer. There's a chance of getting it right.

What is the texture of this extract? Tick the correct box. *[1 mark]*
☐ homophonic   ☐ monophonic   ☐ contrapuntal   ☐ antiphonal

Some Questions Just Need a Short Answer

These questions are only worth a few marks so don't waste time writing your answer out in a nice long sentence — just write down one good word for each mark.

Name two instruments playing the theme in this extract. *[2 marks]*

You'll need to write a bit more if the question's worth 3 or 4 marks.

They Sometimes Give You an Outline of the Music

You'll be given an outline of part of the music called a 'skeleton score'. It will just show part of the music — the melody, rhythm or lyrics, say. The skeleton score will help you with answering the question. You might be asked to fill in the pitch, rhythm or chords of a short section of the music, or to add the appropriate dynamics or tempo instructions.

Fill in the missing notes in bar 4. The rhythm is given above the stave. *[3 marks]*

Some Questions Need a Longer Answer

In these questions you'll need to write a full paragraph as your response. You might be asked to compare two extracts, or describe how the features of an extract create a certain mood. Make sure you cover all the key points of the question in your answer.

Some marks are usually awarded based on how well you construct your argument — there is a * next to the question number if this is the case.

Compare the ways in which both pieces of film music effectively create a sense of heroism and drama. You should mention musical elements, instrumentation and context. *[9 marks]*

EXAM TIP

Shiver me timbers — 'tis the skeleton score...

Concentrate on answering just a few of the questions each time the music's played — it's less confusing. Have a go at the Practice Exam on p.150 to give you an idea of what it'll be like.

The Basics

These two pages give the __essential basics__ you'll need to get through Music GCSE.
Make sure you know everything here before you go on into the rest of the book.

3 TWO LINES OF MUSIC

The top line of music has got a tune — it's the __melody__. The bottom line is the __accompaniment__.

1 CLEF

These symbols at the start of a line tell you how __high__ or __low__ to play the notes. All the different clefs are covered on __page 10__.

2 NOTE

Each note is shown by a separate __oval__. The symbol also tells you how __long__ or __short__ the note is. The symbols are shown on __page 16__.

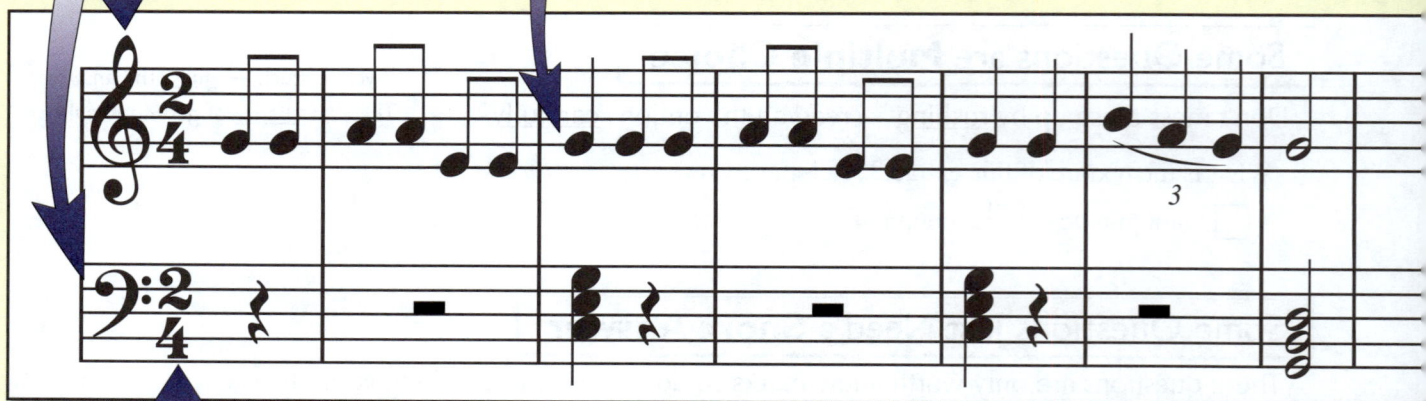

7 TIME SIGNATURE

The numbers tell you about the __beats__ in a __bar__. Time signatures are covered on __page 12__.

9 KEY SIGNATURE

There are no flats or sharps, so this piece is in the __key__ of C. Keys and scales are covered in __Section Three__.

8 BEATS

Each bar has the __same__ number of __beats__. Beats, bars and rhythm are covered on __pages 13, 14, 16 & 17__.

THE PIANO KEYBOARD

Some of the diagrams in this book make more sense if you know what's what on a __piano keyboard__. The white keys play __natural notes__.

Note: The white notes from C to C make the scale of C major (p.24).

The black keys play __SHARPS__ and __FLATS__. Sharps and flats are covered on __page 11__. The C in the middle of a piano keyboard is known as __MIDDLE C__.

The Basics

5 STAVE
The five lines are called a stave. Notes can go on or between the lines, or on separate short lines above or below.

4 BAR
The vertical bar lines split the music into bars.

bar line

6 TRIPLETS
The '3' and the curved line show these notes are triplets. They're explained on page 17.

3

11 PITCH
Notes higher up the stave have a higher pitch. Notes lower down have a lower pitch. Look at page 16 to see where the different notes go.

12 CHORD
More than one note played together makes a chord. See Section Three for more about chords.

13 DOUBLE BAR LINE
You get a double bar line at the end of a piece (or section of a piece).

10 STRUCTURE
The melody's built out of two different tunes — phrases and structures are covered in Sections Three and Four.

TONES AND SEMITONES

Tones and *semitones* are the gaps between notes.

On a piano, a semitone is the gap between any key, black or white, and its immediate neighbour.

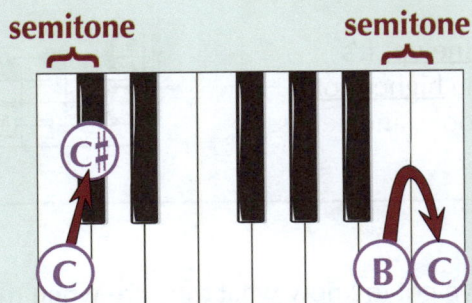

The gap from any key to a key two semitone steps above or below is called a tone.

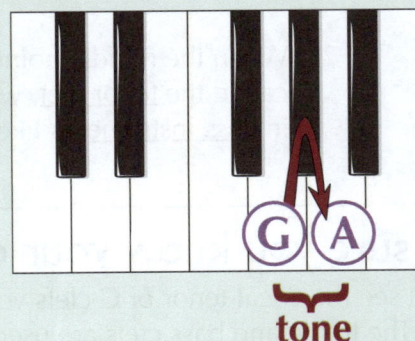

semitone   semitone

C#

C   B C

G A

tone

Clefs

Clefs are the <u>curly symbols</u> that you find right at the <u>start</u> of most written music. The treble clef is used for high-pitched music. The bass and alto clefs are used for lower-pitched music.

The **Treble** Clef is the **Most Common** Clef

1) The treble clef is used for <u>higher-pitched melody instruments</u>, e.g. flute, oboe, clarinet, violin, trumpet and horn.

2) Music for <u>soprano</u> and <u>alto</u> voices is written on the treble clef, too.

3) The sign always goes in the same place on the stave, with the curly bit wrapped around the line for the <u>G above middle C</u>.

The **Bass** Clef is used for **Low-pitched Instruments**

1) The bass clef is used for <u>lower-pitched instruments</u> like the tuba, trombone, bassoon, cello and double bass.

2) It's also used for <u>bass voices</u>.

3) The big blob always goes on the line for the <u>F below middle C</u>, and the two little dots go either side of the line.

The **Vocal Tenor** Clef is for **Tenor** Voices and **Lead Guitar**

1) Each line and gap in the vocal tenor clef stands for exactly the same note as it does in the <u>treble clef</u>, BUT that little '<u>8</u>' underneath means that the notes are played <u>one octave lower</u>.

2) It's used by <u>tenor voices</u> and <u>lead guitar</u> parts.

Here's the 8.

The **C** Clef can **Move** Up and Down on the Stave

The C clef always has its <u>middle point</u> on <u>middle C</u>. It can be used as two different clefs, depending on its <u>position</u> on the stave.

1) When its middle point is on the <u>middle line</u>, it's the <u>alto clef</u> and is used for <u>viola</u> parts.

2) When the middle point is on the <u>fourth line up</u>, it's called the <u>tenor clef</u>, which is used for the <u>higher notes</u> in <u>bass instruments</u> like trombones, bassoons and cellos.

Make sure you know your clefs...

You don't see the vocal tenor or C clefs very often, but you've got to know what they are when they <u>do</u> turn up. The treble and bass clefs are used all the time — aim to get so good at reading and writing them that it's easier than English. The only way is to practise. The notes are written in full on page 16.

Sharps, Flats and Naturals

On a piano, <u>natural</u> notes are the <u>white</u> ones. <u>Sharps</u> are the <u>black</u> notes to the <u>right</u> of the white notes.
<u>Flats</u> are the blacks to the <u>left</u> of the whites. So each black is both sharp <u>and</u> flat.

♯ A **Sharp** Makes a Note One Step **Higher**

1) A sharp sign next to a note tells
you to play it <u>one semitone higher</u>.

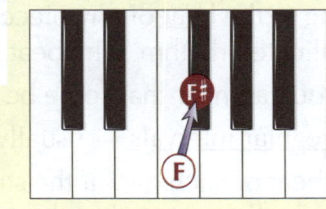

When you're writing on the stave, put sharps, flats and naturals before the note they affect. If you're writing text, put them afterwards — F♯.

2) A <u>double sharp</u> — ✗ — makes a note
<u>two semitones higher</u>. If you see C✗ you
play <u>D</u> — it's the <u>same note</u> going by a
different name. The fancy name for notes
that sound the same but have different
names is <u>enharmonic equivalents</u>.

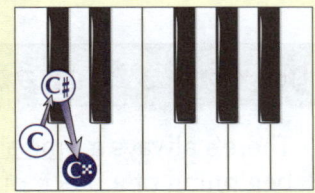

♭ A **Flat** Makes a Note One Step **Lower**

1) A flat symbol next to a note means you
have to play it <u>one semitone lower</u>.

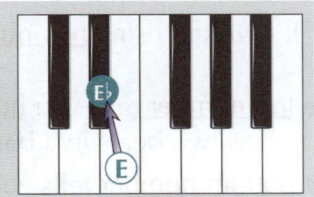

2) A <u>double flat</u> — ♭♭
— makes a note two
semitones (a tone) lower.

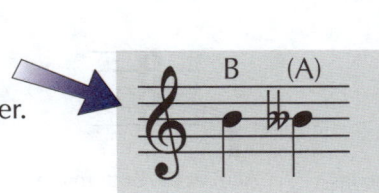

The **Key Signature** is Shown with Sharps or Flats

KEY SIGNATURE

1) Sharps or flats written at the <u>start</u> of a piece,
straight after the clef, tell you the <u>key signature</u>.
2) The key signature makes notes sharp or
flat <u>all the way through</u> a piece of music.
3) Sharps and flats that you see by individual notes — but not in
the key signature — are called <u>accidentals</u>. Once an accidental
has appeared in a bar, it applies to all notes of the same pitch for
the rest of the bar, unless it's cancelled out by a <u>natural sign</u>...

There's more about key signatures on p.24-26.

This key signature's got one sharp
— on the F line. You have to play
every F in the piece as an F♯.

♮ A **Natural** Sign **Cancels** a Sharp or Flat

A <u>natural</u> sign before a note <u>cancels</u> the <u>effect of a sharp or flat</u> sign from earlier in the bar or from a
key signature. You <u>never</u> see natural signs in the key signature, only in the music, as accidentals.

This stuff should all come naturally in no time...

Double sharps and flats are uncommon and quite peculiar — it doesn't seem that <u>logical</u> to write C✗
when you could write D, but sometimes you just have to, I'm afraid. It all depends what key you're in.

Time Signatures

Those <u>two numbers</u> at the beginning of a piece of music tell you <u>how many beats</u> there are in a bar and <u>how long</u> they are. Whatever you're playing, don't ignore them.

Music has a **Regular Beat**

1) You can tap your foot along to the <u>beat</u> of any piece of music, as long as it hasn't got a horribly complicated rhythm. The beat is also called the <u>pulse</u>.
2) If you listen a bit harder, you can hear that some beats are <u>stronger</u> than others.
3) The strong beats come at <u>regular intervals</u> — usually every <u>2</u>, <u>3</u> or <u>4</u> beats.
4) The strong beat is the <u>first</u> beat of each <u>bar</u>. If the strong beat comes every 3 beats, then the piece of music you're listening to has <u>three beats</u> in a bar.

The **Time Signature** Shows **How Many** Beats are in a Bar

1) There's always a <u>time signature</u> at the beginning of a piece of music.
2) It goes to the <u>right</u> of the clef and the key signature.
3) It's written using <u>two numbers</u>.

TOP NUMBER goes between the middle line and the top line

BOTTOM NUMBER goes between the middle line and the bottom line

The <u>top number</u> tells you <u>how many beats</u> there are in each bar, e.g. a '2' means two beats in a bar, a '3' means three beats in a bar and so on.

The <u>bottom number</u> tells you <u>how long</u> each beat is (see <u>page 16</u> for the names of the different notes).

If you see a big 'C' in place of the time signature, it stands for 'common time', which means it's in 4/4. If it's ₵, then it's 'cut common time' — 2/2.

A <u>2</u> at the bottom means each beat is <u>1 minim</u> long.
A <u>4</u> at the bottom means each beat is <u>1 crotchet</u> long.
An <u>8</u> at the bottom means each beat is <u>1 quaver</u> long.
A <u>16</u> at the bottom means each beat is <u>1 semiquaver</u> long.

If the **Beat Changes**, the **Time Signature Changes**

1) The time signature usually <u>stays the same</u> all the way through a piece of music. If it does, it's written just <u>once</u>, at the beginning.

2) Sometimes the beat <u>changes</u> during a piece. If it does, the new time signature's written in the bar where it <u>changes</u>.

3) Not all pieces start on the first beat of the bar — some start on an <u>unaccented beat</u> called an <u>anacrusis</u> (or <u>upbeat</u>).

You can practise listening for the beat any time...
Every time you listen to music, practise <u>listening for the beat</u> and work out the time signature.

Counting the Beat

Counting the beat's fairly easy, but it's a crucial skill. It can help you work out how to <u>play</u> a new piece and how to <u>write a tune down</u> when you've only heard it on a CD or in your head.

In **Simple Time** You Count **All the Beats**

1) <u>Simple</u> time signatures have <u>2</u>, <u>3</u> or <u>4</u> as their <u>top</u> number.

2) In simple time, if you're counting to the music, you count <u>every beat</u>.
For $\frac{4}{4}$ you'd count, "<u>One, two, three, four</u>." For $\frac{3}{2}$, you'd count, "<u>One, two, three</u>."

3) If you want to count out the rhythm of <u>smaller notes</u> as well as the beats, try using "<u>and</u>", "<u>eye</u>" and "<u>a</u>" — it seems to make the rhythm come out just right.

> Count "<u>One and two and</u>" for quavers, and "<u>One eye and a</u>" for semiquavers.

4) Any shorter notes are usually a <u>half</u>, a <u>quarter</u>, an <u>eighth</u> or a <u>sixteenth</u> of the main beat.

In **Compound Time** Only Count the **Big Beats**

1) Compound time signatures have <u>6</u>, <u>9</u> or <u>12</u> as their <u>top</u> number — you can always divide the top number by <u>three</u>.

2) If the music is fairly fast, it's too <u>awkward</u> to count to nine or twelve for every bar. You end up with so many little beats that the rhythm sounds <u>mushy</u>.

3) To make the rhythm <u>clear</u>, you can just count the <u>main beats</u>:

4) If you were counting out the main beats in $\frac{6}{8}$, you'd count "One, two".
$\frac{9}{8}$ would go "One, two, three".

5) To count the <u>in-between notes</u>, use "<u>&</u>" and "<u>a</u>".

6) Shorter notes are made by dividing by three — so they're <u>thirds</u>, <u>sixths</u>, <u>twelfths</u>, etc. of the main beat.

7) Music in compound time <u>sounds different</u> from music in simple time because the beat is divided into threes — <u>practise</u> spotting the difference.

The **Patterns** the Beats Make are Called the **Metre**

Depending on the time signature, the beats make different <u>patterns</u>.
The pattern is known as the <u>metre</u>. Metre can be:

Regular	Irregular	Free
The strong beats make the <u>same pattern</u> all the way through. <u>two</u> beats per bar = <u>duple</u> metre <u>three</u> beats per bar = <u>triple</u> metre <u>four</u> beats per bar = <u>quadruple</u> metre	There could be <u>five</u> beats in a bar grouped in twos and threes, or <u>seven</u> beats in a bar grouped in threes and twos or fours.	Music with <u>no particular metre</u>. This one's fairly unusual.

You can describe a time signature based on its beat and metre — e.g. a piece in $\frac{4}{4}$ is in simple quadruple time, and a piece in $\frac{6}{8}$ is in compound duple time.

One and a, two and a, three and a, four and a...

Counting the beat's not really that hard. The tricky bit on this page is the stuff about <u>metre</u>. You could get asked about the metre of a piece in your listening exam, so learn <u>all three sorts</u>.

Rhythms and Metres

When different rhythms are played at the same time, some of them fit together well, but some of them don't. Rhythms that don't fit can create interesting and crazy effects.

Hemiola Gives the Impression of a Different Metre

1) Hemiola is a rhythmic device used to create contrast within a piece. Music written in duple metre (see p.13) is temporarily accented to make it feel like it's in triple metre, or vice versa.

2) In 6/8 time there are two beats in a bar, each the length of a dotted crotchet. Hemiola is created by playing a bar of three crotchets, giving the impression of 3/4 time instead.

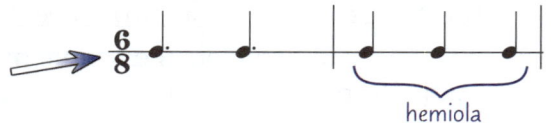

3) In 3/4 time, hemiola is created by accenting every other beat for two bars. This gives the impression of three bars of 2/4 time, rather than two bars of 3/4.

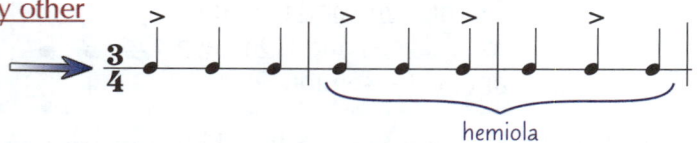

Different Rhythms Can be Played at the Same Time

1) When two or more contrasting rhythms are played at the same time, the music is polyrhythmic. A polyrhythm made up of just two different rhythms is known as a bi-rhythm. Lots of African music is polyrhythmic — see p.111-113.

2) Polyrhythms can be created by a number of performers playing different instruments. A drummer can also create polyrhythms by playing a different rhythm with each hand.

- The rhythms will often have accents in different places. Hemiola might be used in one or more parts, giving the impression of instruments playing in different time signatures (this is known as vertical hemiola).

- Another polyrhythmic device is to use triplets against standard notes, e.g. triplet quavers played at the same time as two normal quavers.

- Cross-rhythm occurs when the accents are 'out of sync' over a number of bars. This can be used to create tension in the music.

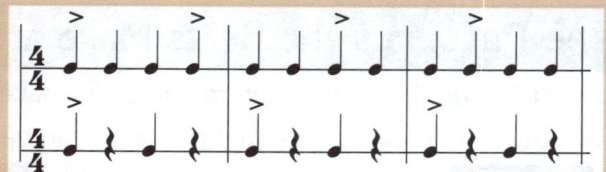

Drum Fills are Little Drum Solos

1) Drum fills are fairly short — they often only last for a few beats.
2) Fills are normally used to build the music up, or to change between sections.
3) They give the drummer a (very short) chance to show off.
4) Most rock, pop and jazz pieces will have drum fills in them.

Rhythms make me very cross...

Listen to 'I Saw Her Standing There' by The Beatles and see if you can pick out the drum fills.

Warm-up and Exam Questions

Now have a crack at some questions to see how much you've learnt so far.

Warm-up Questions

1) Draw the symbols for a treble clef, bass clef, vocal tenor clef and C alto clef.
2) Explain what a sharp sign, a flat sign and a natural sign do.
3) Draw a time signature describing three minim beats per bar.
4) How many beats are there per bar if the time signature is $\frac{9}{8}$?
5) What's the difference between simple and compound time?
6) Name the three main types of metre.

Exam Question

This is the type of question you could get in your listening test. You'll need a track from the CD for this question. Use it to test your understanding of the last few pages and as practice for the real thing.

Play the following extract **four** times. Leave a short pause between each playing of the extract.

Track 1

It's a good idea to read the whole question through before you listen to the track.

a) Fill in the **8 missing notes** from the vocal part, using the rhythm supplied.

Listen carefully for the direction of the notes — this really isn't as difficult as it seems at first.

[8 marks]

b) Draw a circle around the key signature.

[1 mark]

c) Fill in the time signature.

[1 mark]

d) Here is another part of the same extract.
Label the following features:

• the note A#
• two notes a tone apart
• two notes a semitone apart

[3 marks]

Notes and Rests

Let's face it, you'd be a bit lost reading music if you didn't know what all those funny little dots and squiggles meant. Make sure you know all this stuff <u>better than the alphabet</u>.

The **Symbols** Tell You **How Long** Notes and Rests Are

1) <u>Notes</u> tell you how many beats to hold a <u>sound</u> for.

2) <u>Rests</u> tell you how many beats to hold a <u>silence</u> for.

3) Notes and rests have <u>names</u>, depending on how long they are. Two beats is a <u>minim</u> note or rest. A half-beat is a <u>quaver</u> note or rest.

The length of a note or rest is also called its duration.

Learn this table now — you need to know exactly how to <u>write</u> these out, and how to <u>play</u> them.

NAME OF NOTE	NUMBER OF CROTCHET BEATS	NOTE SYMBOL	REST SYMBOL
semibreve	4	o	
minim	2		
crotchet	1		
quaver	½	or if there are 2 or more	
semiquaver	¼	or if there are 2 or more	

The **Position** of the Note Tells You the **Pitch**

<u>Just in case</u> you don't know, this is where the notes go in the <u>bass</u> and <u>treble</u> clefs:

In the <u>bottom</u> half of the stave, the tails on the notes go <u>upwards</u>.

There is some overlap — e.g. these are the same note written in different clefs.

In the <u>top</u> half of the stave, the tails on the notes go <u>downwards</u>.

The tail of the note on the <u>middle line</u> can go <u>up</u> or <u>down</u>.

These lines are called <u>ledger lines</u>. You use them to work out how <u>high</u> or <u>low</u> notes <u>above</u> and <u>below</u> the stave are.

'Leger lines' is an alternative spelling for 'ledger lines'.

There's no excuse for not knowing this stuff...

Those of you who were playing the church organ before you could crawl might be feeling a bit like you know this stuff already and you don't need to be told. It's still worth <u>checking over</u> though, I reckon.

Dots, Ties and Triplets

You can only get so far with the note lengths from page 16. If you use dot, tie and triplet symbols you can create more complicated, interesting and sophisticated rhythms.

A **Dot** After a Note or Rest Makes It **Longer**

1) A dot just to the right of a note or rest makes it half as long again.

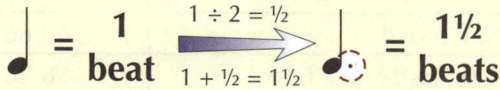

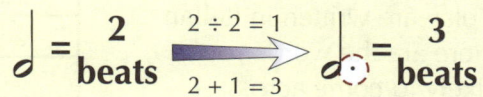

$\quad$ = 1 beat $\quad 1 \div 2 = \frac{1}{2}$ $\quad 1 + \frac{1}{2} = 1\frac{1}{2}$ $\quad$ = 1½ beats $\qquad$ = 2 beats $\quad 2 \div 2 = 1$ $\quad 2 + 1 = 3$ $\quad$ = 3 beats

2) A second dot adds on another quarter of the original note length.

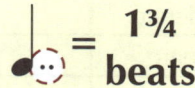

= 1¾ beats $\qquad$ = 3½ beats

Count these really carefully when you're playing — don't just "add a bit on".

3) In dotted quaver rhythms, you have a dotted quaver (worth ½ + ¼ = ¾ of a beat) followed by a semiquaver (worth ¼ of a beat). Dotted quaver rhythms are common in marches. They're usually written like this:

¾ beat $\qquad$ ¼ beat

4) In a Scotch snap, the rhythm is the other way round — the semiquaver is on the beat (and accented), followed by the dotted quaver, like this: Scotch snaps are used in Scottish music (e.g. dances) — hence the name.

A **Tie Joins Two Notes** Together

1) A tie is a curved line joining two notes of the same pitch together.
2) It turns them into one note.
3) Ties are often used to make a long note that goes over the end of a bar.

...sounds the same as...

...sounds the same as...

Ties are not the same as slurs. See page 19.

A **Triplet** is **Three Notes** Played in the Time of **Two**

1) A triplet is three notes, all the same length, squeezed into the time of two.
2) Triplets are marked with a '3' above or below the middle of the three notes. Sometimes there's a square bracket or a curved line as well as the three.

3) The notes don't all have to be played — part of a triplet can be rests.

Stick with it, even the tricky bits...

Triplets look so straightforward on the page, but they can be tricky to get just right. The only way to make sure you're playing them properly is to practise with a metronome. Have a go right now.

Tempo and Mood

Composers don't just tell you the notes — they tell you <u>how fast</u> to play them, and what the <u>atmosphere</u> of the piece should be too. You need to understand all the different <u>terms</u> they use.

The **Tempo** is the **Speed** of the Music

Tempo is Italian for "<u>time</u>". In a lot of music the instructions for how fast to play are written in Italian too. Here are the words you're <u>most</u> likely to come across:

60 beats a minute means each crotchet lasts <u>one</u> second. 120 beats a minute means each crotchet lasts <u>half</u> a second. And so on...

Italian word	What it means	Beats per minute
largo	broad and slow	40-60
larghetto	still broad, not so slow	60-66
adagio	bit faster than largo	66-76
andante	walking pace	76-108
moderato	moderate speed	108-120
allegro	quick and lively	120-168
vivace	very lively — quicker than allegro	168-180
presto	really fast	180-200

This is where you put the <u>tempo</u> and <u>beats per minute</u> on the stave. ♩ = 112 means there are 112 crotchet beats per minute. This is called a <u>metronome marking</u>.

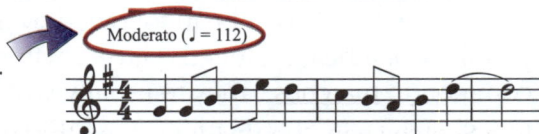

Moderato (♩ = 112)

These words tell you how to <u>vary</u> the speed. The <u>words</u> go <u>underneath</u> the stave. The <u>pause</u> symbol goes <u>above</u>.

Rubato means '<u>robbed time</u>' — you can <u>slow</u> some bits down and <u>speed</u> others up.

Italian word	Abbreviation	What it means
accelerando	accel.	speeding up
rallentando	rall.	slowing down
ritenuto	rit.	holding back the pace
allargando	allarg.	slowing down, getting a bit broader
rubato	rub.	can be flexible with pace of music
𝄐		pause — longer than a whole beat
a tempo		back to the original pace

To give the <u>impression</u> that the tempo has changed (without actually changing it), composers can use <u>augmentation</u> or <u>diminution</u>. Augmentation is where note lengths are <u>increased</u> in a melody (e.g. by <u>doubling</u> the length of every note — so a <u>crotchet</u> becomes a <u>minim</u>). This has the effect of making the music sound <u>slower</u>. Diminution is the <u>opposite</u> — note lengths are <u>shortened</u>, so the music sounds <u>faster</u>.

Mood is the **Overall** Feel of a Piece

The <u>mood</u> of a piece is usually described in Italian too.

Sometimes parts are marked <u>obbligato</u>, which means they are <u>really important</u> and can't be missed out (obbligato means '<u>obligatory</u>').

Italian word	What it means
agitato	agitated
alla marcia	in a march style
amoroso	loving
calmato	calm
dolce	sweetly
energico	energetic

Italian word	What it means
giocoso	playful, humorous
grandioso	grandly
pesante	heavy
risoluto	strong, confident, bold
sospirando	sighing
trionfale	triumphant

To describe the <u>overall mood</u> put the word at the beginning of the piece.

Andante Grandioso (♩=100)

ff

To describe a <u>change of mood</u> write the word under the stave.

p   giocoso

Yes, you do have to learn it all — even the Italian bits...
When you're learning this page, start with words that sound a bit like English — they're easy.

Dynamics and Articulation

More ways for composers to tell players <u>exactly</u> how they want their music to sound...

Dynamic Markings Tell You How Loud or Quietly to Play

Music that was all played at the <u>same volume</u> would be pretty dull.

To get a <u>variety</u> of different volumes you can use these symbols:

Symbol	Stands for	What it means
pp	pianissimo	very quiet
p	piano	quiet
mp	mezzopiano	fairly quiet
mf	mezzoforte	fairly loud
f	forte	loud
ff	fortissimo	very loud
<	crescendo	getting louder
>	diminuendo	getting quieter

You might also see dynamics combined together in other ways. E.g. *fp* means you play a sudden loud bit followed by a sudden quiet bit.

For more extreme dynamics, composers might use *ppp* or *fff* (or even *pppp* or *ffff*).

The markings go <u>underneath</u> the stave.

Crescendos and diminuendos are sometimes called <u>hairpins</u> when they're written like this.

Articulation Tells You How Much to Separate the Notes

In theory all the notes of a bar should add up to one <u>continuous</u> sound — but actually there are <u>tiny gaps</u> between them. If you <u>exaggerate</u> the gaps you get a <u>staccato</u> effect. If you smooth the gaps out, the notes sound <u>slurred</u>.

STACCATO All the dotted notes are played slightly short.

SLUR All the notes below or above the slur are played smoothly, with no breaks between.

<u>Tenuto</u> marks (<u>lines</u> above or below a note) tell you that a note should be held for its <u>full length</u>, or even played slightly <u>longer</u>.

If the articulation goes <u>all the way through</u> a piece, there's an overall instruction at the <u>beginning</u>.

If this piece was marked <u>legato</u> you would have to play smoothly all the way through.

Staccato

Nothing to do with articulated lorries then...

Don't just learn the symbols, learn what they're <u>called</u> too — it'll sound far more impressive if you write about the "dynamics" and "articulation" in your listening exam rather than "loudness and quietness".

More Instructions

Once a composer has told you how <u>fast</u> and how <u>loud</u> to play and how to <u>articulate</u> it, they sometimes put in <u>extra instructions</u>. Things like <u>accents</u>, <u>sforzandos</u> and <u>bends</u> make the music more <u>interesting</u>.

An **Accent Emphasises** a Note

1) An <u>accent</u> is a type of articulation that tells you to <u>emphasise</u> (or <u>stress</u>) a note.
2) On a <u>wind</u> instrument, this is often done by <u>tonguing</u> a note <u>harder</u> than normal.
3) Accents are usually written like this > or like this Λ.
4) If a whole <u>section</u> should be accented, it can be marked '*marcato*' (which means 'marked').

5) A <u>sforzando</u> is a <u>strongly accented</u> note. It's shown by writing *sfz* or *sf* underneath the note.
6) A sforzando is often a <u>sudden</u> accent — e.g. a <u>very loud</u> note in a <u>quiet section</u> of a piece. This makes the music more <u>dramatic</u>.

A **Glissando** is a **Slide** Between Notes

A portamento is similar to a glissando — it's more common in singing and on string instruments.

1) A <u>glissando</u> is a <u>slide</u> from one note to another. Usually you're <u>told</u> which notes to <u>start</u> and <u>finish</u> on.
2) A glissando can be played <u>effectively</u> on a <u>violin</u> (or other <u>string</u> instrument), <u>piano</u>, <u>harp</u>, <u>xylophone</u> (or similar instrument), <u>timpani</u> and <u>trombone</u>. Other instruments can play them too, but they often <u>won't</u> sound as <u>good</u>.
3) On some instruments (e.g. piano, harp and xylophone), <u>every note</u> is played in the glissando. Think about it — if you were to play a glissando on a xylophone, you'd run your beater over every note, so they'd all be played.
4) On other instruments, like the trombone and strings, the notes you hear <u>aren't fixed notes</u> — the glissando covers all the <u>tiny differences</u> in pitch between the two notes. For example, you <u>can't</u> pick out <u>individual notes</u> in a glissando on the trombone.
5) A glissando can be shown by writing *gliss.* underneath the stave, or by putting a <u>line</u> between <u>two notes</u>.

Notes can be **Bent**

1) A <u>bend</u> (or <u>bent note</u>) changes the <u>pitch</u> of the note slightly — it sounds a bit like a <u>wobble</u>.
2) They're often played by starting just <u>above</u> or <u>below</u> the note then <u>bending</u> to it.
3) Bends are often used in <u>jazz music</u>.
4) Bent notes can be played on <u>most</u> instruments — including <u>guitars</u>, <u>trumpets</u>, <u>trombones</u> and <u>harmonicas</u>. <u>Singers</u> can bend notes too.

Roundabouts, swings, climbing frames, glissandi...

All the things on this page are little <u>extras</u> composers can add to their music to make it more <u>interesting</u> — you could try adding some to your compositions too. I do love a good sforzando.

Warm-up and Exam Questions

Get your brain going with these warm-up questions before tackling the exam question below.

Warm-up Questions

1) Draw a 4-beat note, and write down its full name.

2) Draw a 4-beat rest.

3) Name the following notes and give the time value of each of them.

4) Explain the difference between a tie and a slur.

5) Look at the tempo words below. Write them out in order, fastest first.

Andante   **Largo**   **Presto**   **Moderato**   **Allegro**

Exam Question

Here's another exam-style question for you to try.

Play the following extract **three** times. Leave a short pause between each playing of the extract.

Track 2

a)   Listen to the rhythm of the opening melody.
Tick one feature that matches what you hear.

Staccato notes   ☐

Triplets   ☐

Dotted notes   ☐

[1 mark]

Turn over

Exam Question

b) Which word best describes the tempo of this piece of music? Underline your answer.

largo   **adagio**   **andante**   **allegro**

[1 mark]

c) Which word describes the dynamic at the opening? Underline your answer.

pianissimo   **piano**   **forte**   **fortissimo**

[1 mark]

d) Which of the following describes the mood of this extract? Tick the box.

agitato ☐

dolce ☐

energico ☐

pesante ☐

[1 mark]

Revision Summary for Section Two

You'll find a page of questions like this at the end of every section. They're <u>not</u> here just to fill up space — they're here to <u>help you</u> test yourself. The basic idea is, if you can answer all the Revision Summary questions without looking back through the section, you can be pretty sure you've understood and remembered all the important stuff. Look back through the section the first and second time you try the questions (if you must), but by the third time you do the questions, you should be aiming to have all the answers <u>off by heart</u>.

1) Does a clef tell you:
   a) how wide the stave is, b) what instrument it's for, or c) how high or low the notes on it are?
2) Draw a stave with a treble clef at the beginning.
3) Draw a stave with a bass clef at the beginning.
4) Which voices read music from the treble clef?
5) Name two instruments that read music from the bass clef.
6) What's the difference between the symbol for a treble clef and the symbol for the vocal tenor clef?
7) Where does middle C go on a vocal tenor clef?
8) Draw staves showing the C clef in both positions and write the correct name by each one.
9) Draw a sharp sign, a flat sign and a natural sign.
10) What does a sharp do to a note?
11) What does a flat do to a note?
12) Draw each of these signs and explain what you do if you see them by a note:
    a) a double sharp   b) a double flat
13) Draw a treble clef stave and add a key signature with one sharp.
14) What do you call a sharp, flat or natural sign when it's in the music but not in the key signature?
15) One beat in the bar usually feels stronger than the others. Which one?
16) What do you call the two numbers at the start of a piece of music?
17) What does the top number tell you about the beats?
18) What does the bottom number tell you about the beats?
19) When a time signature changes in a piece of music, where's the new one written?
20) What's the difference between simple and compound time?
21) What's the difference between regular and irregular metre?
22) What is meant by a cross-rhythm?
23) Draw the symbol for each of the following notes and write down how many crotchet beats it lasts:
    a) semibreve   b) semiquaver   c) crotchet   d) quaver   e) minim
24) What does a dot immediately after a note or rest do?
25) What's the time value of:
    a) a dotted crotchet   b) a dotted minim   c) a dotted semibreve   d) a double dotted minim?
26) What does a 'tie' do?
27) How much time, in crotchet beats, does a crotchet triplet take up?
28) Where do you put the tempo marking on a stave?
29) Which is slower, *allegro* or *moderato*?
30) Where would you write the word *agitato* on the stave?
31) How does a composer show on the written music that the notes should be played smoothly?
32) How are accents usually indicated in a piece of music?
33) What's a glissando?

Major Scales

There are two main types of scales — <u>major</u> and <u>minor</u>. Once you've got the hang of how scales are put together, you should find keys and chords start to make a lot more sense.

Ordinary Scales have **Eight Notes**

1) An ordinary major (or minor) scale has <u>8 notes</u>, starting and ending on notes of the <u>same name</u>, e.g. C major goes C, D, E, F, G, A, B, C.

The gap between the bottom and top notes of a scale is called an <u>octave</u>. See p.28.

2) Each of the eight notes has a <u>name</u>.

1st note	2nd note	3rd note	4th note	5th note	6th note	7th note	8th note
tonic	supertonic	mediant	subdominant	dominant	submediant	leading note	tonic
I	II	III	IV	V	VI	VII	VIII

3) You can just use the <u>numbers</u> or the <u>Roman numerals</u> to name the notes too.

Major Scales Sound **Bright** and Cheery

Whatever note they start on, all major scales sound <u>similar</u>, because they all follow the same <u>pattern</u>. This pattern is a set order of <u>tone</u> and <u>semitone</u> gaps between the notes:

I → tone → II → tone → III → semitone → IV → tone → V → tone → VI → tone → VII → semitone → VIII

This is how <u>C major</u> goes on a keyboard.

Major scales <u>can start on</u> <u>any note</u>, including the black notes, e.g. C♯ major.

All Major Scales Except C have **One or More Black Notes**

<u>C major</u> is the <u>only</u> major scale with <u>no black notes</u>.
<u>All the others</u> need <u>at least one black note</u> to stick to the 'tone-semitone' pattern.

1) <u>G major scale</u> — you have to change <u>F to F♯</u> to make the notes fit the major scale pattern.

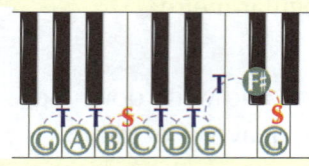

2) <u>F major scale</u> — you have to change <u>B to B♭</u> to make the pattern right.

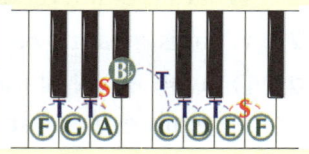

The **Set of Notes** in a **Scale** is Called a **Key**

1) The <u>key</u> tells you what <u>sharps and flats</u> there are (if any).

2) Most music sticks to one key. To show what key it's in, all the <u>sharp</u> or <u>flat</u> signs from the scale are written on the beginning of every stave of the piece. This is called the <u>key signature</u>.

3) A key signature can have <u>sharps or flats</u> but <u>NEVER both</u>.

4) If a piece <u>changes</u> key, it's called a <u>modulation</u> — see p.44.

The key signature goes between the clef and the time signature.

G major's got <u>one</u> <u>sharp</u> note — F♯. You put a <u>sharp</u> symbol on the <u>F line</u>.

Scales — dull but important...

Try playing some major scales starting on <u>different notes</u>. Even if you don't "<u>know</u>" them, you should be able to <u>work out</u> what the notes are, using the <u>tone-semitone</u> pattern and the <u>sound</u>. Give it a go.

Minor Scales

Minor scales have fixed patterns too. There are <u>three</u> different kinds you need to know.

Minor Scales All Sound a Bit Mournful

Minor scales sound <u>completely different</u> from major scales, because they've got a different tone-semitone pattern. There are <u>three</u> types of minor scale, and all of them sound a bit <u>mournful</u>.

1) The Natural Minor has the Same Notes as the Relative Major

These are easy. Start from the <u>sixth</u> note of any major scale. Carry on up to the same note an octave higher. You're playing a <u>natural minor scale</u>.

The sixth note of <u>C major</u> is <u>A</u>. If you play from <u>A to A</u> using the notes of C major, you're playing <u>A natural minor</u> (usually just called '<u>A minor</u>').

Pairs of keys like <u>A minor and C major</u> are called "<u>relative</u>" keys.
A minor is the <u>relative minor</u> of C major.
C major is the <u>relative major</u> of A minor.

<u>All the notes</u> in a natural minor are <u>exactly the same</u> as the ones in the <u>relative major</u>. The <u>key signature's</u> exactly the same too.

2) The Harmonic Minor has One Accidental

1) The <u>harmonic minor</u> has the same notes as the relative major, except for the <u>seventh note</u>.
2) The <u>seventh</u> note is always raised by <u>one semitone</u>.
3) You use the harmonic minor when you're writing <u>harmonies</u>. That <u>sharpened seventh note</u> makes the harmonies work much better than they would with notes from a natural minor. It's probably because it feels like it wants to move up to the <u>tonic</u>.

3) The Melodic Minor has Two Accidentals

1) The <u>melodic minor</u> is just like a natural minor, using the notes from the relative major scale, <u>except for notes 6 and 7</u>.
2) On the way <u>up</u>, notes <u>6</u> and <u>7</u> are each <u>raised</u> by <u>one semitone</u>.
3) On the way <u>down</u>, the melodic minor goes just like the natural minor.

4) The melodic minor is used for writing <u>melodies</u>. The accidental on note 6 makes tunes sound <u>smoother</u> by avoiding the big jump between notes 6 and 7 in the harmonic minor.

And not forgetting the Morris Minor...

All these scales have a <u>minor third</u> between the first and third notes in the scale — that's why they sound melancholy. You need to learn <u>all three</u> — names, notes and what they're used for.

The Circle of Fifths

The circle of fifths looks complicated but it's very <u>useful</u> once you understand how it works — it tells you <u>all the keys</u>, all the <u>relative keys</u> and their <u>key signatures</u>.

The Circle of Fifths Shows All the Keys

1) Altogether there are <u>12 major keys</u>. They're all shown on the <u>circle of fifths</u>.
2) Don't expect to fully get it if this is the first time you've seen it. Just <u>have a look</u>, then read on.

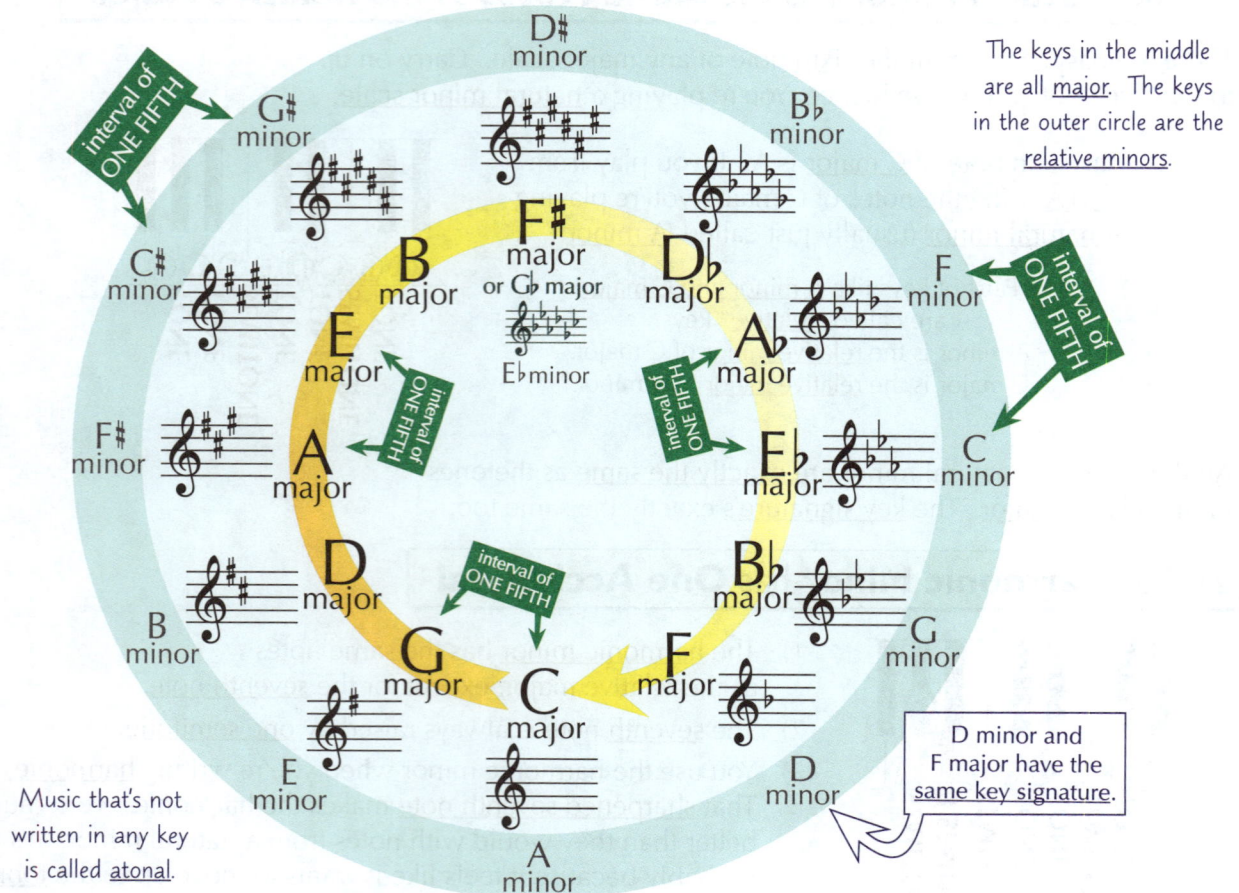

The keys in the middle are all <u>major</u>. The keys in the outer circle are the <u>relative minors</u>.

Music that's not written in any key is called <u>atonal</u>.

D minor and F major have the <u>same key signature</u>.

Each Key Links to the Next One

1) The circle <u>starts</u> with <u>C major</u> at the bottom. The next key round is <u>G</u>. G's the <u>fifth note</u> of C major.
2) The fifth note of G major is D, the <u>next</u> key on the circle. This pattern repeats <u>all the way round</u>. That's why the chart's called the circle of fifths.
3) As you go round the circle the number of <u>sharps</u> in the <u>key signature</u> goes up <u>one</u> for each key.
4) When you get to <u>F♯ major</u> at the top there are <u>six sharps</u>. From here, you start writing the key signature in <u>flats</u> — you don't need as many so it's clearer to read.
5) The number of <u>flats</u> keeps going <u>down</u> until you get back to C major, with no sharps and no flats.

The <u>relative minors</u> in the outer circle work just the same way as the major keys — the <u>fifth note</u> of <u>A minor</u> is <u>E</u> and the next minor key's <u>E minor</u>... and so on. Don't forget you can always work out the relative minor by counting up or down to the <u>sixth note</u> of a major scale (see p.25), or the relative major by counting up to the <u>third note</u> of the minor scale.

REVISION TIP

Don't worry if it's making your head spin...

You need to be familiar with key signatures with <u>up to four sharps</u> or <u>four flats</u> (both <u>major</u> and <u>minor</u>). Don't worry too much about the others (but there's no harm in learning them too).

Modes and Other Types of Scale

Most music uses notes from a <u>major</u> or a <u>minor scale</u> — and they're the <u>most important</u> ones to learn, but there are a few <u>more unusual scales</u> and <u>modes</u> that you need to know about too.

Modes Follow Different Patterns of Tones and Semitones

Just like scales, you can start a <u>mode</u> on any note.

1) The most common mode is the one you get by playing a <u>major scale</u> (e.g. C major — just play the white notes on a keyboard from C to C). The pattern is <u>tone-tone-semitone-tone-tone-tone-semitone</u>.

2) Another mode can be formed by playing the notes of the same major scale, starting from the <u>second note</u>, e.g. D to D:

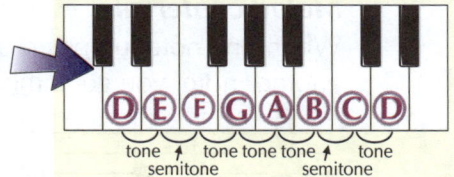

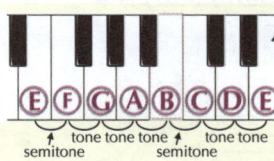

3) Starting on E gives you another mode...

This one is used a lot in flamenco music.

4) ...<u>and so on</u>. Each forms its own semitone / tone pattern and they all have different names. You don't need to know them all though — it's more important that you <u>know what they sound like</u>. (E.g. playing the white notes starting from G forms a mode that sounds quite bluesy.)

5) For some examples of pieces written in modes, have a listen to the folk song <u>Scarborough Fair</u>, the theme tune to <u>The Simpsons</u> and REM's <u>Losing My Religion</u>.

Pentatonic Scales are Used a Lot in Folk and Rock Music

Pentatonic scales use <u>five</u> notes. They're really easy to compose with, because there are <u>no semitone steps</u> — <u>most combinations</u> of notes sound fine. There are <u>two types</u> of pentatonic scale.

1) The <u>major pentatonic</u> uses notes 1, 2, 3, 5 and 6 of a <u>major</u> scale.

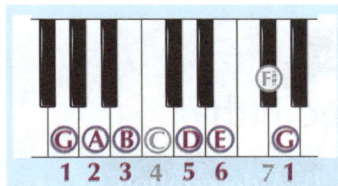

2) The <u>minor pentatonic</u> uses notes 1, 3, 4, 5 and 7 of the <u>natural minor</u> scale.

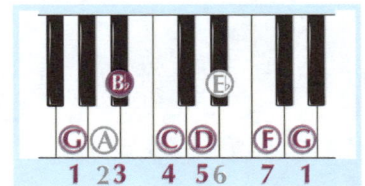

Whole Tone and Chromatic Scales Sound Spooky

Whole tone scales

Whole tone scales are pretty simple to remember — <u>every step is a tone</u>. From bottom to top there are only <u>six notes</u> in a whole tone scale.

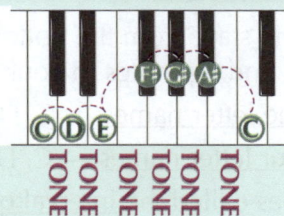

Major and minor scales are known as <u>diatonic scales</u>.

Chromatic scales

Chromatic scales are fairly easy too. On a keyboard you play <u>every white and black note</u> until you get up to an octave above the note you started with. From bottom to top there are <u>12 notes</u>. Basically, <u>every step</u> of a chromatic scale is <u>a semitone</u>.

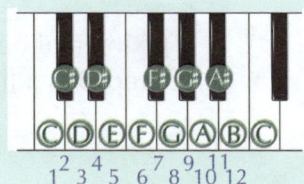

You know the score...

You <u>could</u> get a piece of music in your <u>listening</u> that's written in a <u>mode</u> or one of the other <u>scales</u>. And you could get <u>asked</u> what kind of scale it's written with. So you'd better learn this page.

Intervals

Not the break halfway through a concert, but the distance between two notes.

An **Interval** is the **Gap** Between **Two Notes**

An interval is the musical word for the gap or distance between two notes.
Notes close together make small intervals. Notes further apart make larger intervals.
There are two ways of playing an interval.

Melodic interval
When one note jumps up or down to another note, you get a melodic interval.

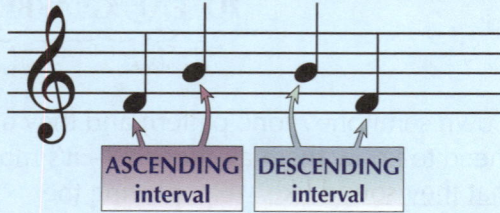

ASCENDING interval | DESCENDING interval

Harmonic interval
When two notes are played at the same time, they make a harmonic interval.

1) You can use the melodic intervals to describe the pattern of a melody.
2) In some melodies, there are only small intervals between the notes — no bigger than a tone.
3) When the notes are close together like this, the melody can be called stepwise, conjunct or scalic (because it moves up and down the notes of a scale).
4) Tunes with big melodic intervals (larger than a tone) are called disjunct.

An Interval has **Two Parts** to its Name...

1) A number

an augmented fifth

2) A description

The **Number** Tells You **How Many Notes** the Interval Covers

1) You get the number by counting up the stave from the bottom note to the top note. You include the bottom and top notes in your counting.
2) C to E is a third because it covers three letter names — C, D and E.
3) C to F is a fourth because it covers four letter names — C, D, E and F.
4) The number of an interval is sometimes called the interval quantity.

The "description" bit is covered at the top of the next page...

The interval between G and D is a fifth.

G	A	B	C	D
1	2	3	4	5

An interval covering eight letters (e.g. A to A) is called an octave.

The interval between D and F sharp is a third (you can just ignore the accidentals when counting).

D	E	F♯
1	2	3

Intervals

The **Description** Tells You How the Interval **Sounds**

There are <u>five names</u> for the five main sounds:

| perfect | major | minor | diminished | augmented |

1) To work out the <u>description part</u> of an interval's name, think of the <u>lower note</u> of the interval as the <u>first</u> note of a <u>major scale</u>.

2) If the top note of the interval is part of that major scale it's either <u>perfect</u> or <u>major</u>:

| PERFECT | MAJOR | MAJOR | PERFECT | PERFECT | MAJOR | MAJOR | PERFECT |
| unison | 2nd | 3rd | 4th | 5th | 6th | 7th | octave |

The perfect intervals are the ones that sound 'best' — the notes go together very cleanly.

3) If the top note <u>doesn't</u> belong to the major scale, then it's <u>minor</u>, <u>diminished</u> or <u>augmented</u>.
If the interval is <u>one semitone LESS</u> than a <u>major interval</u>, then it's <u>minor</u>.
If the interval is <u>one semitone LESS</u> than a <u>minor</u> or a <u>perfect interval</u>, then it's <u>diminished</u>.
If the interval is <u>one semitone MORE</u> than a <u>major</u> or a <u>perfect interval</u>, then it's <u>augmented</u>.

Work Out the **Full Name** of an Interval **Step by Step**

1) **HOW MANY LETTER NAMES DOES IT COVER?**
<u>Six</u> — G, A, B, C, D and E. So the <u>quantity</u> is a <u>sixth</u>.

2) **ARE THE NOTES FROM THE SAME MAJOR SCALE?**
The bottom note's G. E <u>is</u> in G major — it's the <u>sixth</u> note.

3) **WHAT TYPE OF INTERVAL IS IT?**
It's the <u>sixth note</u> of G major, and the sixth note always gives a major interval — so it's a <u>major sixth</u>.

1) **HOW MANY LETTER NAMES DOES IT COVER?**
<u>Three</u> — C, D and E flat. So the <u>quantity</u> is a <u>third</u>.

2) **ARE THE NOTES FROM THE SAME MAJOR SCALE?**
No.

3) **WHAT TYPE OF INTERVAL IS IT?**
A third in the major scale is a <u>major</u> interval.
This interval's one semitone smaller, so it's a <u>minor third</u>.

The **Tritone** Interval **Sounds Odd**

1) The tritone is an interval of <u>three tones</u>. It's <u>dissonant</u> — i.e. it sounds awkward, some would say terrible. It's used in some twentieth century Western art music.

2) <u>Diminished fifths</u> (e.g. G to D flat) and <u>augmented fourths</u> (e.g. G to C♯) are both <u>tritones</u>.

3) Try playing some, so you know what they <u>sound</u> like.

Take it one step at a time and you'll get there in the end...

The tritone interval used to be called 'the Devil's interval' — because it has such an awkward, clashing sound. It's supposed to be unlucky, so use it in your composition at your own risk...

Examples

You need to <u>hear</u> the difference between different types of scales and chords. Tracks 3-9 are practical examples of the theory on pages 24-29. Listen to the tracks as you read the info below.

Examples

Track 3 A <u>major scale</u>, with F# as the tonic, played over two octaves. *(see p.24)*
Try writing out the notes of the scale on a stave. Remember — TTSTTTS.

Track 4 The <u>three</u> different types of <u>minor scale</u> with D as the tonic. *(see p.25)*
a) The <u>natural minor</u> scale
b) The <u>harmonic minor</u>
c) The <u>melodic minor</u>

Track 5 The two different types of pentatonic scale. *(see p.27)*
a) <u>Major pentatonic</u> scale starting on C
b) <u>Minor pentatonic</u> scale starting on A
These are relative scales, and because they're pentatonic all the notes are the same.

Track 6 A <u>whole tone</u> scale. *(see p.27)*
It starts off like the major scale, but the 4th and 5th notes are further apart (<u>harmonically distant</u>) than in a major scale, so it sounds odd.

Track 7 A <u>chromatic</u> scale. *(see p.27)*
This one starts on G, but all <u>chromatic</u> scales use all the notes, so they sound nearly the same.

Track 8 The <u>major</u> and <u>perfect</u> intervals. *(see p.29)*
They're played at the same time so they're <u>harmonic</u>.

Track 9 The <u>minor</u> and <u>diminished intervals</u>. *(see p.29)*
a) Minor 2nd
b) Augmented 2nd / minor 3rd
c) Augmented 4th / diminished 5th
d) Augmented 5th / minor 6th
e) Augmented 6th / minor 7th

Practice Questions

Now check you've got the hang of it all with these practice questions.

Track 10 Listen to the four different types of scale. What are they?

a) ....

b) ....

c) ....

d) ....

You can play these tracks more than once — some of them are quite tricky.

Track 11 What type of scale does this tune use?

....

Track 12 Listen to these harmonic intervals. Write down what each of them is called.

a) ....   b) ....

c) ....   d) ....

e) ....   f) ....

g) ....   h) ....

Track 13 Now name these melodic intervals.

a) ....   b) ....

c) ....   d) ....

e) ....   f) ....

g) ....   h) ....

Warm-up and Exam Questions

Time for another round of questions...

Warm-up Questions

1) How many notes would you find in a normal scale?

2) What does a key or key signature tell you about the music?

3) What do the scales of C major and A minor have in common?

4) Name the **three** types of minor scales.

5) Which scale uses only notes 1, 2, 3, 5 and 6 from the major scale?

6) Why is a chromatic scale unusual?

7) What type of interval is formed when two notes are played together at the same time?

8) Which is smaller, a minor 7th or a diminished 7th?

Exam Question

This exam-style question includes a couple of questions on intervals to test your knowledge.

Play the extract **three** times. Leave a short pause between each playing.

Track 14

a) Here are the first three bars.

Exam Question

i) How many beats are there in a bar?

....

[1 mark]

ii) What is the interval between the notes highlighted in red at letter **a**?

....

[1 mark]

iii) What is the interval between the two lower notes in the left-hand chord indicated at letter **b**?

....

[1 mark]

b) What key is this extract in?

....

[1 mark]

c) What does the mark ‾ above a note tell the performer to do?

....

[1 mark]

Chords — The Basics

A <u>chord</u> is two or more notes played together. Chords are great for writing <u>accompaniments</u>.

Only **Some** Instruments **Play Chords**

<u>Don't play chords.</u>

1) A lot of instruments only play <u>one note at a time</u> — flutes, recorders, trumpets, clarinets, trombones... You can't play a chord with one note, so these instruments <u>don't</u> play chords.

2) You can <u>only</u> play chords on <u>instruments</u> that play <u>more than one</u> note at a time. <u>Keyboards</u> and guitars are both great for playing chords — you can easily play several notes together.

<u>Do play chords.</u>

3) Other <u>stringed instruments</u> like violins and cellos can play chords, but not very easily, so chords are only played from time to time.

Some Chords Sound **Great**, Others Sound **Awful**

1) The notes of some chords <u>go together</u> really well — like apple pie and ice-cream.

When you have nice-sounding chords it's called <u>CONCORDANCE</u> or <u>CONSONANCE</u>.

2) Other chords have <u>clashing notes which disagree</u> — more like apple pie and pickled eggs.

When you have horrible-sounding chords it's called <u>DISCORDANCE</u> or <u>DISSONANCE</u>.

The **Best-Sounding** Chords are Called **Triads**

1) You can play <u>any</u> set of notes and make a chord — but most of them sound <u>harsh</u>.
2) An <u>easy, reliable</u> way of getting nice-sounding chords is to play <u>triads</u>.
3) Triads are chords made up of three notes, with <u>set intervals</u> between them.
4) Once you know the intervals, you can easily play <u>dozens</u> of decent chords.

How to make a triad...

1) On a piano, start with any white note — this is called the <u>root note</u>. You <u>build</u> the triad <u>from the root</u>.
2) Count the root as 'first' and the next white note to the <u>right</u>, as 'second'. The <u>third</u> note you reach is the <u>third</u> — the middle note of the triad.
3) Keep counting up and you get to the <u>fifth</u> — the final note of the triad.
4) The intervals between the notes are <u>thirds</u>.
5) If the root note's a <u>B</u>, then you end up with a <u>B triad</u>. If the root note's a <u>C</u>, you end up with a <u>C triad</u>.
6) You can build triads on black notes too, so long as the intervals between notes are <u>thirds</u>.

FIFTH
THIRD
ROOT

C E G

Good things come in threes...

COMPOSING TIP

The next six pages will be useful when it comes to writing your compositions. You'll need to think about which instruments can play chords, and which notes sound nice together.

Triads

There's more than one type of triad...

Triads Use Major and Minor Thirds

1) All triads have an interval of a third between each pair of notes.
2) The intervals can be major or minor thirds.

A major third is four semitones.

A minor third is three semitones.

1 2 3 4

1 2 3

3) Different combinations of major and minor thirds give different types of triad:

Major triads
- Major triads have a major third followed by a minor third.
- The major third goes between the root and the third.
- The minor third goes between the third and the fifth.

Minor triads
- Minor triads use a major and a minor third too, but in the opposite order.
- The minor third goes between the root and the third.
- The major third goes between the third and the fifth.

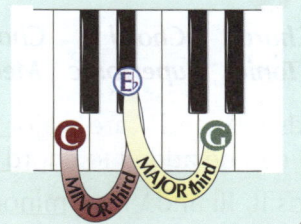

DIMINISHED TRIADS use two minor thirds.
AUGMENTED TRIADS use two major thirds.

These two kinds aren't nearly as common as major and minor triads.

You Can Add a Note to a Triad to Get a 7th Chord

1) 7th chords are triads with a fourth note added — the seventh note above the root.
2) The interval between the root and the 7th can be a major seventh or a minor seventh — see p.29.

These Symbols Stand for Chords

A special notation is used to represent the various chords. For a triad starting on a C:

C = C major

Caug or **C+** = augmented C chord

C7 = C major with added minor 7th

Cmaj7 = C major with added major 7th

Cm = C minor

Cdim or **C-** or **Co** = diminished C chord

Cm7 = C minor with added minor 7th

Cm maj7 = C minor with added major 7th

For chords other than C, just change the first letter to show the root note.

It's not as hard as it looks and it's VERY useful...

If you play the guitar or play in a band you need to learn these symbols right now. Even if you only ever play classical music they're still worth learning — they're really useful as shorthand.

Fitting Chords to a Melody

There are some basic rules about fitting chords to a melody:
No.1: All the notes in the chords have got to be in the same key as the notes in the melody.

The **Melody** and **Chords** Must be in the **Same Key**

1) A melody that's composed in a certain key sticks to that key.

2) The chords used to harmonise with the melody have got to be in the same key or it'll clash.

3) As a general rule each chord in a harmony should include the note it's accompanying, e.g. a C could be accompanied by a C chord (C, E, G), an F chord (F, A, C) or an A minor chord (A, C, E).

There's a Chord for **Every Note** in the **Scale**

You can make dozens of triads using the notes of major and minor scales as the roots. Every note of every chord, not just the root, has to belong to the scale. This is how C major looks if you turn it into chords:

The odd accidental or ornament in a different key is OK — see p.41.

Chord I	Chord II	Chord III	Chord IV	Chord V	Chord VI	Chord VII	Chord I
Tonic	Supertonic	Mediant	Subdominant	Dominant	Submediant	Leading Note	Tonic

1) Chords I, IV and V are major triads. They sound bright and cheery.
A 7th can be added to chord V to give a dominant 7th chord (written V^7).

2) Chords II, III and VI are minor triads. They sound more gloomy.

3) Chord VII is a diminished triad. It sounds different from the major and minor chords. Another name for Chord VII is the leading note chord — it sounds like it should lead on to another chord.

4) Chords built on any major scale, not just C major, follow the same pattern.

5) A series of chords is known as a harmonic progression
(also called a chord progression or chord sequence).

6) The speed at which the chords change is called the harmonic rhythm.

The **Primary Chords** are Most **Useful**

1) The three major chords, I, IV and V, are the most important in any key. They're called primary chords. Between them, the primary chords can harmonise with any note in the scale.

2) This is how it works in C major:

note...	C	D	E	F	G	A	B
goes with...	Chord I	Chord IV	Chord V	Chord I	Chord IV	Chord I	Chord V	Chord IV	Chord V

	C	D	G	C	G	D	C	D
	E	A	B	E	A	E	B	A	B
	C	F	G	C	F	C	G	F	G

Minor Chords Make Harmony **More Interesting**

1) Primary chords can get a bit boring to listen to after a while — the harmonies are fairly simple.

2) Composers often mix in a few of the other chords — II, III, VI or VII — for a change.

3) Instead of just having endless major chords, you get a mixture of minor and diminished chords too.

Section Three — Keys, Scales and Chords

Inversions

Inverting triads means <u>changing the order</u> of the notes. It make accompaniments more <u>varied</u>.

Triads with the **Root at the Bottom** are in **Root Position**

These triads are all in <u>root position</u> — the <u>root note</u> is <u>at the bottom</u>.

● = fifth
● = third
● = root

C chord in <u>root position</u>

F chord in <u>root position</u>

G chord in <u>root position</u>

First Inversion Triads have the **Third** at the **Bottom**

These chords are all in <u>first inversion</u>. The root note's moved up an octave, leaving the <u>third</u> at the bottom.

C chord in <u>first inversion</u>

F chord in <u>first inversion</u>

G chord in <u>first inversion</u>

Second Inversion Triads have the **Fifth** at the **Bottom**

Chords can be played in <u>second inversion</u> too.

From the first inversion, the third is raised an octave, leaving the <u>fifth</u> at the bottom.

C chord in <u>second inversion</u>

F chord in <u>second inversion</u>

G chord in <u>second inversion</u>

7th Chords Can Go into a **Third Inversion**

1) 7th chords can be played in root position, first inversion or second inversion — just like triads.

2) But there's also a <u>third inversion</u> — where the <u>7th</u> goes <u>below</u> the standard triad. They have a third inversion because they're <u>four-note</u> chords.

There's a **Symbol** for Each **Inversion**

This means a C chord with E at the bottom.

ROOT POSITION	...also known as...	5/3 chords	because there's a <u>fifth</u> and a <u>third</u> between the notes	...and in Roman numerals...	Ia	...and in good old chord symbols...	C
FIRST INVERSION		6/3 chords	because there's a <u>sixth</u> and a <u>third</u> between the notes		Ib		C/E
SECOND INVERSION		6/4 chords	because there's a <u>sixth</u> and a <u>fourth</u> between the notes		Ic		C/G
THIRD INVERSION		6/4/2 chords	because there's a <u>sixth</u>, a <u>fourth</u> and a <u>second</u> between the notes		Id		Cmaj7/B

These numbers are used in <u>figured bass</u> — see page 57.

Inversions

So now you know what inversions <u>are</u>. Now get to grips with what to <u>do</u> with them too...

Inversions are Handy for **Moving Between Chords**

When you play chords one after another, it sounds <u>nicer</u> if the notes move <u>smoothly</u> from one chord to the next. Inversions help to smooth out any rough patches...

1) Moving from a <u>C chord in root position</u> to a <u>G chord in root position</u> means <u>all</u> the notes have to jump a <u>long way</u>. It sounds <u>clumsy</u> and not all that nice.

- = fifth
- = third
- = root

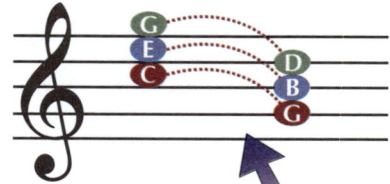

Try playing both sets of chords a few times, until you can hear the difference.

2) If you move from a C chord in root position to a <u>G chord</u> in <u>first inversion</u> instead, the transition is much, much smoother.

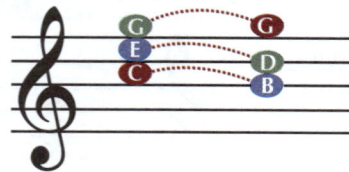

3) You can use <u>second</u> and <u>third inversions</u> too — whatever sounds best.

Unscramble the Inversion to Work Out the Root Note

This isn't exactly a life-saving skill. But it's <u>dead useful</u>...

If you come across an inverted chord you can <u>work out</u> which is the <u>root note</u>. Once you know that, and you know what <u>key</u> you're in, you can tell whether it's chord IV, VII, II or whatever.

1) Basically you have to turn the chord back into a <u>root position triad</u>.
2) Shuffle the order of the notes around until there's a <u>third interval</u> between each one.
3) When the notes are arranged in <u>thirds</u>, the root will <u>always</u> be at the <u>bottom</u>.

B to D is a THIRD, but D to G is a FOURTH. You need to <u>move the G</u> to find the root chord.

G to B is a THIRD so the G goes here — <u>G</u>'s the <u>root note</u>.

4) There are no sharps or flats in the key signature, so the piece is in C major. G's the fifth note of C major, so this is <u>chord V</u>.

Unscramble inversions — go back to your roots...

There's a lot to take in when it comes to inversions. Don't go racing through this page — go over it one bit at a time, letting all the facts sink in. Playing the chords for yourself will help.

Different Ways of Playing Chords

So far, the chords in this section have all been written as three notes. It sounds dull if you do it all the time. To liven things up there are chord figurations — different ways of playing the chords.

Block Chords are the Most Basic

This is probably the easiest way to play chords. The notes of each chord are played all together and then held until the next chord.

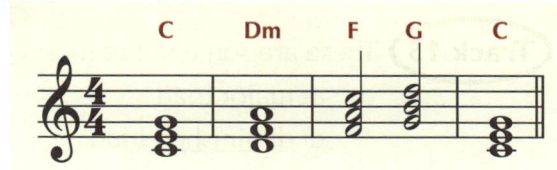

Rhythmic Chords Give You Harmony and Rhythm

1) Rhythmic chords are chords played to a funky rhythm.
2) You play all the notes of each chord at the same time, like you do for block chords.
3) You don't hold the notes though — you play them to a rhythm that repeats in each bar.
4) Rhythm guitar and keyboards often play rhythmic chords.

In Broken and Arpeggiated Chords the Notes are Separate

Accompanying chords don't have to have to be played at all once. You can play the notes separately.

1) Here's one way of doing it — it goes root, fifth, third, root.

2) This pattern was really popular around the time Mozart was alive (last half of the 1700s). It's called Alberti bass after the composer Domenico Alberti — it usually goes root, fifth, third, fifth.

3) The notes of a chord are sometimes played in order (e.g. root, third, fifth, root) going up or coming down. This is called an arpeggio (are-pedge-ee-o).

4) In an arpeggiated chord, you play the notes one at a time, but in quick succession (imagine strumming a harp). On a piano, you hold down each key as you build up the chord. They're usually written with a wiggly line, like this:

5) A walking bass usually moves in crotchets, often either in steps (see p.28) or arpeggios.
6) A drone is a long, held-on note, usually in the bass, that adds harmonic interest.
7) Pedal notes are a bit different — they're repeated notes, again usually in the bass part. However, the harmony on top of a pedal note changes (whereas a drone sets up the harmony for the whole piece).

COMPOSING TIP

Think about using an Alberti bass in your composition...
When you get chord symbols over the music you can play the chords any way you like. Try all these ways of playing chords and think about using them in your compositions.

Examples and Practice

Read on for some more examples of the different kinds of chords.

Examples

Track 15) These are some of the most <u>common</u> chords — learn to recognise them.

a) <u>major</u> triad
b) <u>minor</u> triad
c) <u>diminished</u> triad
d) <u>augmented</u> triad
e) <u>major</u> triad with a <u>major</u> 7th
f) <u>major</u> triad with a <u>minor</u> 7th
g) <u>minor</u> triad with a <u>major</u> 7th
h) <u>minor</u> triad with a <u>minor</u> 7th

Track 16) A <u>sequence</u> of chords, showing different <u>inversions</u>:

What <u>inversion</u> a chord is depends on which note is on the <u>bottom</u> — it doesn't matter how the other notes of the triad are arranged on top.

In these first three chords, chords in the first inversion lead nicely on to root chords a perfect 4th up. The semitone steps in the bass make these progressions sound smooth and logical.

At the end of the sequence, listen out for the third from last note (second inversion of chord I), which leads into the cadence that ends the phrase (see p.42-43 for more on cadences).

How well do you know your chords... Find out by answering these practice questions.

Practice Questions

Track 17) Describe each of the eight chords on the track, using one of the following words:

major	minor	diminished	augmented

You can play these tracks more than once.

a) ....

b) ....

c) ....

d) ....

e) ....

f) ....

g) ....

h) ....

Track 18) For each of the following you'll hear a root note, and then an inversion. Which inversions are they?

a) ....

b) ....

c) ....

d) ....

e) ....

f) ....

g) ....

h) ....

Use Decorations to Vary the Harmony

If you want to <u>liven things up</u> in a harmony you can add a sprinkle of <u>melodic decoration</u>.

Melodic Decoration **Adds Notes** to the Tune

1) <u>Decorative notes</u> are <u>short notes</u> that move between notes or create <u>fleeting clashes</u> (<u>dissonance</u>) with the accompanying chord. They make things sound <u>less bland</u>.

2) Decoration that belongs to the key of the melody (e.g. B in C major) is called <u>diatonic</u>.

3) Decoration that <u>doesn't</u> belong to the key (e.g. F♯ in C major) is called <u>chromatic</u>.

4) There are <u>four</u> main ways of adding melodic decoration.

1) **Auxiliary** Notes are **Higher** or **Lower** than the Notes **Either Side**

1) An auxiliary note is either a <u>semitone</u> or <u>tone</u> <u>above</u> or <u>below</u> the notes either side.

2) The two notes before and after the auxiliary are always the <u>same pitch</u>, and always belong to the accompanying chord.

2) **Passing** Notes **Link** the Notes **Before** and **After**

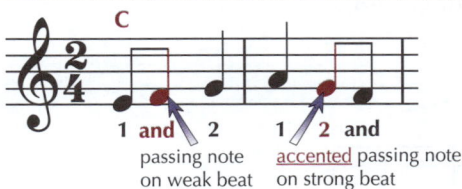

1) A passing note <u>links</u> the notes before and after. They either belong to the same chord or link one chord with another.

2) They're usually put on <u>weak beats</u>. When they <u>are</u> on the strong beat they're called '<u>accented passing notes</u>'.

3) **Appoggiaturas Clash** with the Chord

1) An appoggiatura <u>clashes</u> with the accompanying chord. It's written as a <u>little note</u> tied to the note of the chord, and takes <u>half the value</u> of the note it's tied to.

2) The note <u>before</u> it is usually quite a <u>leap</u> away (jumps between notes of more than a <u>2nd</u> are called <u>leaps</u>).

3) The note after the appoggiatura is always <u>just above</u> or <u>below</u>. It's called the <u>resolution</u>. The <u>resolution</u> has to be from the <u>accompanying chord</u>.

4) Appoggiaturas usually fall on a <u>strong beat</u>, so the resolution note falls on a <u>weaker beat</u>.

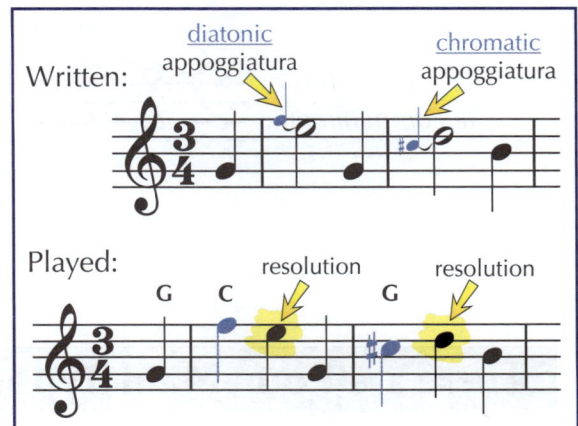

4) **Suspensions Clash** then Go Back to **Harmonising**

A suspension is a series of three notes called the <u>preparation</u>, <u>suspension</u> and <u>resolution</u>.

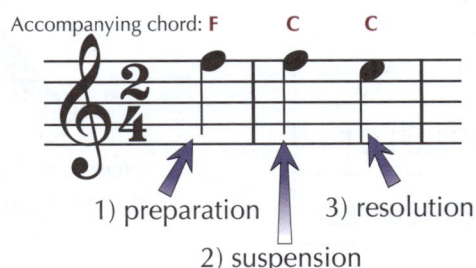

1) The <u>preparation</u> note belongs to the accompanying chord. It's usually on a weak beat.

2) The <u>suspension</u> is the <u>same pitch</u> as the preparation note. It's played at the same time as a <u>chord change</u>. It <u>doesn't go</u> with the new chord, so you get <u>dissonance</u>.

3) The <u>resolution</u> note moves up or down (usually down) from the suspension to a note in the accompanying chord. This <u>resolves</u> the dissonance — everything sounds lovely again.

Section Three — Keys, Scales and Chords

Phrases and Cadences

Notes in a melody fall into 'phrases' just like the words in a story are made up of sentences.
A cadence is the movement from the second-to-last to the last chord of a phrase — it finishes it off.

A **Phrase** is Like a Musical **'Sentence'**

There should be clear phrases in any melody. A tune without phrases would
sound odd — just like a story with no sentences wouldn't make much sense.

1) Phrases are usually two or four bars long.

2) Phrases are sometimes marked with a curved
line called a phrase mark, that goes above
the stave. Not all music has phrase marks but
the phrases are always there. Don't confuse
phrase marks and slurs. A phrase mark
doesn't change how you play the notes.

Cadences Emphasise the End of a Phrase

1) A cadence is the shift between the second-to-last chord and the last chord in a phrase.

2) The effect you get from shifting between the two chords works like a comma or a full stop.
It underlines the end of the phrase and gets you ready for the next one.

This is the tune...

Twin- kle   twin- kle   litt- le   star

...and this is the accompaniment.

C chord   C chord   F chord   C chord

These last two chords make the cadence.

There are **Four Main Types** of Cadence

These pairs of chords are only cadences when they come at the end of a phrase.
Anywhere else in a phrase, they're just chords.

Second Last Chord	Last Chord	Cadence
Chord V	Chord I	PERFECT
Chord IV	Chord I	PLAGAL
Chord I, II or IV	Chord V	IMPERFECT
Chord V	any except Chord I, (usually Chord VI)	INTERRUPTED

More on these on the next page...

Cadences

Learning the <u>names</u> of the different cadences is no use unless you also learn what they're <u>for</u>.

Perfect and Plagal Cadences Work Like Full Stops

1) A <u>perfect cadence</u> makes a piece of music feel <u>finished or complete</u>.
2) It goes from <u>Chord V</u> to <u>Chord I</u> — in C major that's a <u>G chord</u> to a <u>C chord</u>.
3) This is how a perfect cadence goes at the <u>end</u> of 'Twinkle, Twinkle, Little Star':

Here's the <u>perfect cadence</u>.

4) A <u>plagal cadence</u> sounds really different from a perfect cadence but it has a <u>similar effect</u> — it makes a piece of music sound finished.
5) A plagal cadence in C major is an <u>F chord</u> (IV) to a <u>C chord</u> (I). Play it and see what it sounds like. The plagal cadence gets used at the <u>end</u> of lots of <u>hymns</u> — it's sometimes called the '<u>Amen</u>' cadence.

Imperfect and Interrupted Cadences are Like Commas

<u>Imperfect</u> and <u>interrupted</u> cadences are used to end <u>phrases</u> but <u>not</u> at the end of a piece. They work like <u>commas</u> — they feel like a <u>resting point</u> but not an ending.

An <u>imperfect cadence</u> most commonly goes from chord <u>I</u>, <u>II</u> or <u>IV</u> to <u>V</u>. Here's one going from <u>chord I</u> to <u>chord V</u> at the end of the <u>third line</u> of 'Twinkle, Twinkle':

Here's the <u>imperfect cadence</u>.

In an <u>interrupted cadence</u> chord V can go to any chord except I, but it usually goes to chord VI. You expect it to go to chord I — so it sounds "interrupted". In C major an interrupted cadence may go from a <u>G chord</u> (V) to an <u>Am chord</u> (VI).

Some Minor pieces Finish with a Tierce de Picardie

1) If a piece of music is in a <u>minor key</u>, you'd expect it to <u>finish</u> with a <u>minor chord</u>.
2) However, some composers (especially <u>Baroque</u> composers) finish a <u>minor piece</u> with a <u>major chord</u>, by using a <u>major third</u> in the last chord. This is known as a <u>Tierce de Picardie</u> (or <u>Picardy third</u>).

This extract is from <u>Scarlatti's Piano Sonata in G Minor (Cat's Fugue)</u>. Even though the piece is in <u>G minor</u>, it finishes with a <u>G major chord</u>.

You need to listen to cadences to understand them...

Cadences probably won't make much sense unless you try playing them. <u>Play</u> the cadences for yourself (or listen to Track 19 — see p.48) until you can <u>hear</u> the differences between them.

Modulation

Most of the notes in a piece of music come from one key — but to vary the tune or harmony you can <u>modulate</u> (change key). It can happen just once, or a few times. It's up to the composer.

The **Starting Key** is Called '**Home**'

1) The key a piece <u>starts out in</u> is called the <u>home key</u> or <u>tonic key</u>.
2) If the music's modulated it goes into a <u>different key</u>.
3) The change of key is usually only <u>temporary</u>. The key <u>goes back</u> to the home key after a while.
4) However much a piece modulates, it usually <u>ends</u> in the home key.

There are **Two** Ways to Modulate

1) Modulation by **Pivot Chord**

1) A pivot chord is a chord that's in the home key <u>and</u> the key the music modulates to.
2) <u>Chord V</u> (G, B, D) in <u>C major</u> is exactly the same as <u>chord I</u> in <u>G major</u> — so it can be used to <u>pivot</u> between C major and G major.
3) Sometimes, the <u>key signature</u> changes to show the new key. More often, <u>accidentals</u> are written in the music where they're needed.

The home key here is <u>C</u>. At the end of the <u>first bar</u> the accompaniment uses the chord <u>G, B, D</u> to pivot into G major:

This is called a V/I pivot because it uses <u>V</u> from the home key and <u>I</u> from the key it modulates to.

<u>Pivot</u> chord

F♯ belongs to G major.

Related keys...

1) It sounds best if you modulate to <u>related keys</u>.
2) The <u>closest</u> keys are (major) keys <u>IV</u> and <u>V</u> and the <u>relative minor</u>.
3) The <u>next closest</u> are the relative minors of keys IV and V.

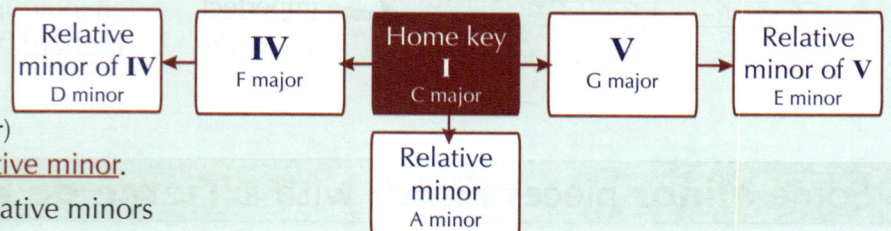

Relative minor of **IV** — D minor | **IV** F major | Home key **I** C major | **V** G major | Relative minor of **V** — E minor

Relative minor — A minor

2) **Abrupt** Modulation

1) In abrupt modulation there's <u>no pivot chord</u>, and no other preparation either. It just happens.
2) Often the modulation is between two keys just <u>one semitone apart</u>, e.g. from <u>C major</u> to <u>C♯ major</u>.
3) <u>Pop songs</u> often modulate <u>up</u> one semitone. It creates a <u>sudden</u>, <u>dramatic effect</u> — it's meant to give the music an <u>excited</u>, <u>uplifting</u> feeling.

You can choose related keys but you can't choose your family...

If you see <u>accidentals</u> it often means the music's modulated, but <u>not always</u>. The accidental could also be there because: 1) the music's written in a <u>minor key</u> — harmonic or melodic (see p.25); or 2) the composer fancied a spot of <u>chromatic</u> decoration (see p.41). That's composers for you...

Texture

Here's one last way composers vary the harmony — by changing the texture. Texture's an odd word to use about music — what it means is how the different parts (e.g. chords and melody) are woven together.

Texture is How the parts Fit Together

1) An important part of music is how the different parts are woven together. This is known as texture — it describes how the melody and accompaniment parts fit together.
2) Monophonic, homophonic and polyphonic are all different types of texture.
3) Some textures are made up of the same melodic line that's passed round different parts. Imitation and canons are good examples of this.

Monophonic Music is the Simplest

1) In monophonic music there's no harmony — just one line of tune (e.g. a solo with no accompaniment).
2) Parts playing in unison or doubling each other (i.e. the same notes at the same time) are also monophonic.
3) Monophonic music has a thin texture.

Polyphonic Music Weaves Tunes Together

1) Polyphonic music gives quite a complex effect because there's more than one tune being played at once.
2) It's sometimes called contrapuntal music.
3) Parts that move in contrary motion (one goes up and another goes down) are polyphonic.
4) Two-part music (with two separate melodic lines) is also polyphonic.

In Homophonic Music, the Parts Move Together

1) If the lines of music move at more or less the same time, it's homophonic music.
2) A melody with accompaniment (the accompaniment is often chordal) is a good example of homophonic music.
3) Parallel motion (when parts move with the same interval between them, e.g. parallel 5ths) is also homophonic.

Melody

Accompaniment

In Heterophonic Music the Instruments Share the Tune

Flute

Oboe

In heterophonic music there's one tune. All the instruments play it, but with variations, and often at different times.

Polyphonic, homophonic and heterophonic music all have quite a thick texture.

EXAM TIP

You might have to write about texture in the exam...
Texture is one of those things that examiners love to ask about. Make sure you know the proper words to describe texture, and that you can tell the difference between the different types.

Texture

When there's <u>one</u> part, the music's <u>pure</u> and <u>simple</u>, but put <u>more parts in</u> and it's much more <u>complex</u>.

Imitation — Repeat a Phrase With **Slight Changes**

1) In <u>imitation</u> a phrase is repeated with <u>slight changes</u> each time.
2) It works particularly well if one instrument or voice imitates <u>another</u> and then <u>overlaps</u>.

original phrase   *original phrase, one octave higher*

imitation with modulation   *overlap starts in relative minor*

Canon — **Same Melody** Different Parts

1) In a <u>canon</u>, each part plays the <u>same melody</u>, but they come in <u>separately</u> and at <u>regular intervals</u>. The parts <u>overlap</u>.
2) A canon is also known as a <u>round</u>. There are some really well-known rounds, e.g. '<u>London's Burning</u>'.
3) Canons are an example of <u>contrapuntal</u> (or <u>polyphonic</u>) music (see previous page).
4) Composers from the <u>Baroque</u> period (1600-1750) like <u>Bach</u> and <u>Vivaldi</u> used lots of canons.

This extract comes from 'Spring' from Vivaldi's Four Seasons. The solo violin and first violin often play in canon.

Another common Baroque texture is the <u>continuo</u> (or <u>basso continuo</u>) — see p.57.

Solo Violin / First Violin / Solo Violin / First Violin

Looping and Layering are **Modern Techniques**

1) In the <u>1960s</u> and <u>70s</u>, composers like <u>Steve Reich</u> started developing <u>new techniques</u> in their music.
2) They took recordings of sections of <u>music</u>, <u>words</u>, <u>rhythms</u> and <u>other sounds</u> and <u>repeated</u> them over and over again. These are called <u>loops</u>.
3) The loops were often created by <u>cutting</u> pieces of <u>tape</u> and <u>sticking</u> the ends together so they could be played over and over again — this is <u>looping</u>.
4) If there are lots of <u>different loops</u> being played at the <u>same time</u> it's called <u>layering</u>.

A layer of fruit, a layer of sponge, a layer of custard...

There are a few more words on this page that'll be useful if you need to write about musical texture in the listening exam — imitation, canon, looped and layered. Make sure you know what they mean.

Texture

Composers use <u>different textures</u> to <u>vary</u> their music. They can change the <u>number</u> of instruments and whether they play the <u>same notes</u> or in <u>harmony</u>. They can also <u>split</u> tunes between <u>different instruments</u>.

More Than One Part Can Play the Same Melody

1) If there's just <u>one part</u> playing with <u>no accompaniment</u>, there's just a <u>single melody line</u>.

2) If there's <u>more than one</u> instrument playing the <u>same melody</u> at the <u>same pitch</u>, they're playing in <u>unison</u>.

3) If there's <u>more than one</u> instrument playing the <u>same notes</u> but in <u>different ranges</u>, they're playing in <u>octaves</u>.

All of these are examples of <u>monophonic</u> textures.

Some Instruments Play Accompanying Parts

1) The instruments that <u>aren't</u> playing the tune play the <u>accompaniment</u>. Different <u>types</u> of accompaniment give different <u>textures</u>.

2) If the accompaniment is playing <u>chords</u> underneath the melody (or the <u>same rhythm</u> of the melody but <u>different notes</u>), the texture is <u>homophonic</u>. It sounds <u>richer</u> than a single melody line, unison or octaves.

3) If there are <u>two choirs</u> singing at <u>different times</u>, the music is <u>antiphonal</u>. The two choirs will often sing <u>alternate phrases</u> — like <u>question and answer</u> or <u>call and response</u>. A lot of <u>early religious vocal music</u> was antiphonal. You can also get the same effect with two groups of <u>instruments</u>.

Group 1

Group 2

4) If there's <u>more than one</u> part playing <u>different melodies</u> at the <u>same time</u>, the music is <u>contrapuntal</u> (or <u>polyphonic</u>). Contrapuntal parts <u>fit together</u> harmonically.

The examples on this page use the melody from Handel's 'Water Music'.

REVISION TIP

Would you care to accompany me to the cinema...

Quite a few tricky <u>textures</u> to learn on this page. Listen to the different types, and try and <u>recognise</u> what they sound like so that you can describe them if they come up in the <u>exam</u>.

Section Three — Keys, Scales and Chords

Examples

Track 19 should help you get a better idea about cadences, and Track 20 gives you some different examples of modulation. Listen to them lots of times until you can recognise them straight away.

Examples

Track 19 You'll hear this bar played **four** times, followed by a different cadence each time.

a) The perfect cadence sounds totally complete — perfect, in fact. You can't imagine it moving on to any other chord.

V   I
a   a

b) The plagal cadence is sometimes called the "amen cadence" — it sounds peaceful and reassuring.

IV   I
a   a

c) The imperfect cadence is the opposite of the perfect cadence. Instead of bringing things to a close, it seems to open up loads of possibilities.

I   V
c   a

d) The interrupted cadence starts off like a perfect cadence but ends with a more open, melancholy feel.

V   VI
a   a

Track 20 Listen to these **three** short extracts. Each one is a different example of a modulation from one key to another. In each extract the pattern goes like this:

Note 1 Original key

Note 2 Original key

Note 3 Pivot chord (in the original key and the new key)

Note 4 New key

Practice Questions

Practise your hard-won knowledge of chords, modulation and texture with the questions on this page and the next. Listen to each track a few times to make sure you've heard it properly.

Practice Questions

Track 21 This question is about identifying cadences.
You will hear eight phrases, a)-h), all starting like this:

Write down whether the final cadence is perfect, plagal, imperfect or interrupted.

a) ....

b) ....

c) ....

d) ....

e) ....

f) ....

g) ....

h) ....

Track 22 For each of the following tracks, fill in the missing notes in the melody, then answer the questions.

a)

b) The chord in the fourth bar has an A in the bass.
What inversion of chord I is this?

....

c) What type of cadence does the passage end with?

....

Track 23 a)

b) In this passage, the harmony tends to move in time with the melody.
What is the name of this type of musical texture?

....

c) What type of cadence does the passage end with?

....

d) Which note is sustained in the bass in the second-to-last bar?

....

Practice Questions

Practice Questions

Track 24 a)

b) The first chord in bar 2 is the major of chord II.
Which note in this chord is not in the scale of the home key?

....

c) What type of cadence does the passage end with?

....

Track 25 a)

b) Circle each auxiliary note in the passage, and say whether each is diatonic or chromatic.

c) Which one of the following best describes the chord in bar 4?
Ring your answer.

1st inversion   **harmonic**   **relative minor**   **suspension**

Track 26 a)

b) What key does this passage start in?

....

c) What key does it finish in?

....

d) The B flat chord at the start of bar 3 comes before the dominant chord of the new key. Give the name of a chord in this position in a modulation.

....

e) Fill in the blanks in the following sentence with the appropriate Roman numerals:

The B flat chord is chord .... in the home key

and chord .... in the final key.

Warm-up and Exam Questions

Warm-up Questions

1) Name **two** instruments that are frequently used to play chords.

2) Which **three** chords in a major key produce major triads?

3) If the *root* of a chord is on the top, and the *third* of the chord is on the bottom, which inversion is the chord in?

4) Name **three** different ways of playing chords.

5) What do you call a melodic decoration that belongs to the same key as the main melody?

6) List **three** ways melodies can be decorated to help vary the harmony within a piece of music.

7) At what point in a piece of music would you expect to find an imperfect or interrupted cadence?

8) What's another name for the texture known as polyphonic?

Exam Question

Now practise your exam technique with the question below and over the page.

Track 27

Play the extract **four times** then answer the questions on the next page.

Leave a short pause for writing time before each playing.

Here is the complete score for the extract:

Exam Question

a) What instrument is playing this piece?

....

[1 mark]

b) How would you describe the way the left hand is playing at **1**?

....

[1 mark]

c) Which of the following best describes the cadence at **2**?
Circle your choice from the options below.

perfect   plagal   imperfect

[1 mark]

d) Which key is this extract in?

....

[1 mark]

e) Look at the key of the piece. How would you explain the sharpened note at **3**?

....

[1 mark]

f) What term is used to describe the dots above the notes at **4**?

....

[1 mark]

g) Which of these options best describes the texture of this music?
Circle your choice.

monophonic   homophonic   heterophonic

[1 mark]

Revision Summary for Section Three

There's a lot to remember here: four types of triad, four types of triad inversion, cadences, different ways of using decoration with chords, modulation, the something-phonic words... It's too much to tackle all in one go. Test yourself a page at a time and make sure you really know it. You'll know you've done it properly when you can answer all these questions <u>without</u> looking back.

1) How many notes are there in a major scale? How many notes are there in a minor scale?
2) Write out the names of the notes of a scale in words, numbers and Roman numerals.
3) Write down the tone-semitone pattern for a major scale.
4) Which major scale only uses the white notes on the keyboard?
5) What does a key signature tell you?
6) How do you find the 'relative minor' of a major scale?
7) D major has two sharps — F and C. What's the key signature of the relative minor?
8) Write out A minor in each of the three types of minor scale and label the tone and semitone gaps.
9) How many major scales are there altogether?
10) How many minor scales are there altogether?
11) Write down all the major scales in order around the circle of fifths, starting with C major.
12) Write out two common modes.
13) What's a pentatonic scale? What types of music often use pentatonic scales?
14) What are the notes in a G major pentatonic scale?
15) What's a chromatic scale? How many notes are there in a chromatic scale?
16) What's a whole tone scale?
17) What's the difference between a melodic and a harmonic interval?
18) Give the name and number of each of these intervals: a) A to C   b) B to F   c) C to B   d) D to A
19) What's a tritone?
20) What do you call chords with: a) clashing notes   b) notes that sound good together?
21) What are the two most common types of triad? Describe how you make each one.
22) What makes a 7th chord different from a triad?
23) Write down the letter symbols for these chords:
    a) G major   b) A minor   c) A minor with a major 7th   d) D diminished triad
24) Draw the scale of G major on a stave, then build a triad on each note. *(Don't forget the F sharps.)*
25) Which three chords of any major or minor scale are known as the 'primary' chords?
26) Write out the notes of the three primary chords in C major, G major and D major.
27) Where do the root, third and fifth go in: a) a first inversion chord   b) a second inversion chord?
28) Are these chords in root position, first inversion, second inversion or third inversion?
    a) 6/4   b) C/E   c) IVa   d) 6/4/2
29) Name and describe four different chord figurations.
30) What's the difference between a 'diatonic' decoration and a 'chromatic' decoration?
31) Explain the following terms: a) auxiliary note   b) passing note   c) appoggiatura
32) What is a musical phrase and what job does a cadence do in a phrase?
33) How many chords make up a cadence?
34) Write down the four different types of cadence and which chords you can use to make each one.
35) What do you call it when a piece in a minor key ends on a major chord?
36) What do people mean when they talk about the 'texture' of music?
37) Explain the difference between monophonic music, homophonic music and polyphonic music.

Common Melodic Devices

Melodic devices are methods that composers use to construct melodies.
You need a few good technical words to describe them — like conjunct, disjunct, triadic and scalic.

Melodies can be Conjunct or Disjunct

1) Conjunct (or stepwise) melodies move mainly by step — notes that are a tone or a semitone apart.

2) The melody doesn't jump around, so it sounds quite smooth.
   This example shows a conjunct melody:

This extract's from 'The Silver Swan' by Orlando Gibbons.

3) Disjunct melodies move using a lot of jumps — notes that are more than a major 2nd (a tone) apart.

4) The melody sounds quite spiky as it jumps around a lot.

5) Disjunct melodies are harder to sing or play than conjunct ones.
   This example shows a disjunct melody:

This one's from 'Nessun Dorma' by Puccini.

6) The distance between the lowest and highest notes in any melody is called the range (or compass).

Triadic Melodies Use the Notes of a Triad

1) Triads are chords made up of two intervals of a third on top of each other — so triadic melodies usually move between the notes of a triad. (There's more on triads on page 35.)

2) For example, a C major triad is made up of the notes C, E and G. There's a major third between C and E, a minor third between E and G and a perfect fifth between C and G. There's more on intervals on pages 28-29.

3) This example shows a triadic melody:

This extract is from the first movement of Haydn's Trumpet Concerto.

Scalic Melodies Use the Notes of a Scale

1) A scalic melody moves up and down using the notes of a scale.

2) Scalic melodies are similar to conjunct melodies, but they can only move to the next note in the scale. Conjunct melodies can have a few little jumps in them.

3) Like conjunct melodies, scalic melodies sound quite smooth. Here's an example of a scalic melody (it's also from the first movement of Haydn's Trumpet Concerto):

Some melodies contain all of these melodic devices...

These different types of melody are pretty easy to spot if you have the music in front of you, but it's a bit harder if you're listening to them. Listen out for them in all types of music and practise identifying them.

Common Melodic Devices

Call and response is used a lot in blues, rock and pop, as well as African and Indian music
— so it's important that you know what it is. It's used in both instrumental and vocal music.

Call and Response is Like a Musical Conversation

1) Call and response is a bit like question and answer. It takes place either between
   two groups of musicians, or between a leader and the rest of the group.

2) One group (or the leader) plays or sings a short phrase. This is the call.
   It's then answered by the other group. This is the response.

3) The call ends in a way that makes you feel a response is coming
   — e.g. it might finish with an imperfect cadence (see page 43).

4) Call and response is very popular in pop and blues music. Often the lead singer
   will sing the call and the backing singers will sing the response.

In a 12-bar blues structure (see p.136), the usual pattern of a call and response would be A, A1, B:

A is the call (4 bars)

A1 is the call repeated
with slight variations (4 bars)

B is the response (4 bars).

4 bars	4 bars	4 bars
A — CALL	A1 — CALL WITH VARIATION	B — RESPONSE

To make things more complicated,
sections A and B can have a 2-bar
call and response of their own:

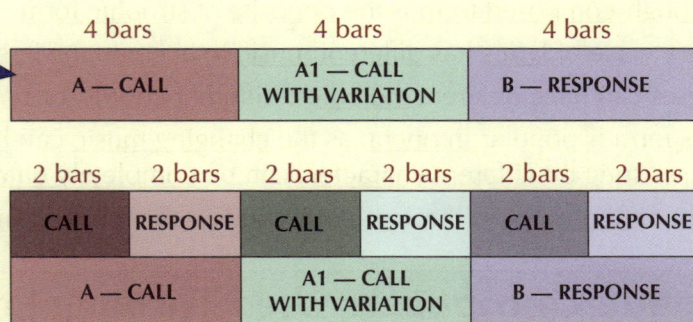

2 bars	2 bars	2 bars	2 bars	2 bars	2 bars
CALL	RESPONSE	CALL	RESPONSE	CALL	RESPONSE
A — CALL		A1 — CALL WITH VARIATION		B — RESPONSE	

Indian and African Music Use Call and Response

1) In Indian music, call and response is usually used in instrumental music. One musician
   will play a phrase and it'll either be repeated or improvised upon by another musician.

2) African music uses call and response in religious ceremonies and community events.
   The leader will sing first and the congregation will respond.

3) Call and response is also used in African drumming music (see p.111-113).
   The master drummer plays a call and the rest of the drummers play an answering phrase.

Some Melodies Form an Arch Shape

1) If a melody finishes in the same way it started, then the tune has an arch shape.

2) The simplest example of this is ABA — where the first section is the same as the last section
   of the piece. This is extended in some pieces to ABCBA, or even ABCDCBA.

3) This gives a symmetrical melody because
   the sections are mirrored. It makes the
   whole piece feel more balanced.

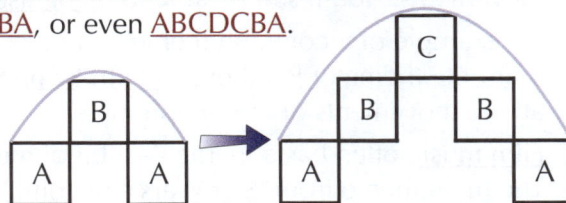

Call and response is used in a lot of music...

EXAM TIP

... so make sure you can spot it if it comes up in the listening exam — remember to listen out for
it in both instrumental and vocal music. Keep your ears pricked for arch-shaped melodies too.

Common Forms

Form or structure is the way a piece of music is organised as a whole. Strophic form, through-composed form and da capo arias are all song structures. Cyclic form is found in large works like symphonies.

In **Strophic Form** Each **Verse** has the **Same Tune**

1) In strophic form, the same section of music is repeated over and over again with virtually no changes.
2) Strophic form is used in Classical, folk, blues and pop music.
3) In strophic songs, the music for each verse is the same, but the lyrics change in every verse. Hymns are a good example of this.
4) Strophic form can be thought of like this: A, A1, A2, A3, etc. — the same section is repeated but with a small change (the lyrics).
5) The first part of Led Zeppelin's 'Stairway to Heaven' is in strophic form.

In **Through-Composed Form** Each **Verse** is **Different**

1) Through-composed form is the opposite of strophic form — the music changes in every verse.
2) Every verse of lyrics has different music to accompany it, so there's no repetition.
3) Verses can have different melodies, different chords, or both.
4) This form is popular in opera, as the changing music can be used to tell stories. Verses sung by different characters can be completely different.
5) A lot of film music is through-composed — the music changes to reflect what's happening on-screen.

'Bohemian Rhapsody' by Queen is a through-composed pop song.

Baroque Composers Used **Ternary Form** in **Arias**

1) An aria is a solo song form that appeared in operas.
2) Arias from the Baroque period (1600-1750) are often in ternary form (see p.82). Arias like this are called 'da capo arias'. Handel wrote lots of these.

After repeating Section A and Section B you come to the instruction da capo al fine. It means "go back to the beginning and play to where it says fine". The fine is at the end of Section A. That's where the piece finishes.

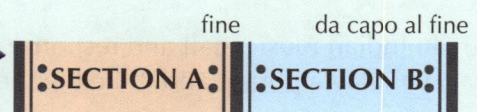

fine   da capo al fine

║: SECTION A :║ ║: SECTION B :║

Works in **Cyclic Form** Have a **Common Theme**

1) Pieces in cyclic form have common themes in all the movements. These themes link the movements together.
2) Big works like sonatas, symphonies and concertos are sometimes in cyclic form.
3) The linking themes vary in different ways, e.g. they might be played on different instruments, played faster or slower, or played in a different key in different movements. You'll still be able to recognise them though.
4) An example of a common theme in a piece in cyclic form is the four-note theme of Beethoven's Fifth Symphony. It appears in all the movements of the symphony.
5) Film music often has a theme — a bit of melody that keeps popping up throughout the film. The main theme from 'Star Wars®' by John Williams is really easy to recognise.

Don't mind me — I'm just passing through...

Make sure you're completely sorted with the definitions and proper names of all these forms.
Have a listen to the suggested pieces, and check you can spot the features of the forms they're written in.

Common Forms

Continuo and ground bass are both types of bass part. A cadenza is played by a soloist.

A **Continuo** is a **Bass Part**

1) A continuo (or basso continuo) is a continuous bass part. Most music written in the Baroque period has a continuo that the harmony of the whole piece is based on. They are a feature of both the solo concerto (see p.86) and the concerto grosso (see p.87).

2) The continuo can be played by more than one instrument, but at least one of the continuo group must be able to play chords (e.g. a harpsichord, organ, lute, harp, etc.). A cello, double bass or bassoon could also be used. The most common combination was a harpsichord and a cello.

3) Continuo parts were usually written using a type of notation called figured bass. Only the bass notes were written on the stave, but numbers underneath the notes told the performers which chords to play. The continuo players would then improvise using the notes of the chord.

4) If there weren't any numbers written, the chord would be a normal triad (the root, the third and the fifth). A 4 meant play a fourth instead of the third, and a 6 meant play a sixth instead of the fifth. A 7 meant that a 7th should be added to the chord.

means

Some versions of Handel's Water Music still have the continuo written in figured bass.

5) The improvisation is called a realization — the performer would 'realize' a continuo part.

Ground Bass Pieces Have **Repetition AND Variety**

1) A ground bass is a repeated bass part that's usually four or eight bars long. It can be played by the left hand on a harpsichord or piano, or by the cello and double bass in a chamber orchestra. A ground bass is a type of ostinato — a short pattern of notes repeated throughout a piece of music.

2) The tune is played over the ground bass part. First you hear the main tune, then a load of variations. The variations are played as one continuous piece — there are no gaps between them.

3) The ground bass part can be varied too. You change the starting note but keep the pattern the same.

First time round, the ground bass tune starts on C.   *Later on you get the same tune starting on G.*

4) The ground bass piece gets more and more complex as it goes on. It can be developed by adding extra, decorative notes to the melody, using more advanced harmonies and adding more instruments to give a richer texture.

A **Cadenza** is Where a **Soloist** can **Show Off**

1) A cadenza is a bit of music that's played by a soloist, usually in the middle of a concerto.

2) Almost all concertos have a cadenza — it allows the soloist to show off their technique.

3) Cadenzas started out as improvisations on the main themes of a piece, but now most of them are written out by the composer. However, different musicians will interpret the cadenza in their own way.

SUGGESTED LISTENING

This page is done — better continuo onto the next one...

Listen to a couple of different performances of Haydn's Trumpet Concerto in E♭ major — the cadenzas will sound different in each one, even though the soloists are playing the same notes.

Popular Song Forms

It's not just <u>Classical</u> music that follows set <u>structures</u> — <u>pop songs</u> do as well.

Pop Songs Usually Have an Intro

Pop tunes almost always start with an <u>intro</u>. It does <u>two jobs</u>:

- It often uses the best bit from the rest of the song to <u>set the mood</u>.
- It grabs people's <u>attention</u> and makes them <u>sit up and listen</u>.

Most Pop Songs Have a Verse-Chorus Structure

<u>After</u> the intro, the structure of most pop songs goes <u>verse-chorus-verse-chorus</u>.

- All the verses usually have the <u>same tune</u>, but the <u>lyrics change</u> for each verse.
- The chorus has a <u>different tune</u> from the verses, usually quite a catchy one. The lyrics and tune of the chorus <u>don't change</u>.
- In a lot of songs the verse and chorus are both <u>8 or 16 bars long</u>.

'Livin' on a Prayer' by Bon Jovi has a verse-chorus structure.

The old verse-chorus thing can get repetitive. To avoid this most songs have a <u>middle 8</u>, or <u>bridge</u>, that sounds different. It's an <u>8-bar section</u> in the <u>middle</u> of the song with <u>new chords</u>, <u>new lyrics</u> and a whole <u>new feel</u>.

The song ends with a <u>coda</u> or <u>outro</u> that's <u>different</u> to the verse and the chorus. You can use the coda for a <u>big finish</u> or to <u>fade out gradually</u>.

Pop Songs Can Have Other Structures Too

For example:

CALL AND RESPONSE
This has <u>two bits</u> to it. <u>Part 1</u> is the call — it asks a musical <u>question</u>. <u>Part 2</u>, the response, responds with an <u>answer</u> (p.55).

RIFF
A <u>riff</u> is a <u>short section</u> of music that's <u>repeated</u> over and over again (a bit like an <u>ostinato</u> — see p.84). Riffs can be used to build up a <u>whole song</u>. <u>Each part</u>, e.g. the drums or bass guitar, has its own riff. All the riffs <u>fit together</u> to make one section of the music. They often <u>change</u> for the <u>chorus</u>.

'Wind Beneath my Wings' by Bette Midler is a pop ballad.

BALLADS
These are songs that tell <u>stories</u>. Each verse usually has the <u>same rhythm</u> and <u>same tune</u>.

32-BAR SONG FORM
This breaks down into <u>four 8-bar sections</u>. Sections 1, 2 and 4 all have the <u>same melody</u>, but may have different lyrics. Section 3 has a <u>contrasting melody</u>, making an AABA structure. The 32 bars may be repeated. The song 'Somewhere Over the Rainbow' from the film 'The Wizard of Oz' has this form.

Verse — chorus — verse — chorus — tea break — chorus...

Turn on the radio and listen to a pop song — see if you can identify some of the things covered on this page. Verses and choruses are fairly easy to identify, but it could be trickier to spot a bridge or a 32-bar song form.

Improvisation

Improvisation isn't just making up whatever you like. There's actually quite a bit more to it.

Lots of Jazz is Improvised

1) Improvisation is where a performer makes up music on the spot.
There's often an improvised solo section in jazz pieces.

2) The improvisations aren't totally random though — the soloist will be told which
chords to improvise over. This is often a 12-bar blues chord pattern (see p.136).
Some improvisations use a mode (see page 27) instead of a chord pattern.

3) The soloist will know which notes are in each chord, but sometimes they'll play clashing notes to
keep the solo interesting. If they're using a mode, they'll use the notes of the mode in their solo.

4) They might also use bits of the main melody of the piece as a starting point,
then develop it into a much more complex phrase.

5) Some performers pinch bits of other tunes in their solos
— it keeps the audience entertained when they spot them.

6) Rock songs will often include an improvised guitar solo — e.g. Queen's 'We Will Rock You'.

Improvisation Uses Lots of Different Techniques

1) Performers use lots of different musical ideas and techniques in their solos
— it gives them a chance to show off.

2) Improvisations will often be syncopated to make them feel 'jazzy'.
Triplets and dotted rhythms can help the melodies flow (see p.17).

3) Ornaments (like passing notes and appoggiaturas) make the melodies more exciting
(see p.41). Blue notes (see p.136) are often used in jazz improvisations.

4) A wide range of dynamics (see p.19) and accents (see p.20) also help keep the solos interesting.

Indian Music Uses Improvisation Too

1) Improvisation isn't just used in Western music —
it's an important part of Indian music as well (see p.104-106).

2) The improvisations are based on a raga — a set of notes (usually between 5 or 8)
that are combined to create a particular mood. There are hundreds of different ragas.
Each one is named after a different time of day or season and is supposed to create an
atmosphere like the time or season it's named after.

3) Raga performances are improvised, but based on traditional melodies and rhythms.

4) These are never written down — they are passed on from generation to generation aurally (by ear).

5) The improvised melody is often played on an Indian instrument called a sitar (see p.104),
but it's sometimes performed by a singer instead. They only use the notes of the raga.

6) The melody is played over a drone — a long held-on note that provides the harmony (see p.39).

These are the notes of the rag desh, a night-time raga for the rainy season. The melody would be improvised using these notes over a drone.

I'll improvise my way through the listening exam...

In 'Dancing Men', a number of instruments have improvised solos (often the saxophone, trombone and drums). Have a listen to recordings of this piece by Buddy Rich, Simon Phillips and Dennis Chambers — you'll notice that the solos are completely different each time.

Warm-up and Exam Questions

Warm-up Questions

1) Describe each of the following melody structures:

      Conjunct   **Disjunct**   **Triadic**   **Scalic**

2) What is through-composed form?

3) What is a ground bass, and what instruments often play these parts?

4) Give two examples of types of music where improvisation is used.

Exam Question

If there are bits you get stuck on in this question, reread the last few pages, then try again.

Play the extract **four** times, leaving a short pause between each playing.

Track 28

a) i) The key signature of the extract is shown below.
What key is the extract in?

[1 mark]

  ii) What is the interval between the notes shown on the right?
Circle your answer.

    Major third   **Minor third**   **Diminished fourth**

[1 mark]

b) At the very beginning of the extract, the singer's lines are answered by a group of instruments. What is this back-and-forth movement called?

[1 mark]

c) Which of these examples is the music that these answering instruments play?
Tick the box next to your choice.

A:

B:

[1 mark]

Exam Question

Play the extract **four** times, leaving a short pause between each playing.

Track 29

a) What musical period was this piece composed in?

....
[1 mark]

b) Name two instruments that play in the extract.

....

....
[2 marks]

c) The melody at the start of the extract is shown below.

i) Fill in the missing notes in bars 3 and 4.
The rhythm is given above the stave.

[7 marks]

ii) Which word best describes the melodic style in this excerpt?
Circle your choice from the options below.

Conjunct   **Disjunct**   **Triadic**

[1 mark]

d) What type of bass part is used in this piece?

....
[1 mark]

e) Give one instrument that plays the bass part.

....
[1 mark]

Revision Summary for Section Four

*You need to know a lot more about melodies and structures than being able to whistle a few tunes —
you'll need to be familiar with all the terms used in this section so you can use them when you need to
describe melodies and musical structures in the exam. If you're not sure about any, go back and have
another look over the section. And then to really cement this knowledge into your head, go through
these questions until you can answer them without looking back.*

1) Explain what is meant by each of the following words that are used to describe melodies:
   a) conjunct,
   b) disjunct,
   c) triadic,
   d) scalic.
2) What is call and response?
3) Name two types of music that use call and response.
4) Explain what is meant by an arch-shaped melody.
5) What's the difference between strophic and through-composed form?
6) Give an example of a type of music that's often written in through-composed form,
   and explain why this form is used.
7) What's a da capo aria?
8) What is cyclic form?
9) What is basso continuo?
10) Explain how figured bass works.
11) Describe the structure of a ground bass piece.
12) What's a cadenza?
13) Why do pop songs have an introduction?
14) Describe verse-chorus structure.
15) What is a bridge?
16) What is a riff?
17) What is the structure of a song in 32-bar form?
18) Name two structures (other than 32-bar form) often used in pop songs.
19) Name three things performers can do to keep improvised solos interesting.

Brass Instruments

You probably know a lot about <u>your</u> instrument. It's also a good idea to know about the instruments other people play so you can understand what they're up to. <u>Brass</u> first.

Brass Instruments are All Made of Metal

1) Brass instruments include <u>horns</u>, <u>trumpets</u>, <u>cornets</u>, <u>trombones</u> and <u>tubas</u>.

2) They're all basically a length of <u>hollow metal tubing</u> with a <u>mouthpiece</u> (the bit you blow into) at one end and a <u>funnel shape</u> (the <u>bell</u>) at the other.

3) The different <u>shapes</u> and <u>sizes</u> of these parts gives each brass instrument a different tone and character.

4) Brass instruments often play <u>fanfares</u> (short musical <u>flourishes</u>) in orchestral pieces. They're most commonly played on the <u>trumpet</u>, and can be accompanied by <u>percussion</u>. A fanfare might also be played as part of a <u>ceremony</u>.

trumpet

French horn

trombone

tuba

You Get a Noise by 'Buzzing' Your Lips

1) To <u>make a sound</u> on a brass instrument, you have to make the air <u>vibrate</u> down the tube.

2) You do it by 'buzzing' your lips into the <u>mouthpiece</u>. You <u>squeeze</u> your lips together, then <u>blow</u> through a tiny gap so you get a <u>buzzing noise</u>.

3) You have to squeeze your lips together <u>tighter</u> to get <u>higher notes</u>.

4) Notes can be <u>slurred</u> (played together <u>smoothly</u>) or <u>tongued</u> (you use your tongue to <u>separate</u> the notes).

Brass Instruments Use Slides and Valves to Change Pitch

1) Squeezing your lips only gets a <u>limited range</u> of notes. To get a decent range, brass instruments use <u>slides</u> (like on a trombone) or <u>valves</u> (like on a trumpet).

2) The <u>slide</u> on a trombone is the <u>U-shaped tube</u> that moves in and out of the main tube. Moving it <u>out</u> makes the tube <u>longer</u> so you get a <u>lower</u> note. Moving it in makes the tube <u>shorter</u> so you get a <u>higher</u> note.

3) <u>Horns</u>, <u>trumpets</u> and <u>cornets</u> use three buttons connected to <u>valves</u>. The valves <u>open</u> and <u>close</u> different sections of the tube to make it <u>longer</u> or <u>shorter</u>. Pressing down the buttons in <u>different combinations</u> gives you all the notes you need.

Brass Players use Mutes to Change the Tone

1) A <u>mute</u> is a kind of <u>bung</u> that's put in the <u>bell</u> of a brass instrument. It's used to make the instrument play more <u>quietly</u> and change the <u>tone</u>. You wouldn't usually use one all the way through a piece — just for a <u>short section</u>.

2) <u>Different shapes</u> and <u>sizes</u> of mute change the tone in different ways, e.g. the <u>wah-wah</u> mute gives the instrument a wah-wah sound.

EXAM TIP

Brass instruments aren't always made of brass...

If you get brass in a listening test and need to say what instrument it is, remember that bigger instruments generally play lower notes and smaller instruments usually play higher notes.

Woodwind Instruments

Some people get woodwind and brass muddled up. If you're one of them, learn the difference.

Woodwind Instruments Used to be Made of Wood

Woodwind instruments got their name because they all use air — wind — to make a sound and once upon a time were all made of wood. Nowadays some are still made of wood. Others are made of plastic or metal. These are the main ones:

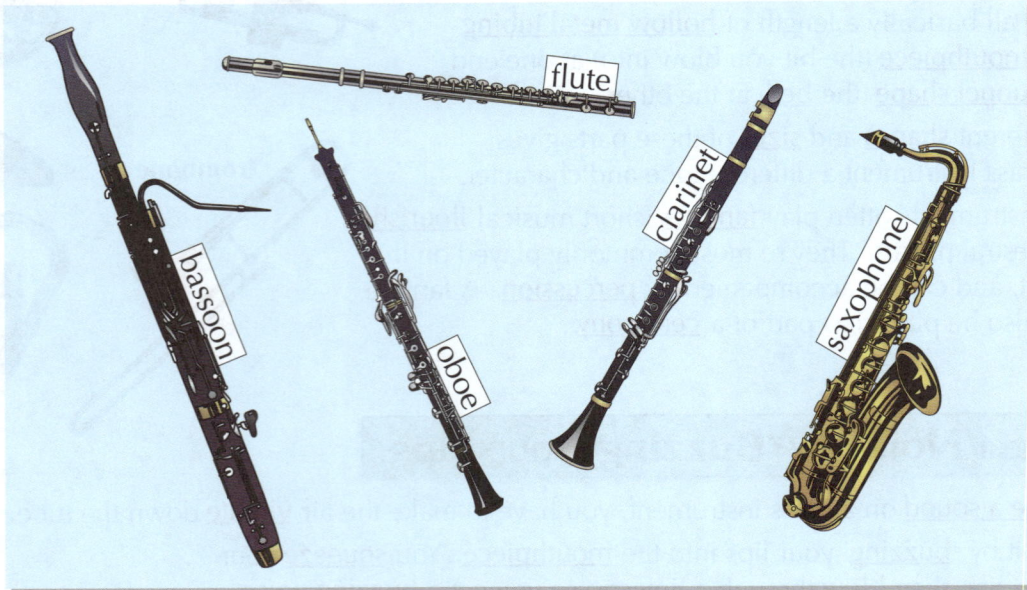

Woodwind Instruments Make Sound in Different Ways

To get a sound from a wind instrument, you have to make the air in its tube vibrate. There are three different ways woodwind instruments do this:

1) Edge-tone instruments — flutes and piccolos. Air is blown across an oval-shaped hole. The edge of the hole splits the air. This makes it vibrate down the instrument and make the sound.

2) Single-reed instruments — clarinets and saxophones. Air is blown down a mouthpiece which has a reed (a thin slice of wood/reed/plastic) clamped to it. The reed vibrates, making the air in the instrument vibrate, and creating the sound.

3) Double-reed instruments — oboes and bassoons. The air passes between two reeds, tightly bound together and squeezed between the lips. The reeds vibrate and you get a sound.

Like brass instruments, woodwind instruments can be slurred or tongued as well.

Different Notes are Made by Opening and Closing Holes

1) Wind instruments are covered in keys, springs and levers (or just holes for some instruments). These operate little pads that close and open holes down the instrument.

2) Opening and closing holes effectively makes the instrument longer or shorter. The shorter the tube, the higher the note. The longer the tube, the lower the note.

I can't see the woodwind for the clarinets...

Flutes and saxophones are made of metal but they're still woodwind instruments. If you're still confused, remember that woodwind instruments sound more breathy than brass instruments.

Orchestral Strings

Orchestral strings are the <u>heart</u> of the orchestra — or so string players would have you believe.

The **Double Bass**, **Cello**, **Viola**
and **Violin** are Very Alike

These are all <u>made</u> and played in a <u>similar way</u>.
The main differences are the <u>size</u> and <u>pitch</u>.

The <u>bigger</u> the instrument is, the <u>lower</u> the sounds
it makes. So the double bass plays the lowest
notes and the violin plays the highest.

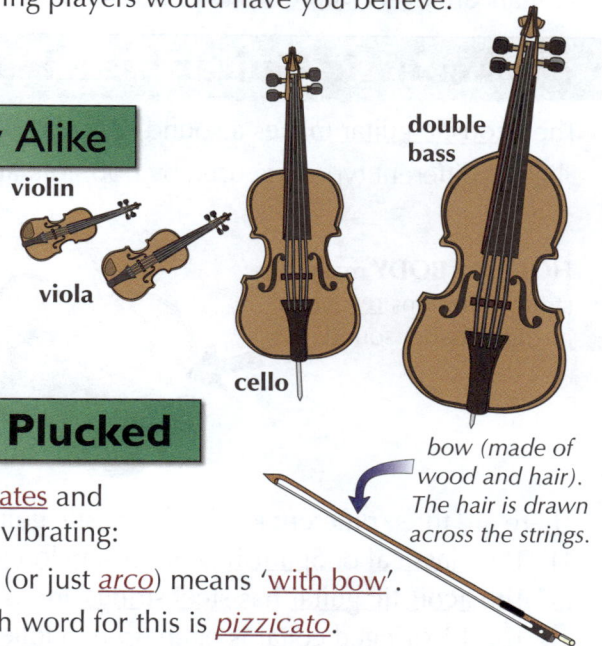

violin

viola

cello

double
bass

bow (made of
wood and hair).
The hair is drawn
across the strings.

Stringed Instruments can be **Bowed** or **Plucked**

When the <u>strings vibrate</u>, the air inside the instrument <u>vibrates</u> and
amplifies the <u>sound</u>. There are two ways to get the strings vibrating:

1) <u>Bowing</u> — drawing a bow across the string. *Con arco* (or just *arco*) means '<u>with bow</u>'.

2) <u>Plucking</u> the string with the tip of your finger. The posh word for this is *pizzicato*.

The **Strings** are 'Stopped' to Make **Different Notes**

1) You can get an "<u>open note</u>" just by plucking or bowing one of the four strings.

2) To get all the other notes, you have to change the <u>length</u> of the strings.
   You do this by <u>pressing down</u> with your finger. It's called <u>stopping</u>.

3) If you stop a string <u>close to the bridge</u>, the string's short and you get a <u>high</u> note.

4) If you stop a string <u>further away</u> from the bridge, the string's longer and you get a <u>lower</u> note.

5) <u>Double-stopping</u> is when <u>two</u> notes are played at the same time. Both strings are <u>pressed</u> (not open).

6) If you just <u>touch</u> a string <u>lightly</u> at certain points (instead of stopping), you
   can produce a series of <u>higher</u>, <u>fainter-sounding notes</u> called <u>harmonics</u>.

You Can Get **Very Varied** Effects with Stringed Instruments

1) **Tremolo**   The bow's moved <u>back and forth</u> really <u>quickly</u>. This makes the notes
   sort of trembly. It's a great effect for making music sound <u>spooky</u> and <u>dramatic</u>.

2) **Col legno**   The <u>wood</u> of the bow (instead of the hair) is tapped on the strings.
   This makes an <u>eerie</u>, <u>scraping</u> sound.

3) **Con sordino**   A <u>mute</u> is put over the <u>bridge</u> (the piece of wood that supports the
   strings). It makes the strings sound <u>distant</u> and <u>soft</u>. Mutes are made of <u>wood</u>, <u>rubber</u> or <u>metal</u>.

4) **Vibrato**   By <u>wobbling</u> the finger used to stop a string, a player varies the <u>pitch</u> slightly,
   creating a <u>rich tone</u>. This technique is also used on the <u>guitar</u> (see next page).

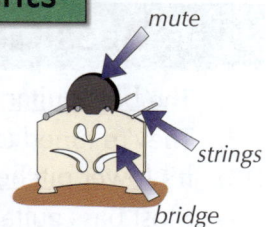

mute

strings

bridge

The **Harp** is Different...

1) The harp's <u>always plucked</u> — not bowed.

2) Most have <u>47</u> strings. Plucking each string in order on a
   concert harp is like playing up the <u>white notes</u> on a piano.

3) It has <u>seven pedals</u>. Pressing and releasing these lets you play <u>sharp</u> and <u>flat</u> notes.

4) You can play <u>one</u> note at a time, or play <u>chords</u> by plucking a few strings together.

EXAM TIP

Don't stop now, there are lots more instruments to come...

Make sure you learn the different string effects — you might need to identify them in the exam.

66

Guitars

Guitars are everywhere so it's best to know a bit about how they work.

An **Acoustic Guitar** has a **Hollow Body**

The acoustic guitar makes a sound the same way as the orchestral strings — by vibrating air in its belly. Slightly different types are used by pop, folk and classical guitarists, but the basic design is similar.

HOLLOW BODY makes the string vibrations resonate, giving a louder sound.

STRINGS tuned to the notes E(low)-A-D-G-B-E(high). Low E is the string nearest your head as you're playing. Played with fingers or a plectrum.

FRETS (the little metal strips on the fingerboard/neck) help the player find the correct finger position for different notes.

acoustic guitar

There are three different kinds of acoustic guitar:
1) The classical or Spanish guitar has nylon strings (the thickest three are covered in fine wire).
2) The acoustic guitar has steel strings and is used mainly in pop and folk music.
3) The 12-stringed guitar is often used in folk music. There are two of each string, giving a 'thicker' sound which works well for accompanying singing.

Some guitar music is written in tablature (tab for short) — the numbers tell guitarists which frets to place their fingers at for each string.

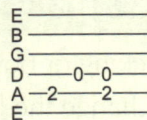

```
E
B
G
D-----0-0
A--2-----2
E
```

This means play the 2nd fret on the A string, then the open D string, then both at the same time.

Electric Guitars Use an Amplifier and a Loudspeaker

electric guitar

1) An electric guitar has six strings, just like an acoustic guitar, and is played in a similar way.
2) The main difference is that an electric guitar has a solid body. The sound's made louder electronically, using an amplifier and a loudspeaker.
3) A combo (short for combination) is an amplifier and loudspeaker 'all in one'.

The **Bass Guitar** has **Four Strings**

1) The bass guitar works like a guitar except it usually has four strings, not six.
2) They're tuned to the notes E-A-D-G (from lowest note to highest).
3) It's lower pitched than other guitars because it has thicker and longer strings.
4) Most bass guitars have frets, but there are some (imaginatively named fretless basses) that don't.

Like ordinary guitars, you can get electric or acoustic basses.

Guitar Strings are **Picked** or **Strummed**

1) Plucking one string at a time is called picking. Classical and lead guitarists pick the notes of a melody. Bass guitarists almost always pick out the individual notes of a bass line. They hardly ever strum.
2) Playing two or more strings at a time in a sweeping movement is called strumming. It's how chords are usually played. Pop and folk guitarists tend to play accompaniments rather than tunes, so they do more strumming than picking.
3) A plectrum is a small, flat piece of plastic that guitarists can use to pluck or strum with.
4) 'Hammer-on' and 'pull-off' are techniques that allow a guitarist to play notes in quick succession — they create a smoother, more legato sound than picking.

The guitar's a really popular instrument...
Make sure you learn the different types of guitar, and the proper words for the various playing techniques.

Section Five — Instruments

Keyboard Instruments

The actual <u>keyboard</u> looks much the same on most keyboard instruments, but the wires and mysterious levers <u>inside</u> vary quite a bit. That means the <u>sounds</u> they make vary too.

Harpsichords, Virginals and Clavichords Came First

harpsichord

1) Harpsichords were invented long before pianos. They're still played today but they were <u>most popular</u> in the <u>Baroque</u> and <u>early Classical</u> periods.

2) Harpsichords have quite a <u>tinny</u>, <u>string</u> sound. When you press a key a string inside is <u>plucked</u> by a lever. You can't vary the <u>strength</u> of the pluck, so you <u>can't</u> vary the <u>dynamics</u>.

3) A <u>virginal</u> is a <u>miniature</u> table-top version of a harpsichord. In the <u>sixteenth century</u>, virginals were really popular in England.

4) The <u>clavichord</u> is another early keyboard instrument. Clavichords are small and have a <u>soft</u> sound. The strings are <u>struck</u> with hammers (called "blades"), not plucked, so you can <u>vary</u> the dynamics a <u>little bit</u>.

The Most Popular Keyboard Instrument Now is the Piano

1) The piano was invented around <u>1700</u>. The <u>technology</u> is <u>more sophisticated</u> than it was in earlier keyboard instruments. When a key's pressed, a hammer hits the strings. The <u>harder</u> you hit the key, the <u>harder</u> the hammer hits the strings and the <u>louder</u> the note — there's a big range of <u>dynamics</u>.

2) Pianos have a wide range of <u>notes</u> — up to <u>seven and a half octaves</u>.

3) Pianos have <u>pedals</u> that let you change the sound in different ways.

The <u>soft</u> pedal on the left <u>mutes</u> the strings, making a softer sound.

The <u>sustain</u> pedal on the right <u>lifts</u> all the <u>dampers</u>. This lets the sound <u>ring on</u> until you release the pedal.

For more detail on the piano, have a look at page 98.

<u>Grand pianos</u> have a <u>middle pedal</u> too. This lets the player <u>choose</u> which notes to sustain. Modern pianos might have an extra mute pedal for <u>very quiet</u> practising.

Traditional Organs Use Pumped Air to Make Sound

1) The traditional organ (the <u>massive instrument</u> with hundreds of metal pipes that you see in churches and concert halls) is one of the most <u>complicated</u> instruments ever designed.

2) Sound is made by <u>blowing air</u> through sets of pipes called <u>ranks</u>. The air is pumped in by <u>hand</u>, <u>foot</u> or, on more recent organs, <u>electric pumps</u>.

3) The pipes are controlled by <u>keyboards</u> (called <u>manuals</u>) and lots of <u>pedals</u> which make a keyboard for the player's feet.

4) <u>Pressing</u> a key or pedal lets air pass through one of the pipes and play a note. <u>Longer</u> pipes make <u>lower</u> notes. <u>Shorter</u> pipes make <u>higher</u> notes.

5) Organs can play <u>different types of sound</u> by using differently designed pipes. Buttons called <u>stops</u> are used to select the different pipes. One stop might select pipes that make a <u>trumpet</u> sound, another might select a <u>flute</u> sound...

6) Modern <u>electronic organs</u> don't have pipes. Sound is produced <u>electronically</u> instead. These organs are much <u>smaller</u> and <u>cheaper</u> to build.

REVISION TIP

You've got to learn it all...

Listen to music played on each of these instruments so you know how they all sound — harpsichords have a more <u>jangly</u> tone than pianos, and organs are fairly easy to spot as well.

Percussion

A percussion instrument is anything you have to <u>hit</u> or <u>shake</u> to get a sound out of it. There are <u>two types</u>: those that play tunes are called <u>tuned percussion</u>, and the ones you just hit are <u>untuned</u>.

Tuned Percussion Can Play Different Notes

<u>XYLOPHONES</u> have <u>wooden</u> bars. The sound is '<u>woody</u>'.

<u>GLOCKENSPIEL</u> — Looks a bit like a xylophone but the bars are made of <u>metal</u>. Sounds <u>tinkly</u> and <u>bell-like</u>.

<u>CELESTA</u> — a bit like a glockenspiel except that you use a <u>keyboard</u> instead of whacking it with a hammer.

<u>TUBULAR BELLS</u> — Each of the <u>hollow steel tubes</u> plays a different note. Sounds a bit like <u>church bells</u>.

<u>TIMPANI</u> — also called <u>kettledrums</u>. The handles on the side or the foot pedal can be used to tighten or relax the skin, giving <u>different notes</u>.

<u>VIBRAPHONE</u> — This is like a <u>giant glockenspiel</u>. There are long tubes called <u>resonators</u> below the bars to make the notes <u>louder</u> and <u>richer</u>. <u>Electric fans</u> can make the notes <u>pulsate</u>, giving a warm and gentle sound.

There are Hundreds of Untuned Percussion Instruments

<u>Untuned percussion</u> includes any instrument that'll <u>make a noise</u> — but <u>can't</u> play a tune. These are the instruments that are used for <u>pure rhythm</u>. It's pretty much <u>impossible</u> to learn <u>every</u> untuned percussion instrument, but try and remember the names of these.

cymbals
bass drum
tambourine
maracas
triangle
castanets
sleigh bells
timbale
bongos
bodhrán
snare drum

Percussion instruments make different sounds depending on what you hit them with. e.g. hard wooden drumsticks, mallets, beaters (sticks with hard or soft round heads), brushes...

Remember — xylophones are wooden, glockenspiels are metal...

In a band, the drummer's job is to make a song sound like it's going somewhere and keep everyone in <u>time</u>. In an orchestra, percussion emphasises the <u>rhythm</u> of the piece and also adds <u>special effects</u> — you can imitate thunder with a drum roll on the timpani, or the crashing of waves with clashes of the cymbals.

The Voice

There are special names for male and female voices and groups of voices.

Female Singers are Soprano, Alto or Mezzo-Soprano

1) A singer with a particular type of voice is expected to be able to sing a certain range of notes.
2) The range of notes where a particular singer is most comfortable is called the tessitura. This term can also describe the most commonly used range of notes within a vocal or instrumental part of a piece.
3) A high female voice is called a soprano. The main female parts in operas are sung by sopranos.
4) A lower female voice is called an alto — short for contralto.
5) Mezzo-sopranos sing in the top part of the alto range and the bottom part of the soprano range.

Male Voices are Tenor or Bass

1) Higher male voices are called tenors.
2) Low male voices are called basses (it's pronounced "bases").
3) Baritones sing the top part of the bass range and the bottom part of the tenor range.
4) Men who sing in the female vocal range are called countertenors.
5) Some tenors, baritones and basses can push their voices higher to sing some of the same notes as a soprano. This is called falsetto singing.

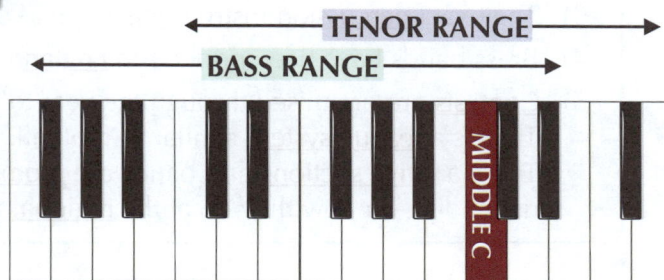

Children's Voices are Either Treble or Alto

1) A high child's voice in the same range as a soprano is called a treble.
2) A low child's voice is called an alto. They sing in exactly the same range as an adult alto.
3) Girls' voices don't change much as they get older. Boys' voices drop to a lower range when they hit puberty.

When Several Voices Sing Each Part It's a Choir

1) A choir is a group of singers. Each part is performed by more than one singer.
2) A mixed voice choir has sopranos, altos, tenors and basses (SATB for short).
3) An all-male choir has trebles, altos, tenors and basses — a treble has the same range as a soprano, so it's basically SATB.
4) A male voice choir is slightly different — it tends to have two groups of tenors, as well as baritones and basses (TTBB for short), with no higher parts.
5) An all-female choir has two groups of sopranos and two groups of altos (SSAA for short).
6) When a choir sings without an instrumental accompaniment, this is known as 'a cappella'.
7) Music written for a choir is called choral music.

These are the names for smaller groups:
2 singers = a **duet**
3 singers = a **trio**
4 singers = a **quartet**
5 singers = a **quintet**
6 singers = a **sextet**

No excuses — get on and learn all the voices...

The different voices don't just sound different in pitch — they've got different characters too, e.g. sopranos usually sound very clear and glassy, and basses sound more rich and booming.

Wind, Brass and Jazz Bands

In your listening exam, you'll get marks for saying what type of <u>group</u> (or <u>ensemble</u>) is playing. <u>Wind</u>, <u>jazz</u> and <u>brass</u> bands can sound quite <u>similar</u>, so make sure you know the differences.

Wind Bands have Woodwind, Brass and Percussion

1) Wind bands are <u>largish groups</u>, made up of 'wind' instruments — woodwind and brass — and percussion instruments.
2) There's <u>no string section</u>. If there was it would be an orchestra...
3) <u>Military bands</u> are wind bands. They tend to play <u>marches</u> — pieces with a <u>regular rhythm</u> (usually $\frac{4}{4}$ or $\frac{2}{4}$ time) that can be marched to.

Brass Bands have Brass and Percussion

1) A brass band is a group of <u>brass</u> and <u>percussion</u> instruments.
2) A typical brass band would have <u>cornets</u>, <u>flugelhorns</u>, <u>tenor</u> and <u>baritone horns</u>, <u>tenor</u> and <u>bass trombones</u>, <u>euphoniums</u> and <u>tubas</u>.
3) The exact <u>percussion instruments</u> depend on the piece being played.
4) Brass bands have been popular in <u>England</u> for <u>years</u>.
5) <u>Contests</u> are organised through the year to find out which bands are 'best'. There's a <u>league system</u> similar to football. The divisions are called <u>sections</u>. There are <u>five sections</u> and bands are <u>promoted</u> and <u>demoted</u> each year depending on how they do at the <u>regional</u> and <u>national</u> contests.

Jazz Bands are Quite Varied

1) Jazz bands have <u>no fixed set of instruments</u>.
2) Small jazz groups are known as <u>combos</u>. A typical combo might include a <u>trumpet</u>, <u>trombone</u>, <u>clarinet</u>, <u>saxophone</u>, <u>piano</u>, <u>banjo</u>, <u>double bass</u> and <u>drum kit</u> — but there's no fixed rule. Combos play in small venues like <u>clubs</u> and <u>bars</u>.
3) Larger jazz bands are known as <u>big bands</u> or <u>swing bands</u>. Instruments are doubled and tripled up so you get a <u>much bigger sound</u>. Big bands were really popular in the <u>1930s</u> and <u>1940s</u>. They played live at <u>dance halls</u>.
4) A large jazz band with a string section is called a <u>jazz orchestra</u>.

Jazz Bands have a Rhythm Section and a Front Line

In a jazz band, players are either in the <u>rhythm section</u> or the <u>front line</u>.

1) The <u>rhythm section</u> is the instruments responsible for <u>keeping the beat</u> and <u>adding the harmony parts</u>. The rhythm section's usually made up of the <u>drum kit</u> with a <u>double</u> or <u>electric bass</u>, <u>electric guitar</u> and <u>piano</u>.
2) The instruments that <u>play the melody</u> are the <u>front line</u>. This is usually <u>clarinets</u>, <u>saxophones</u> and <u>trumpets</u>, but could also be guitar or violin.

Keep at it — there are more groups to come...

You need to know the differences between wind, brass and jazz bands — if you reckon you've got it sorted, test yourself by covering up the page and writing down the instruments that play in each type of band.

Chamber Music

Chamber music is music composed for <u>small groups</u> and it's pretty formal stuff.

Chamber Music was Originally 'Home Entertainment'

1) '<u>Chamber</u>' is an old word for a room in a posh building like a palace or a mansion.

2) <u>Rich people</u> could afford to <u>pay musicians</u> to come and play in their 'chambers'. Musical families could play the music for themselves. The music written for these private performances is called <u>chamber music</u>.

3) Nowadays, you're more likely to hear chamber music in a <u>concert hall</u> or on a <u>CD</u> than live at someone's house. Let's face it — most people haven't got the cash to hire musicians for the evening, and they can download any music they want to listen to.

Chamber Music is Played by Small Groups

1) The rooms where musicians came to play were nice and <u>big</u> — but <u>not enormous</u>. Limited space meant that chamber music was written for a <u>small number</u> of musicians — between <u>two</u> and <u>eight</u>.

2) There's a <u>name</u> for each size of group:

Duet = two players
Trio = three players
Quartet = four players
Quintet = five players
Sextet = six players
Septet = seven players
Octet = eight players

Have a look at the names for singing groups on p.69 — they're much the same.

These instruments make up a 'piano trio' — see below.

3) With so <u>few people</u> in chamber groups, you <u>don't</u> need a conductor. Instead, one of the players <u>leads</u>. The others have to <u>watch</u> and <u>listen</u> carefully, to make sure the <u>timing</u>, <u>dynamics</u> and <u>interpretation</u> are right.

4) Each part in the music is played by <u>just one person</u>.

Some Chamber Groups are Extra-Popular with Composers

Chamber music is written <u>more often</u> for some instrumental groups than others.
These are some of the most <u>popular</u> types of chamber group:

String trio	— violin, viola, cello
String quartet	— first violin, second violin, viola, cello
Piano trio	— piano, violin, cello (<u>not</u> three pianos)
Clarinet quintet	— clarinet, first violin, second violin, viola, cello (<u>not</u> five clarinets)
Wind quintet	— usually flute, oboe, clarinet, horn and bassoon

Chamber groups are small...

Learn the instruments that play in all the different chamber groups. Keep a special eye out for the piano trio and clarinet quintet — they're not what you'd expect. And finally, don't forget there's no conductor.

The Orchestra

If you go to a classical concert, more often than not there'll be an <u>orchestra</u> up there on stage. Loads and loads of classical music has been written for orchestras.

A **Modern Orchestra** has **Four** Sections

If you go and see a <u>modern symphony orchestra</u>, it'll have <u>four sections</u> of instruments — strings (p.65), woodwind (p.64), brass (p.63) and percussion (p.68). The strings, woodwind, brass and percussion always sit in the <u>same places</u>.

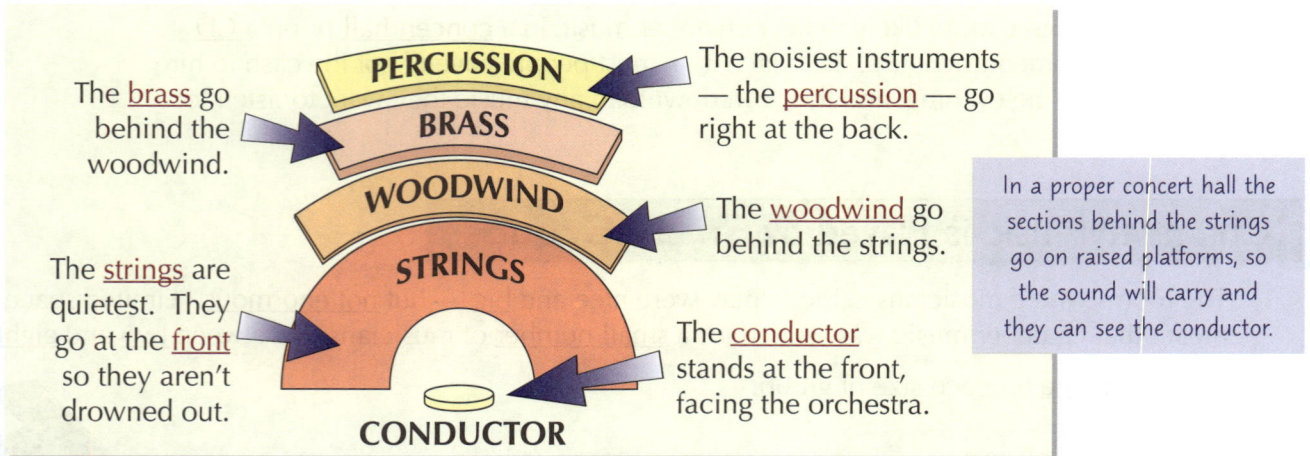

The <u>brass</u> go behind the woodwind.

PERCUSSION
BRASS
WOODWIND
STRINGS
CONDUCTOR

The noisiest instruments — the <u>percussion</u> — go right at the back.

The <u>woodwind</u> go behind the strings.

In a proper concert hall the sections behind the strings go on raised platforms, so the sound will carry and they can see the conductor.

The <u>strings</u> are quietest. They go at the <u>front</u> so they aren't drowned out.

The <u>conductor</u> stands at the front, facing the orchestra.

The **Conductor** has a **Complete Overview**

1) The conductor has a <u>score</u> — a version of the piece with <u>all the parts</u>. The <u>parts</u> are arranged in a <u>standard order</u>, one on top of the other, so that it's easy to see what any part is doing at any time. Woodwind parts are written at the <u>top</u>, followed by brass, percussion, and strings at the <u>bottom</u>.

2) The conductor <u>controls the tempo</u> by beating time with their hands, or a <u>baton</u> — a pointy white stick that's easy to see. There's a different way of beating time for each <u>time signature</u>.

3) The conductor '<u>cues in</u>' musicians — especially helpful for <u>brass</u> and <u>percussion</u>, who sometimes don't play anything for <u>hundreds of bars</u>, then suddenly have to play a <u>really loud, important bit</u>.

4) The conductor <u>interprets</u> the music. A conductor can decide whether to play one bit <u>louder</u> than another, whether to play a section in a <u>moody</u> or a <u>magical</u> way, and whether to make a piece sound very <u>smooth</u> or very <u>edgy</u>. They're a bit like a <u>film director</u> deciding the best way to <u>tell a story</u>.

An **Orchestra** is Any **Large Group with Strings**

<u>Symphony orchestras</u> (above) are the biggest type of orchestra. There are <u>other</u> smaller kinds too:

1) <u>String orchestra</u> — an orchestra with <u>stringed instruments</u> only.
2) <u>Chamber orchestra</u> — a <u>mini-orchestra</u>. It has a small string section, a wind and brass section with <u>one or two</u> of each instrument (but <u>no</u> tubas or trombones) and a small percussion section.
3) <u>Jazz orchestra</u> — a largish jazz group with an added string section.

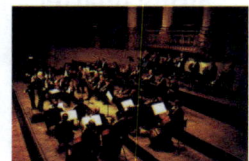

You have to do what the conductor tells you...

Copy out the diagram of the orchestra, but don't copy the labels. Close the book and see if you can fill in the different instrument sections in the right places. Then learn all about the conductor.

Music Technology

Modern <u>technological</u> and '<u>virtual</u>' instruments allow a huge variety of sounds to be created.

MIDI lets you Connect Electronic Musical Instruments

1) <u>MIDI</u> was invented in 1983. It stands for <u>Musical Instrument Digital Interface</u>. It's a way of <u>connecting</u> different electronic instruments.

2) MIDI equipment is connected by <u>MIDI cables</u>.

3) <u>MIDI data</u> is digital information (i.e. in <u>zeroes</u> and <u>ones</u>). It's sent down the MIDI cables. MIDI <u>instruments</u> turn MIDI <u>information</u> into <u>sound</u> (or vice versa).

4) One important <u>advantage</u> of MIDI is that it allows <u>musical equipment</u> to be <u>linked</u> with <u>computers</u>, opening up a whole <u>new world</u> of music-making.

Synthesizers Let You Make New Sounds

<u>Synthesizers</u> come in <u>different forms</u> — some have <u>keyboards</u> and some <u>don't</u>. The most common ones today are <u>virtual synthesizers</u>, which are <u>software-based</u> (see below). The <u>point</u> of them is to let you <u>create</u> sounds, which often <u>imitate</u> musical instruments. There are <u>different types</u> of synthesizers:

1) <u>Analogue synthesizers</u> were mainly made in the <u>70s</u> and <u>early 80s</u>. They've often got lots of <u>knobs</u> and <u>sliders</u> — you use these to <u>change</u> the sound.

2) <u>Digital synthesizers</u> started to be popular in the <u>80s</u>. Most modern synthesizers are digital, though some of them try to <u>mimic</u> analogue synths. Digital synths usually have <u>fewer</u> knobs and sliders than analogue ones.

3) <u>Software synths</u> started to become popular in the <u>late 90s</u>. Software synths are <u>computer programs</u> (often <u>linked</u> to a <u>sequencer</u> — see below). They often have <u>graphical sliders</u> and <u>knobs</u> that you can move with a <u>mouse</u>. Some of them try to be like analogue and early digital synthesizers. They also try to <u>recreate</u> classic <u>electric instruments</u> like the <u>Hammond organ</u>.

Sequencers Let You Record, Edit and Replay Music

1) <u>Sequencer</u> is the posh word for equipment that can <u>record</u>, <u>edit</u> (mess about with) and <u>replay</u> music stored as <u>MIDI</u> or <u>audio</u> information. A "<u>sequenced composition</u>" is musical piece produced mainly from synthesized sounds using a sequencer.

2) Modern sequencers are usually <u>computer programs</u>, which often include <u>synthesizers</u> and <u>samplers</u>.

3) Most sequencers can record <u>audio</u> (real sounds) as well as the <u>MIDI</u> stuff, so you can create <u>synthesized</u> music and then record your own <u>voice</u> or <u>instruments</u> along with it. If you're unhappy with part of a recording, it's easy to replace that section with a <u>re-take</u>.

4) Modern sequencers are <u>multi-track recorders</u>. This allows the various lines of music, such as those played by different instruments, to be recorded on <u>separate tracks</u>. The individual tracks can then be <u>edited separately</u> to achieve the perfect <u>balance</u> of sounds.

5) One of the big <u>advantages</u> of a sequencer is that it shows your music as actual <u>notation</u> or as <u>representative boxes</u> — this makes it much easier to change and try out new ideas.

6) <u>Drum machines</u> are special sequencers that play back rhythm patterns using built-in drum sounds.

This can all be a bit confusing...

Some of this stuff is quite <u>technical</u> — but don't panic. You <u>don't</u> need to have an <u>in-depth understanding</u> of how the different types of technology work — as long as you know <u>what</u> they do and what people <u>use them for</u>. You can even have a go at using them in your <u>compositions</u>.

Music Technology

Sampling is a very popular way of putting different sounds into your music.
Samples can be fiddled with and looped to make long repeated sections.

Samplers let you 'Pinch' Other People's Sounds

1) A sampler is a piece of equipment that can record, process (change) and play back bits of sound.

2) These sections of sound are called samples.

3) Samplers are often used to take a bit of a piece of music that's
already been recorded to use in some new music.

4) You can sample anything from instruments to birdsong — even weird things like a car horn.

5) Today, samplers are most often used to reproduce the sound of real instruments,
such as strings or piano. Most pop music is sampled.

6) Pop stars often use samples of other people's music in their own music
— anything from other pop songs to bits from Classical pieces. For example:

- Madonna used a sample of ABBA's 'Gimme! Gimme! Gimme! (A Man After Midnight)'
  in her 2005 hit 'Hung Up'.
- Take That sampled 'Dies Irae' from Verdi's *Requiem* in 'Never Forget' (1995).
- Fallout Boy used a sample of 'Tom's Diner' by Suzanne Vega in their song 'Centuries' in 2014.

Samples Can be Added to Other Pieces

1) You don't have to create a piece made up entirely of samples — you can just add one or
two, or use a whole range to create a collage of sound. The collage can then be put over
the top of a repeating drum and bass loop.

2) DJs and producers often do this when they make a dance remix of a piece.

> REMIX is a term used for a different version of a piece of music.
> They're often used to turn pop or rock tunes into dance music
> — e.g. by speeding them up and giving them a fast drum beat.

3) Samples can be added to a piece by over-dubbing — adding tracks over the top of other tracks.
You can record a drum track, then overlay the guitar part, then the vocal part, etc.

DJs Choose, Play and Alter Music

1) DJs (disc jockeys) choose which tracks (lines of music) to play, and change bits of them
(e.g. by adding samples). Some DJs also rap over the top of the music.

2) DJs play music in clubs and on the radio.

3) At a live performance in a club, the DJ sometimes adds extra sounds
using samples, keyboards or a drum machine to build the piece up.

4) DJs use a mixing desk to combine different tracks and add extra sounds to the music,
and a set of decks to play their music.

5) The amplification is important — DJs need to make sure the right parts stand out,
and that all parts can be heard. The amplification can be changed in live performances.

There's even a dance remix of Beethoven's 5th Symphony...

Again, there's lots of technical bits on this page. You might choose to use some samples in your own
compositions, but even if you don't, you need to know how other people (like DJs) might use them.

Timbre

When you're listening to music, you can pick out <u>individual instruments</u> because of their <u>unique sound</u> — e.g. a trumpet sounds nothing like a violin. This is all down to a little thing called <u>timbre</u>.

Every Instrument Has its Own **Timbre**

1) <u>Timbre</u> is the <u>type of sound</u> that different instruments make. It's also known as <u>tone colour</u>.

2) <u>Musical notes</u> (and all sounds) are made by <u>vibrations</u>. Different instruments produce vibrations in <u>different ways</u>. For example, on a <u>string</u> instrument, the <u>bow</u> is drawn across the <u>string</u> to make it vibrate. On a <u>brass</u> instrument the vibrations are produced when the player '<u>buzzes</u>' their lips. The different <u>vibrations</u> make the <u>timbres</u> different.

3) The <u>size</u> and <u>material</u> of the instrument alter the timbre as well — e.g. a <u>cello</u> has a different timbre to a <u>violin</u> because it's <u>bigger</u>, and <u>wooden</u> flutes sound different from <u>metal</u> ones.

4) The same instrument can sound <u>different</u> depending on who's playing it. The <u>tone</u> (or quality) of the sound is affected by an individual's <u>playing style</u> and can be described as <u>rich</u>, <u>full</u>, <u>strong</u>, etc.

5) The overall nature of the sound produced by an instrument is called its <u>sonority</u>. <u>Timbre</u> and <u>tone</u> contribute to this, along with the <u>dynamics</u> and <u>articulation</u> of the music.

Instruments From the **Same Family** Have **Similar Timbres**

Even though each instrument has a <u>unique</u> timbre, it can still sometimes be <u>hard</u> to tell ones from the <u>same family</u> apart. Different families of instruments <u>change</u> the <u>timbre</u> in <u>different ways</u>:

STRING INSTRUMENTS

- String instruments (like the <u>violin</u>, <u>viola</u>, <u>cello</u> and <u>double bass</u>) have a <u>warm</u> sound. Notes are produced by making the <u>strings vibrate</u>, either using a <u>bow</u> or the <u>fingers</u>.
- All string instruments can be played *con arco* (with a bow), *pizzicato* (plucked), *con sordino* (muted) or *sul ponticello* (close to the bridge).
- <u>Double stopping</u> is when <u>two strings</u> are pressed at the <u>same time</u>, so <u>two notes</u> can be played at once.
- <u>Tremolo</u> sounds like <u>trembling</u> — the bow is moved <u>back and forth</u> very quickly.

PIANO

- When you press the <u>keys</u>, a <u>hammer</u> hits the strings inside the piano, making them <u>vibrate</u>.
- The timbre of the piano can be <u>changed</u> by using the <u>soft</u> or <u>sustain pedals</u>.

There's more on families of instruments and types of ensembles on pages 63-72.

WOODWIND INSTRUMENTS

- Wind instruments (e.g. <u>flute</u>, <u>clarinet</u>, <u>oboe</u> and <u>bassoon</u>) have a <u>soft</u>, <u>mellow</u> sound.
- <u>Edge-tone</u> instruments (e.g. flutes) make a <u>softer</u>, <u>breathier</u> sound than <u>reed</u> instruments (e.g. clarinets).
- Clarinets and oboes can <u>alter</u> their timbre by using a technique called '<u>bells up</u>', where the player <u>points</u> the end of the instrument <u>upwards</u>. This produces a <u>harsher</u> sound.

BRASS INSTRUMENTS

- Brass instruments (like the <u>trumpet</u>, <u>French horn</u>, <u>trombone</u> and <u>tuba</u>) have a <u>bright</u>, <u>metallic</u> sound.
- Playing <u>with a mute</u> (*con sordino*) can change the timbre.

PERCUSSION INSTRUMENTS

- Percussion instruments (e.g. <u>drums</u> and <u>xylophones</u>) make a sound when they're <u>struck</u>.
- What you hit them with can <u>change</u> the <u>timbre</u> — e.g. whether you use <u>sticks</u>, <u>brushes</u> or your <u>hands</u>.

SINGERS

- Singers produce notes when their <u>vocal cords</u> vibrate.
- The <u>speed</u> that they vibrate changes the <u>pitch</u> and the <u>timbre</u> — e.g. <u>bass</u> voices sound very <u>different</u> to <u>sopranos</u>.
- Techniques like <u>vibrato</u> (making the note <u>wobble</u>) can give a <u>richer</u> sound.
- <u>Falsetto</u> singing produces a much <u>thinner</u> sound.

I'm picking up good vibrations...

You may be asked to <u>describe</u> the timbre of different instruments that crop up in your exam.

Timbre

Electronic effects can be used to alter the timbre of an instrument or voice.

There are Lots of Different Electronic Effects

1) There are loads of different ways to change the sound of an instrument.
2) These effects are often used with electric guitars — they're really popular with rock bands, especially during guitar solos. Guitarists use pedals (e.g. a wah-wah pedal) to alter the tone or pitch.
3) The effects can also be used to change the sound of recorded music during mixing or post-processing.
4) Electronic effects (also called studio effects) include:

- **DISTORTION** distorts the sound.
- **REVERB** adds an echo to the sound.
- **CHORUS** makes it sound as if there's more than one player or singer — copies of the original sound are mixed together, with slight changes in timing and pitch.
- **PHASER** creates a 'whooshing' effect (a bit like the noise an aeroplane flying overhead makes).
- **FLANGER** similar to a phaser, but makes a more intense sound. The effect is created by combining the original sound with a copy, and varying the delay between them. It's used a lot in sci-fi programmes.
- **PITCH SHIFTING** used to bend the natural note or add another harmony.
- **OCTAVE EFFECTS** creates octaves above or below the note being played.

Synthesized Sounds have Different Timbres to Real Sounds

1) The natural sound of an instrument can be digitally reproduced to create a synthesized sound.
2) Electronic keyboards have different settings, so they can be made to sound like pretty much any instrument, from violins to percussion.

One big difference between real and synthesized sounds is what happens to the timbre when the volume changes. When a real instrument is played louder, it has a different timbre to when it's played quietly. However, a synthesized sound has the same timbre at any volume — it's just the loudness that changes.

Sampling Uses Recordings of Real Instruments

1) The most effective way to recreate the sounds of real instruments is to use sampling (see p.74).
2) Sampling is where you record an instrument and use the recording (called a sample) in your music.
3) The samples can be altered to create different effects — there are lots of different computer programs that help you do this.
4) Samples can be looped (played over and over again), and other samples can be added over the top.
5) Most electronic music produced today uses looping, especially drum patterns.
6) It's not just instruments that can be sampled — you can take samples of anything you like, e.g. traffic noises or doorbells.
7) Lots of pop songs use samples — see if you can spot any in your favourite songs.

I'd like a sample of that cake please...

Have a listen to the 2005 hit 'Gold Digger' by Kanye West — he uses a sample of 'I Got A Woman' by Ray Charles (which was released more than 50 years earlier, in 1954).

Warm-up and Exam Questions

The questions on these pages are great for finding out what you know — don't ignore them.

Warm-up Questions

1) For each of the words below, name an instrument that links with the word:

   slide   **single reed**   **double reed**   **pizzicato**   **wooden bars**

2) Explain each of these words and phrases:

   tremolo   **con sordino**   **tenor**   **falsetto**

3) Name the **three** main types of guitar and briefly describe each of them.

4) In which period was the harpsichord the most popular keyboard instrument?

5) Explain the difference between a military band, a brass band and a jazz band.

6) List all the instruments that play in a piano trio and a clarinet quintet.

7) Define the following terms:

   MIDI   **sampler**   **remix**   **sequencer**

Exam Question

Brush up on your exam technique with this question.

This question is about two extracts, Track 30 and Track 31.
First play Track 30 **three** times, leaving a short pause for writing time between each playing.

Track 30

a) Name the solo woodwind instrument that plays at the beginning.

....

[1 mark]

b) What is the other instrument that plays in the extract?

....

[1 mark]

Exam Question

c) Tick **one** box to indicate which shape best represents the opening of the melody played by the solo instrument.

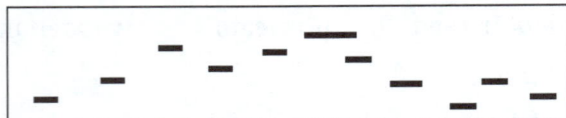

Shape A ☐

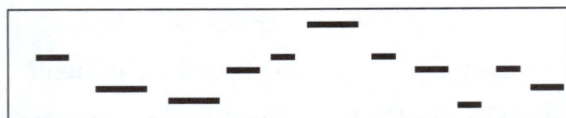

Shape B ☐

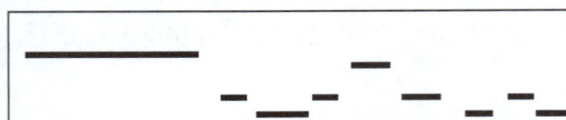

Shape C ☐

[1 mark]

d) Describe the relationship of the two instruments heard here. Refer to the **texture** and any other interesting features.

....

....

[2 marks]

Two marks available means you need to make two points. Don't forget to write about <u>texture</u>.

Track 31

Now play Track 31 **three** times, leaving a short pause for writing time between each playing.

e) Name the two solo woodwind instruments which play the melody at the beginning of this excerpt.

....

....

[2 marks]

Make sure you write about the <u>melody</u>, not the accompaniment.

Exam Question

f) Name the family of instruments playing throughout this excerpt.

....

[1 mark]

g) Ring the word that describes the scale used throughout the excerpt.

major   minor   chromatic

[1 mark]

h) Tick one of the following to represent the backing melody played by the two wind instruments.

[1 mark]

i) Ring **one** feature that you can hear in this excerpt.

accelerando   crescendo   ritardando

[1 mark]

Revision Summary for Section Five

This section should be easy where it's talking about your own instruments. Don't ignore the other instruments. You'll need to know enough about them to be able to describe them in the listening test. And you might need to write parts for other instruments for your composition — it'll be a big help to know what they can and can't do. Go through the questions and check you can answer them all.

1) Name three brass instruments.

2) How do you vary the pitch on a brass instrument?

3) Are all woodwind instruments made of wood?

4) Name three woodwind instruments.

5) What are the three different mouthpieces used on woodwind instruments called? How do they work?

6) What are all those little keys, springs and levers for on a woodwind instrument?

7) What's the smallest orchestral string instrument?

8) What's the biggest string instrument that you play with a bow?

9) How do you make different notes on a string instrument?

10) What makes a harp different from the other string instruments? Give three differences.

11) Where would you put a mute on a bowed string instrument and what effect would it have?

12) How many strings are there on:
   a) an acoustic guitar   b) an electric guitar   c) a bass guitar?

13) What do you call those metal bits on the fingerboard of a guitar? Do you get them on a bass?

14) What's the proper word for twanging a guitar string with a plectrum?

15) Name three different keyboard instruments.

16) What's the biggest type of keyboard instrument?

17) What's the most popular keyboard instrument?

18) How could you tell you were listening to a church organ and not a harpsichord?

19) Name three tuned percussion instruments and six untuned percussion instruments.

20) What's the highest type of singing voice?

21) What's the lowest type of singing voice?

22) What do you call a boy's voice when it's got the same range as a soprano?

23) How can you tell the difference between a wind band and a brass band?

24) How can you tell the difference between a wind band and a jazz orchestra?

25) What are the two sections of a jazz orchestra called, and what are their jobs?

26) Why's chamber music called chamber music?

27) How many people are there in: a) a trio   b) a sextet   c) a quartet   d) an octet?

28) How many clarinets are there in a clarinet quintet?

29) Sketch a plan of a standard symphony orchestra. Label the different sections and the conductor.

30) What sections are there in a string orchestra, chamber orchestra and jazz orchestra?

31) How is MIDI information stored?

32) What do sequencers do?

33) What are samples? How can they be used in tracks?

34) Explain how the sound is produced on:
   a) a string instrument   b) a piano   c) a brass instrument?

35) Name four different electronic effects.

The Baroque Style

'The Concerto Through Time' is one of your areas of study. You need to know about the concerto between 1650 and 1910, and how the style of music evolved during that time. Let's start with Baroque music.

Baroque has a Recognisable Sound

The Baroque period was from about 1600-1750. Key composers include Bach, Handel, Vivaldi and Purcell. Baroque music is pretty easy to recognise. These are the main things to look out for:

1) The melodies are built up from short musical ideas (called motifs), so you get quite a bit of repetition.

2) The harmonies are simple, with a fairly narrow range of chords — mainly I and V.

3) The melody is packed with ornaments, added in to make it sound more interesting (see p.85).

4) The music often involves counterpoint — where two or more different lines of melody are played at the same time. This texture is described as contrapuntal (or polyphonic — see p.45).

5) The dynamics change suddenly. Each bit is either loud or soft — this is called terraced or stepped dynamics. You won't hear any gradual changes in volume (no crescendos or diminuendos). This is mainly due to the prominence of the harpsichord in Baroque music — harpsichords could either play loud or soft, but couldn't change gradually between the two.

6) Baroque music is tonal:

> • From about 1600, Western composers used major and minor keys to write tonal music — this replaced modal music (see p.27).
>
> • Composers used modulation to switch between keys (see p.44) — this created contrast in their music.
>
> • Compositions were often made up of sections in different keys, with modulation between them. New structures were developed for organising pieces of music with a number of sections, e.g. binary and ternary forms (see next page).

String and Keyboard Instruments Played Key Roles

1) String instruments were dominant in a Baroque orchestra (just like today) — violins, violas, cellos and double basses were all used. (If you see 'violone' in the score, it's played by a double bass today.)

2) Keyboard instruments such as the harpsichord and organ were also very important in Baroque music.

3) Woodwind instruments such as the flute, recorder, oboe and bassoon were also used.

4) The instruments available were much more limited than in the later musical periods. There were some early forms of brass instruments, such as trumpets and horns, but they didn't have any valves so could only play a limited range of notes.

5) Orchestras were generally small compared to modern orchestras. The size of an orchestra depended on the resources available, and the performance space. Music was often performed by chamber groups (see p.71) with a small number of musicians, but there were larger orchestras too.

Baroque Music Often Had a Basso Continuo

> 1) A basso continuo is a continuous bass part (see page 57). It's played throughout a piece, and the chords are based on it.
>
> 2) It was often played on an organ or harpsichord, but could also feature additional instruments — e.g. cellos, double basses or bassoons.

EXAM TIP

'Baroque Around the Clock' was a huge hit...
You might have to spot key features of Baroque music in the exam, so make sure you learn them.

Baroque Structures

Large compositions, such as <u>concertos</u>, are usually broken down into sections called movements. The movements themselves can be <u>structured</u> in a variety of <u>different ways</u>.

There Were **Two Types** of **Baroque Concerto**

<u>Concertos</u> are works for <u>orchestra</u> and <u>soloist</u>(s). They're made up of a number of <u>movements</u>, with common <u>themes</u> but contrasting <u>tempos</u>, <u>keys</u>, <u>moods</u>, etc. There are <u>two types</u> of Baroque concerto:

1) In a <u>solo concerto</u>, a <u>single solo instrument</u> is <u>accompanied</u> by an <u>orchestra</u>.

2) In a <u>concerto grosso</u>, a small <u>group</u> of soloists (called the <u>concertino</u>) is contrasted with the rest of the orchestra (the <u>ripieno</u>) and the <u>basso continuo</u>. See p.86-87 for more detail on both concerto types.

Baroque Composers Used **Standard Structures**

Binary and **Ternary Forms** are Made Up of **Different Sections**

1) <u>Binary</u> means something like '<u>in two parts</u>' — <u>binary form</u> has <u>two sections</u>.

2) Binary form is usually used for <u>Baroque dances</u>, e.g. bourrée, menuet, gavotte, sarabande and gigue.

3) Each section is <u>repeated</u>. You play Section A twice, and then Section B twice, so it goes <u>AABB</u>.

4) Section B <u>contrasts</u> with Section A — the two bits should sound <u>different</u>.

5) The contrast is often made by <u>modulating</u> to related keys. Pieces in a <u>minor</u> key usually modulate to the <u>relative major</u>, e.g. A minor to C major. Pieces in a <u>major</u> key usually modulate to the <u>dominant</u> key (V), e.g. C major to G major.

1) <u>Ternary form</u> has <u>three sections</u>. The general structure is <u>ABA</u>, but the sections are often <u>repeated</u>, producing structures such as <u>AABBAA</u>.

2) Section A ends in the <u>home key</u>, normally with a <u>perfect cadence</u> (see pages 42-43). This makes it sound like a <u>complete piece</u> in itself.

3) In Section B the music often modulates to a <u>related key</u>, like the <u>dominant</u> or <u>relative minor</u>, and then <u>goes back</u> to the <u>home key</u> before it ends.

4) The last section can be <u>exactly the same</u> as Section A, or a slightly <u>varied</u> version. If it <u>is</u> varied, you call it <u>A1</u> instead of A.

In a <u>ritornello</u>, the same musical <u>idea</u> or <u>theme</u> is repeated at various points in the piece. The theme might be <u>shortened</u> or <u>developed</u> in some way when it is heard again. A more formal structure of this type is a <u>rondo</u>, where a <u>main theme</u> (A) is <u>repeated</u>, separated by a number of different <u>sections</u>, creating forms such as <u>ABACA</u> (see p.94).

A **Fugue** Has a **Subject** and **Counter-Subject**

1) A <u>fugue</u> is based around a <u>short musical phrase</u> called the <u>subject</u>. The <u>melodic line</u> immediately following the subject is called the <u>counter-subject</u>.

2) If there's more than one instrument, <u>each</u> plays the subject one after another, in <u>imitation</u> (see p.84). The subject, or a <u>variation</u> on it, <u>reappears</u> throughout the piece.

3) <u>J.S. Bach</u> used this structure in many of his works, including the <u>Brandenburg Concertos</u> (see p.87).

4) In '<u>The Well-Tempered Clavier</u>', Bach wrote a collection of <u>fugues</u> for solo keyboard instruments. Here, each fugue was coupled with a piece called a <u>prelude</u>. In the <u>Baroque</u> period, a <u>prelude</u> was a <u>short</u>, relatively <u>simple</u> piece of music which served as an <u>introduction</u> to one or more pieces.

This topic is in binary form — get ready for the second section...

Make sure you've got all the structures on this page fixed in your brain — there are a few more to come.

Baroque Structures

Variations are pieces which start with one pattern or tune, and then change it in different ways. There are two main structures for variations. They're called 'theme and variation' and 'ground bass'.

Theme and Variation Form Varies the Melody

1) In theme and variation form, the theme's usually a memorable tune.

2) The theme is played first. There's a short pause before the first variation is played, then another pause before the next variation. Each variation is a self-contained piece of music. There can be as many or as few variations as the composer wants.

3) Each variation should be a recognisable version of the main theme, but different from all the others.

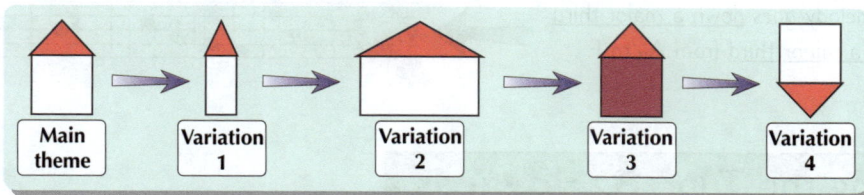

You can vary a tune in loads of simple ways:

1) Start off with a basic theme...

2) Add notes to make the tune more complex.

3) Remove notes to simplify the tune.

4) Change the metre — e.g. from 2 beats in a bar to 3.

5) Add a countermelody — an extra melody over the top of the theme.

6) You can also change the tempo, change the key (from major to minor or vice versa), change some or all of the chords or add a different type of accompaniment instead of block chords.

> A fantasia is a composition with an improvised feel — the composer uses their imagination and skill to compose a piece that doesn't follow a set structure. Fantasias often involve variations on a theme.

Ground Bass Form Varies Ideas Over a Fixed Bass Part

> Ground bass is a continuous set of variations — there are no pauses. The main theme (called the ground) is a bass line which repeats throughout the piece — it is also known as basso ostinato (see p.84). Varying melodies and harmonies which become gradually more complex are played over the ground. There are two types of Baroque dance that are in ground bass form — the chaconne and passacaglia. They're quite slow and stately.

Freshly ground bass — it goes all powdery...

Theme and variation form crops up a lot so make sure you get it sorted now. In concertos throughout the Baroque, Classical and Romantic eras, key themes are stated and then developed as the pieces progress.

Baroque Melody Patterns

Composers often create a melody by starting with a <u>key phrase</u>, then <u>adapting</u> it using different <u>techniques</u>.

Melodic Inversion — Turning the Tune **Upside Down**

With <u>melodic inversion</u> you keep the <u>same intervals</u> between the notes, but they go in the <u>opposite direction</u>, i.e. down instead of up, and up instead of down. Basically you turn the tune on its head.

The first melody goes <u>up a major third</u> from C to E, then <u>up a minor third</u> to G.

In the inversion the melody goes <u>down a major third</u> to A♭, then <u>down a minor third</u> from A♭ to F.

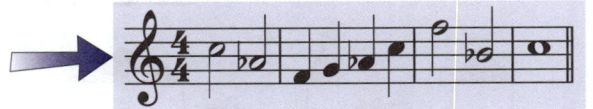

Retrograde — Playing the Tune **Backwards**

Playing the notes <u>in reverse order</u> but with the same rhythm is called <u>retrograde</u>. This is the retrograde version of the first melody (above).

If you switch the notes so they're in reverse order <u>and</u> inverted, you get a <u>retrograde inversion</u>. This is the retrograde inversion of the first melody.

Sequencing — Repeat a **Pattern**, Vary the **Pitch**

1) Repeat the <u>pattern</u> of a phrase but start on a <u>different note</u>, higher or lower. This is called a <u>sequence</u>.
2) <u>Ascending</u> sequences go up in pitch. <u>Descending</u> sequences go down.

Imitation — Repeat a Phrase With **Slight Changes**

1) In <u>imitation</u>, a phrase is repeated with <u>slight changes</u> each time.
2) It works really well if one instrument or voice imitates <u>another</u> and then <u>overlaps</u>.
3) There is imitation right at the <u>start</u> of the <u>3rd Movement</u> of Brandenburg Concerto No. 5 (see p.87).

original phrase

original phrase, one octave higher

imitation with modulation

overlap starts in relative minor

Ostinato — Keep **One Pattern** the **Same**, Change the Rest

1) An ostinato is a pattern that's played <u>over and over</u> again.
2) The rest of the piece <u>changes around it</u>.
3) An ostinato is usually in the <u>bass</u> line, but it can be in other parts too.
4) <u>Ground bass form</u> (p.83) features ostinato <u>phrases</u> in the bass line — the repeated phrases can be quite <u>long</u>.

Here's the repeating pattern

Section Six — The Concerto Through Time

Ornaments in Baroque Music

Ornaments are short extra notes that liven up the main melody — Baroque composers used them a lot in their music. There are a few different types of ornament...

A Trill is Lots of Tiny Quick Notes

1) In Baroque music, the trill starts one note above the written note then goes quickly back and forth between the written note and the note you started on.

2) Sometimes a trill ends with a turn (see below).

3) If the note above the written note doesn't belong to the key signature, there'll be a sharp, flat or natural sign above the trill symbol.

4) A trill is slightly different in Classical music — it starts on the written note and goes up to the note above.

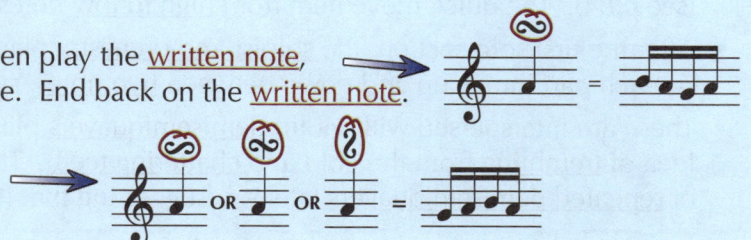

This is how you play a trill in Baroque music...

The trill lasts the same length of time as the written note.

An Appoggiatura is an Extra Note in a Chord

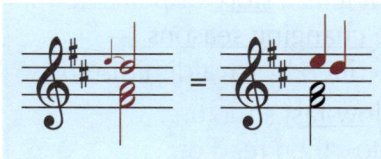

1) The appoggiatura starts on a note that clashes with the chord, then moves to a note that belongs in the chord (this is called the resolution).

2) The two notes are usually just one tone or semitone apart.

3) It normally takes half the time value of the note it 'leans' on.

Squeezing in a Tiny Note is Called Acciaccatura

"Acciaccatura" means crushing in. An acciaccatura is a note that's squeezed in before the main note and played as fast as possible.

Mordents and Turns are Set Patterns of Notes

MORDENTS

Mordents start off like trills.

The difference is they end on the written note, which is played a bit longer than the trilled notes. There are loads of different mordents but these two are the most common.

upper mordent

lower mordent

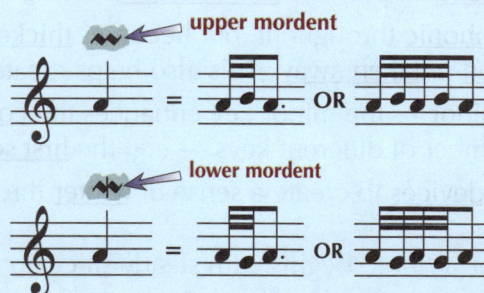

TURNS

Start on the note above the written note, then play the written note, followed by the note below the written note. End back on the written note.

For an inverted turn play the note below the written note, the written note, the note above that and finally the written note.

I've done my bit — now it's your turn...

COMPOSING TIP

Take a look at p.41 for more on decoration. You might even want to add some of these ornaments to your compositions to make them more exciting (don't go overboard though).

The Baroque Solo Concerto

Now it's time to look at underlined concertos (the focus of this area of study) in a bit more detail. First up, it's the Baroque solo concerto — not to be confused with the concerto grosso, which comes on the next page.

A Solo Concerto Shows Off an Instrument

1) In a solo concerto, a single solo instrument is 'showcased', allowing its performer to demonstrate the instrument's capabilities and show off their own skills. The soloist is accompanied by an orchestra.

2) A concerto consists of a number of different movements. In the Baroque period it was common for there to be three movements — a fast one, a slow one and another fast one. Not all concertos followed this pattern, but it became more standard in the Classical period (see p.93).

3) Many famous Baroque composers wrote solo concertos — Handel wrote them for the oboe, organ and violin. J.S. Bach wrote solo concertos for the violin, and for the harpsichord too. Vivaldi wrote around 350 solo concertos, mostly for the violin — including the famous 'Four Seasons'.

- Vivaldi's 'Four Seasons' is a set of four solo concertos for the violin, with a string orchestra and basso continuo (usually an organ or harpsichord, but sometimes a cello or double bass would play this part too). The basso continuo realises a figured bass (see p.57).

- The work is an early example of programme music — music that tells a story or paints a picture. The 'Four Seasons' is meant to capture the mood of the changing seasons — each concerto is based on a poem about that season (possibly written by Vivaldi himself).

- Each of the four concertos has three movements, with the fast-slow-fast structure. Have a listen to the first movement of Winter (the fourth concerto), then read on...

'Winter' Paints a Picture of Snow, Ice and Wind

1) The first movement of 'Winter' alternates between orchestral sections and violin solos (accompanied or unaccompanied). The themes played by the orchestra recur throughout the movement, giving it ritornello form (see p.82).

2) The solo passages are fast and difficult to play — they show off the violinist's skill. Sections where the soloist and orchestra all play the same rhythm also have a big impact (such as the last four bars).

3) The texture is homophonic throughout, but becomes thicker or thinner as instruments are added or taken away. This also helps create dynamic contrast.

4) The home key is F minor — the minor key enhances the cold mood of the piece. There are modulations to a number of different keys — e.g. the first solo is in C minor (the dominant key).

5) Vivaldi uses various devices to create a sense of winter through the music:

- The first movement of 'Winter' begins with steady staccato quavers (some with trills) — they build up in the string orchestra, and are joined by the soloist. This timbre creates the idea of sharp, icy rain.

- The solo violin plays fast demisemiquavers in scale and arpeggio patterns, with lots of sequences (see p.84). The quick movement from high to low notes gives the idea of swirling winds in a blizzard.

- After the first solo section, the soloist and orchestra play repetitive semiquaver patterns — each part jumps up and down between two notes, suggesting stamping feet.

- These are interspersed with violin demisemiquavers played on a single note, creating the idea of trembling from the cold and chattering teeth. There are more extended phrases of repeated demisemiquavers later on, suggesting that it's getting increasingly cold.

Learn the key features of a Baroque solo concerto...

SUGGESTED LISTENING

Have a listen to Vivaldi's 'Winter' and see if you can pick out the features described above (you don't need to know all the details off by heart, but you could get a similar piece in the exam).

The Baroque Concerto Grosso

And now for the second type of Baroque concerto — the concerto grosso.

A **Concerto Grosso** has a **Small Group of Soloists**

1) In a concerto grosso there is a small group of solo instruments called the concertino.
2) The rest of the orchestra (usually strings) is called the ripieno. There is also a basso continuo.
3) Musical ideas are passed back and forth between the concertino and ripieno.
4) Handel, Corelli and J.S. Bach all wrote concerto grossi (plural of grosso).

Bach's **Brandenburg Concertos** are Famous **Concerto Grossi**

1) The Brandenburg Concertos are a set of six concerto grossi — they were written by J.S. Bach for the Margrave of Brandenburg around 1721.
2) The first concerto has four movements, but the other five concertos all have three movements, following the fast-slow-fast structure.
3) Bach used a wide variety of instruments — the violin, viola, cello, oboe, flute, recorder, bassoon, trumpet, horn and harpsichord all feature as part of the concertino in at least one of the concertos. The use of some of these instruments as soloists was unusual for the period — e.g. the harpsichord in Concerto No. 5, and the viola and cello in Concerto No. 6.
4) Certain members of the concertino were showcased more than others. E.g. in Concerto No. 4 the concertino is a violin and two flutes or recorders, but the violin gets the most virtuosic material.
5) Bach used ritornello form (see p.82) in at least one movement of each concerto. E.g. in Concerto No. 4, the recorders state a theme at the start of the first movement. The recorders and solo violin then repeat the theme throughout the movement.
6) The texture of each concerto is mainly contrapuntal. Bach used the form of the fugue (see p.82) in Concertos No. 2, 4 and 5, creating a rich polyphonic texture. In Concerto No. 5, it's the third movement that takes this form:

- In Brandenburg Concerto No. 5, the concertino consists of a flute, violin and harpsichord. The ripieno is a string orchestra, and the continuo is played by the harpsichord (when it's not playing a solo part), cello and double bass.
- The concertino starts the 3rd movement, with the solo violin, flute and harpsichord playing the fugue subject one after the other in imitation.

- After this, the ripieno (string orchestra) enter and play the fugue subject themselves. The subject is restated throughout the movement, and often passes back and forth between the ripieno and concertino. Sometimes one instrument starts playing the subject before the previous one has finished — this overlapping is known as 'stretto'.
- Of the three concertino instruments, the movement showcases the harpsichord in particular. Its part is very complex at times, and has a completely unaccompanied solo for 14 bars.
- The overall structure of the movement is ternary or ABA (see p.82). Section A is in D major, section B is in B minor (the relative minor), and the final section is back in D major.
- The movement is in ritornello form — the main melodic section (the first 29 bars) is repeated throughout the piece (in full or in part), with contrasting sections in between. It also incorporates elements of a gigue (a lively 17th century dance).
- Bach used various musical devices — these include sequences (see p.84), e.g. the flute part at bar 137, and pedal point (or pedal note — see p.39), e.g. the cello part in bars 90-95.

Pedal as fast as you can...

Listen to the piece a few times, until you can spot all the features and musical devices mentioned above.

Warm-up and Exam Questions

That's it for Baroque concertos, but there are Classical and Romantic ones still to come. Here's a little breather for you in the form of some questions — there are some quick-fire ones to start off with.

Warm-up Questions

1) Describe how dynamics were used in the Baroque period.

2) In a concerto grosso, what is:
   a) the concertino?
   b) the ripieno?

3) In a fugue, what is the name of the main musical idea?

4) What is an ostinato?

5) What is an appoggiatura?

6) How many movements did most Baroque solo concertos have?

7) What is Bach's set of six concerto grossi called?

Exam Question

Have a go at this exam-style question.

Track 32 is an extract from a Baroque concerto.
Play the extract **three** times, leaving a short pause for writing time between each playing.

Track 32

a) i) Name the two different instruments playing at the beginning of the extract.

   ....

   ....
   [2 marks]

   ii) Name one of the instruments that plays the basso continuo
   once the orchestra has started playing.

   ....
   [1 mark]

b) At the start of the extract, what is the interval between the first two notes of the melody?

   Major third ☐

   Perfect fourth ☐

   Perfect fifth ☐

   Octave ☐

   [1 mark]

Exam Question

c)   How would you describe the texture of the music? Tick the correct answer.

Contrapuntal ☐

Homophonic ☐

Monophonic ☐

Heterophonic ☐

[1 mark]

d)   i) Is this extract from a solo concerto or a concerto grosso?

....

[1 mark]

ii) Give a reason for your answer.

....

....

[1 mark]

e)   Suggest a suitable composer for this concerto.

....

[1 mark]

f)   Suggest a suitable tempo for this extract.

....

[1 mark]

g)   Are the dynamics of this extract typical of the Baroque period? Explain your answer.

....

....

....

....

....

....

[4 marks]

From Baroque to Classical

Classical music came from Baroque, so it's similar but not the same...

Tastes Moved Towards a Simpler Sound

Classical
1750–1820

1) The Classical period of music was from around 1750 to 1820. Mozart, Haydn and Beethoven were key composers during this time.

2) The style of music didn't just change overnight — the Classical style developed from the Baroque style as tastes changed and instruments became more versatile.

3) Towards the end of the Baroque era, many composers moved away from the polyphonic sound (see p.45) that had been a key feature of the period. They began to write more homophonic music with a clear melody line and fewer ornaments (see p.85).

4) This development can be seen in the compositions of J.S. Bach's sons, C.P.E. Bach and J.C. Bach. They were influenced by new styles as well as their father's compositions, and they composed much more homophonic music than their father.

5) There was also a move towards more subtle dynamics. Composers began to use crescendos and diminuendos rather than sudden changes in volume — this was partly due to the invention of the piano (see below).

Forms and Structures Developed Too

1) Baroque forms and structures changed over time, and grew into popular Classical structures:

- The solo concerto became more popular than the concerto grosso (see p.87) — it became an important form in the Classical period.
- The Baroque trio sonata consisted of a number of movements played by three instruments plus a harpsichord continuo. This developed into the Classical sonata, a form consisting of three or four movements, usually composed for a solo instrument (see p.93).
- In the Baroque period, operas often began with an 'Italian overture' — an orchestral piece consisting of three sections — a fast section followed by a slow section, followed by another fast section. These pieces were often performed independently of the opera. The Classical symphony (see p.93) developed from this (although Classical symphonies tended to have four movements).

2) Other forms that were popular in the Baroque period continued to be used — binary form, ternary form and theme and variation form (see p.82-83) were still important in the Classical era. New structures such as sonata form (p.94) were also developed.

The Invention of the Piano had a Big Impact

1) The piano was invented in about 1700. It became more popular than the harpsichord because it was able to create a much greater variety of tones — the notes could be played in a legato or staccato style and the dynamics could be varied depending on how hard the keys were pressed. The full name of the piano is actually 'pianoforte', which means 'soft-loud'.

2) C.P.E. Bach and J.C. Bach both composed for the piano and were influential in increasing its popularity. The piano became very widely used in Classical music.

3) Other instruments (such as the clarinet) were developed, and this led to important changes in the structure of the orchestra — see the next page.

Souvenir shops suffered terribly as the use of ornaments declined...

Remember, Classical music developed from Baroque music, so many of the features you've come across in Baroque music still make an appearance. But there's lots of new stuff to get to grips with too...

The Classical Orchestra

Orchestras <u>got bigger</u> during the Classical period as new instruments were developed.
The <u>set-up</u> of an orchestra (i.e. which instruments were included) became more <u>standardised</u>.

Orchestral Music was Written for **Wealthy Audiences**

1) At the start of the Classical period, composers worked for <u>royalty</u> and <u>aristocrats</u>. They were <u>paid</u> to write music for <u>official events</u>, <u>church services</u> and plain old <u>entertainment</u>. Composers had to write music that their <u>patrons</u> (employers) would <u>approve of</u>.

2) <u>Later</u> in the Classical period, society <u>changed</u>. Middle-class people had more <u>money</u> and wanted entertainment. <u>Public concert halls</u> were built, where people could go to listen to music.

3) Famous Classical composers like <u>Haydn</u> and <u>Mozart</u> worked for patrons, but they also put on concerts in the new concert halls.

4) By the <u>1800s</u>, composers could earn quite a bit of money from ticket sales at concert halls. This gave them more <u>freedom</u> — they could write for the tastes of <u>concert-goers</u> instead of just pleasing their patrons.

Orchestras **Grew** During the **Classical Period**

1) At the start of the Classical period, composers wrote for <u>smallish</u> orchestras — mainly <u>strings</u>, with <u>horns</u>, <u>flutes</u> and <u>oboes</u>. There'd be <u>two</u> horns and <u>one</u> or <u>two</u> woodwind.

2) Later on, the <u>woodwind</u> section <u>grew</u> — <u>clarinets</u> were developed during the Classical period and were included in the orchestra. <u>Mozart</u> was the first composer to use the clarinet in a symphony.

3) <u>Brass</u> instruments were used more widely. <u>Horns</u> were developed so they could produce <u>more notes</u> and play in a greater <u>variety of keys</u>.

4) The <u>percussion</u> section grew too — <u>timpani</u> became a standard fixture, and some orchestras used <u>bass drums</u>, <u>snare drums</u>, <u>triangles</u> and <u>cymbals</u> as well.

5) In some <u>early</u> Classical music, there'd be a <u>harpsichord</u> (see p.67), but after a while composers <u>stopped</u> using it. The harpsichord was there to fill in the <u>harmonies</u>, but it wasn't really needed once the extra woodwind had been added.

6) This is a fairly <u>typical layout</u> for a later Classical orchestra:

PERCUSSION	
FRENCH HORNS	TRUMPETS
FLUTES	CLARINETS
OBOES	BASSOONS
SECOND VIOLINS	VIOLAS	DOUBLE BASSES
FIRST VIOLINS	CELLOS

Classical Orchestras Mostly Use **String Instruments**

1) The most <u>important</u> section in a Classical orchestra is the <u>strings</u>. They're the <u>dominant sound</u> in most Classical music. The <u>violins</u> generally play most of the <u>melodies</u>.

2) The <u>wind</u> instruments play extra notes to fill out the <u>harmony</u>. When they do get the tune, they mostly <u>double</u> the string parts.

3) You do hear the occasional wind <u>solo</u>. Classical <u>concertos</u> (see p.93) feature one or two <u>solo instruments</u> accompanied by an orchestra.

4) In later Classical music, the woodwind section started to have a more <u>independent role</u>. They'd sometimes play the melody <u>alone</u>, and there'd be more solos. The strings were still really important though.

You need to know what instruments were used in the Classical era...

Orchestras grew in size because composers in the Classical period began to include more parts for different instruments. This gave rise to a greater variety of music later in the Classical period.

The Classical Style

A whole page about the features of Classical music... enjoy.

Classical Melodies Have a **Clear, Simple Structure**

Classical music sounds clearer and simpler than music from other periods. This is partly because the melodies are structured in a very straightforward way, with short, balanced 2- or 4-bar phrases.

Here's an extract from Haydn's *Clock Symphony*:

4-bar question phrase / *4-bar answer phrase*

And here's the opening of Mozart's *Piano Sonata No. 16 in C major* with two-bar phrases:

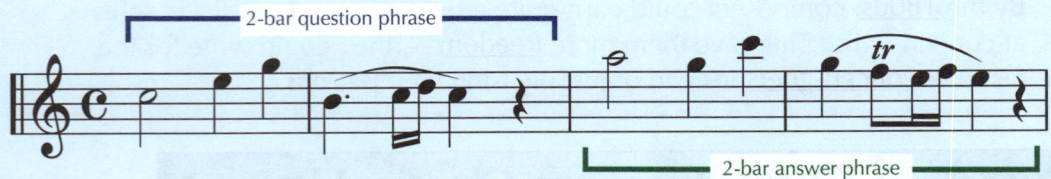

2-bar question phrase / *2-bar answer phrase*

Classical **Textures** are Mainly **Melody** and **Chords**

1) Most Classical music has just one melody with accompanying chords. This makes the tune really stand out. It's called homophonic texture (see page 45).
2) These accompanying chords can be played in different ways:

These are block chords...

... and these are broken chords

3) Polyphony (where several tunes weave in and out of each other) is used too, but not as often.

Classical Music Uses **Major** and **Minor Keys**

1) Classical music is always in either a major or minor key — the tonality is major or minor.
2) Bright, cheery bits are in major keys and gloomy, sad bits are in minor keys.
3) Classical harmony is what's known as diatonic — nearly all the notes belong to the main key.

The **Beat** is Obvious and **Easy to Follow**

1) The metre in Classical music is very regular. You can happily tap your foot in time to the music.
2) The tempo stays constant — the speed of the beat stays pretty much the same all the way through, without massively speeding up or slowing down.

> **REVISION TIP**
> ## Classical style — a wig, tailcoat and breeches...
> Make sure you're happy with all the key features of the Classical period. Make a list of them all, then learn your list. Keep going back over it to check you know them off by heart.

Classical Structures

Concertos, sonatas and symphonies were all popular forms in the Classical period. Your area of study is about concertos, but it's useful to have a brief look at the others, to put it all in context.

Classical Concertos are Played by a Soloist and Orchestra

1) The Classical concerto developed from the Baroque solo concerto — in a classical concerto the soloist has most of the tune, and can really show off. They're accompanied by the orchestra (though the orchestra does get the tune too).

2) The structure of concertos became more standardised in the Classical period — the vast majority of Classical concertos have three movements, following a quick-slow-quick pattern. The three movements traditionally take the following forms:

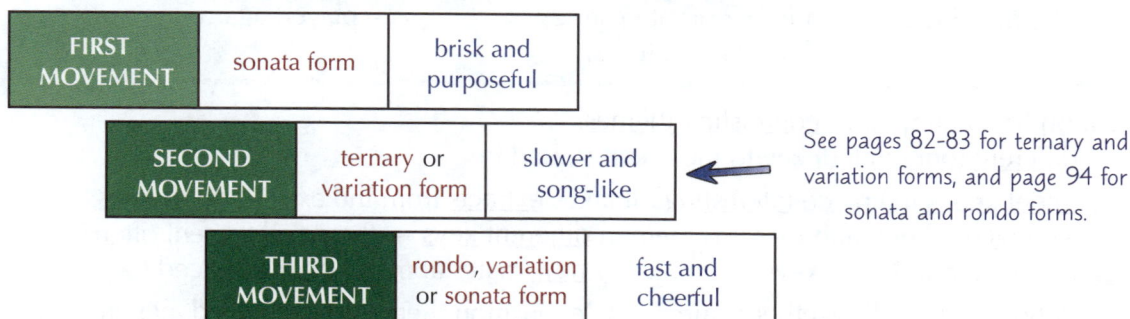

FIRST MOVEMENT	sonata form	brisk and purposeful

SECOND MOVEMENT	ternary or variation form	slower and song-like

See pages 82-83 for ternary and variation forms, and page 94 for sonata and rondo forms.

THIRD MOVEMENT	rondo, variation or sonata form	fast and cheerful

3) Classical concertos often have a bit called a cadenza (p.57), where the orchestra stops and the soloist can show everyone how brilliant they are. A cadenza is sometimes improvised.

4) Famous examples of Classical concertos include Haydn's Trumpet Concerto in E♭ major and Mozart's Horn Concerto No. 4 in E♭ major.

Composers Also Wrote Symphonies, Sonatas and Overtures

- A SYMPHONY is a big piece for the full orchestra — they can last more than an hour.
- Symphonies usually have four movements (but some have three, and they can have more than four). The contrast between the movements is important.
- In a four-movement symphony, the structure is similar to a concerto (see above), but with an additional movement between the slow movement and the final fast movement.
- This additional movement (the third movement) uses minuet or scherzo form — see p.94.
- Examples of symphonies include Haydn's Surprise Symphony and Beethoven's Eroica Symphony.

- SONATAS are usually written for one instrument. Some are written for two instruments (either the same or different), with each one playing a different part.
- A sonata usually has three or four movements. If it has three movements, it follows the same pattern as a concerto. For a four-movement sonata, the structure is the same as in a symphony.
- Piano sonatas were very popular — Haydn alone wrote 62. Mozart's Piano Sonata in C Major, Haydn's Piano Sonata in C Major and Beethoven's Sonata Pathétique are famous examples

- An OVERTURE is a one-movement piece for orchestra, written as an introduction to a larger work such as an opera or ballet. Overtures use musical themes from the main work to prepare the audience. For an example, have a listen to Mozart's overture to his opera *The Magic Flute*.
- A SUITE is another offshoot of ballets and operas — it's an orchestral arrangement of the music used to accompany the action on stage. It would be played as a stand-alone piece at concerts.

Classical Structures

Let's have a look at the forms taken by the individual movements of Classical works in a bit more detail.

Sonata Form has Three Main Sections

The first movement of a concerto is almost always in sonata form, and the final movement sometimes takes this form too (see previous page). The movements are themselves made up of a number of different sections — sonata form has three main sections:

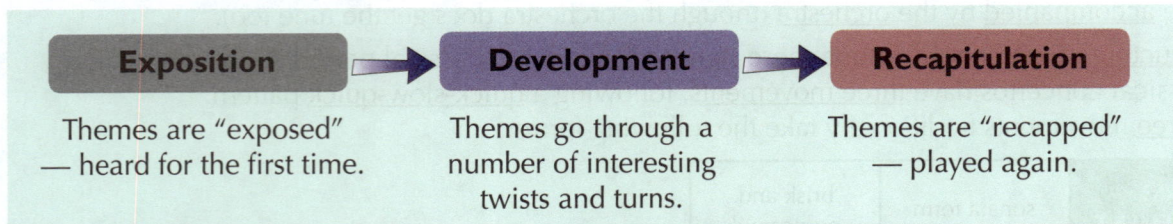

Exposition	→	Development	→	Recapitulation
Themes are "exposed" — heard for the first time.		Themes go through a number of interesting twists and turns.		Themes are "recapped" — played again.

1) The exposition has a number of contrasting themes. It ends in a different (but related) key to the one it started in.

2) The development keeps the piece interesting. It takes extracts from the exposition themes, explores variations on them, and presents them in different keys — the development often modulates through a number of keys. Completely new material might be introduced too.

3) The recapitulation pulls it all together again — the exposition themes are repeated, generally in the same order as in the exposition. They're usually changed a bit — the composer might add ornaments (see p.85) or shorten them. Some themes are heard in a different key — a theme that was in the relative key in the exposition usually moves to the tonic key in the recapitulation.

4) Composers usually add a coda to finish off the piece neatly as well.

5) In any musical work, composers drop hints when they're moving to a new theme or section. The end of a section is usually marked with a cadence (p.42-43), and bridge sections create a smooth transition to the next, often modulating through a number of keys to reach the key of the new section.

Rondo Form Can Have Any Number of Sections

1) The final movement of a concerto, sonata or symphony is often a rondo.

2) Rondo means going round. A rondo starts with a main idea in Section A, moves into a new section, goes round again to A, moves into another new section, goes round again to A, etc., etc. The new section after each Section A always contrasts with A.

3) Section A is known as the main theme or refrain. The contrasting sections are called episodes.

SECTION A	SECTION B	SECTION A	SECTION C	SECTION A
main theme	contrasting episode	main theme	another contrasting episode	main theme

4) The main theme is always in the home key, with modulations to related keys for the contrasting sections.

A Minuet and Trio is in Ternary Form

1) A minuet is a French dance with three beats in a bar. Minuets were used in the third movement of sonatas and symphonies (see previous page).

2) The movement is structured as a 'minuet and trio', with ternary form. A minuet is played, followed by a trio (another minuet, usually written for three instruments), and then the first minuet is repeated.

3) A scherzo and trio is sometimes used instead. A scherzo (which means 'joke' in Italian) is faster and more light-hearted than a minuet. Beethoven was one of the first to use a scherzo like this.

ABACADAEAFAGAHA — my rondo got a bit out of hand...

Remember, sonata form doesn't just crop up in sonatas — it's used for the first movement of a concerto.

The Classical Concerto

You've already seen the structure of the Classical concerto, and learnt about the sonata form used for its first movement (see p.93-94). Over the next couple of pages we'll look at the differences between Classical and Baroque concertos in a bit more detail, and see some examples of Classical concertos.

The Concerto Developed from Baroque to Classical

The Classical concerto features a solo instrument that's contrasted with, and accompanied by, an orchestra. The form emerged from the Baroque solo concerto, but the musical developments of the Classical period mean that Classical concertos differ from Baroque concertos in many ways.

- Classical concertos featured newly invented or developed instruments as solo instruments — Mozart composed a clarinet concerto and Beethoven wrote five concertos for the piano. Haydn wrote a trumpet concerto for the new 'keyed trumpet', which was capable of playing many more notes than the 'natural trumpet' it was developed from.
- The new instruments also meant composers could write for larger orchestras (see p.91).
- Concertos became longer, and structures such as sonata form and rondo form (see p.94) encouraged composers to develop their themes further.
- Soloists were given more prominence — the soloist could show off their skills and the capabilities of their instrument in the cadenza.

Sonata Form Contrasts the Soloist with the Orchestra

1) As you saw on page 93, concertos usually have three movements (quick, slow, quick). The first movement is in sonata form, which is made up of three main sections: the exposition, the development and the recapitulation (see p.94). Composers used sonata form to create variety and contrast between the soloist and orchestra.

2) In a Classical concerto, the exposition section tends to be a double exposition. The orchestra plays first (usually without the soloist), and introduces the main themes. The soloist then restates these themes (accompanied by the orchestra) — but often with some variation or new ideas.

3) In the first exposition, the orchestra usually plays each theme in the tonic (home) key. The soloist begins the second exposition in the tonic key, but modulates to a different key after the first theme — usually the dominant key if the tonic is major, or the relative major if the tonic is minor.

4) There aren't so many rules for the development and recapitulation — they normally include episodes where the soloist and orchestra are heard separately, and bits where they play together.

5) The recapitulation is generally followed by the cadenza, played by the soloist. This was often improvised, but sometimes written out too. In many of Mozart's works, the only indication of the cadenza is a pause sign above the orchestral parts, but he did write some out — e.g. for his Piano Concerto No. 5. Cadenzas would often be based on themes from elsewhere in the movement.

6) After the cadenza, there's a final orchestral section called the coda, which ends the movement.

Double Exposition		Development	Recapitulation	Cadenza	Coda
Exposition 1	Exposition 2				
Orchestra	Soloist (with orchestra)	Both	Both	Soloist	Orchestra

In a concerto, one exposition just isn't enough...

Have a listen to some Classical concertos, and see if you can spot the features described above. Mozart and Beethoven both wrote lots of concertos — there's more detail on two of them on the next page.

The Classical Concerto

Annoyingly, composers don't always stick exactly to the script when it comes to sonata form. Below are a couple of examples which mostly follow the standard structure, with just one or two differences...

Mozart Wrote a Famous Clarinet Concerto

1) In the Classical period, there were three types of clarinet — C, A and B♭. Each was best suited to playing in the major key it was named after, but could also play in related keys such as the dominant. The C clarinet isn't played today, but the A and B♭ clarinets are both still used.

2) Mozart's Clarinet Concerto in A major is for the A clarinet. It is a transposing instrument — when it plays a written note C, the sound it makes is an A.

3) In the concerto, the solo clarinet is accompanied by an orchestra — this is dominated by the strings, but there are also parts for flutes, bassoons and horns.

4) The concerto has three movements, with the quick, slow, quick structure. The first movement is in sonata form (see p.94), the second movement is in ternary form (see p.82), and the final movement is in rondo form (see p.94). Let's have a look at the first movement in a bit more detail:

- The first movement has a double exposition (see previous page), with the orchestra playing the first exposition. This first exposition has two main themes — they're both in A major (the tonic key).

- The solo clarinet introduces the second exposition, initially accompanied only by the violins. The first theme is restated, and the second theme is played in E major (the dominant key). New material is appears between these two themes — some of this is in A minor (the tonic minor).

- The clarinet adds ornamentation to the original themes — two matching bars from the first theme of each exposition are shown here.

- The soloist doesn't always have the melody — near the end of the exposition section, the clarinet accompanies the orchestra with an Alberti bass (see p.39).

- Unusually, there is no cadenza after the recapitulation. However, there is a pause in the orchestral part during the recapitulation, where the soloist can improvise.

Beethoven's Piano Concerto No. 1 has an Unusual Exposition

1) Beethoven's Piano Concerto No. 1 in C major also follows the standard three-movement structure, with the movements taking the same forms as the Mozart concerto above.

2) The concerto is for solo piano, accompanied by an orchestra of strings, woodwind, brass and timpani.

3) The orchestral exposition in the first movement introduces two main themes. The first theme has the regular rhythmic feel of a march, with lots of staccato notes. In contrast, the second theme has a more legato, flowing melody.

4) The orchestral exposition is very long — the piano soloist doesn't enter until bar 106. Rather than repeat the orchestra's themes, the piano plays a completely new theme, unaccompanied for the first 8 bars. In this way, Beethoven does not follow the standard sonata form structure.

5) He does, however, include a cadenza in the expected place after the recapitulation. Beethoven played the piano at the first performance of this piece, and would have improvised at this point. However, he later wrote out a few different cadenzas (other composers have also written their own).

6) The piece includes lots of variation in dynamics — they range from **pp** to **ff**, with sudden **fp** changes and **sf** accents, plus more gradual crescendos and diminuendos. Dynamics like these are common in Romantic music (see p.97) — Beethoven bridged the Classical and Romantic eras.

If you've got a spare minute, why not write your own cadenza...

I can't promise that these pieces will come up in the exam, but you will definitely be played an extract from a concerto and asked about its features — things like the key, instrumentation, dynamics, texture, etc.

The Romantic Period

The Romantic period was about how passionate emotions can be expressed through art and music.

The **Romantic Period** was in the **19th Century**

1) The Romantic period was from about 1820-1900 (though there's always a bit of an overlap between different musical periods).
2) Writers, artists and composers at this time were portraying contrasting emotions and ideas, such as love and hate, happiness and grief, and life and death.
3) They were inspired by the natural world too, and were fascinated by supernatural ideas.
4) Composers wrote programme music — music based on a poem or painting, or that tells a story.
5) Tchaikovsky, Wagner and Chopin were all Romantic composers. Some of Beethoven's later pieces also fitted into the Romantic period.

Romantic Music is More **Dramatic** Than Classical

1) Romantic music used a wide range of dynamics. Sudden changes made the music very dramatic — it could go from *ppp* to *fff* and back again within a bar. Sforzandos and accents added to the drama.
2) To make the music more expressive, composers gave extra instructions — as well as tempo markings, they would include instructions like *dolce* (sweetly), *amoroso* (lovingly) or *agitato* (agitated).
3) There were more tempo changes — a piece might change speeds lots of times within the same section. Musicians in this period used *rubato* as well — it means 'robbed time' and it's when performers speed up a little in one phrase and slow down in another to make up for it. It gives them the freedom to be more expressive.
4) Composers added extra notes to chords to make the harmonies more interesting — they used 7ths, 9ths, 11ths and 13ths (9ths, 11ths and 13ths are just 2nds, 4ths and 6ths but an octave higher). They helped create dissonance (clashing notes), which let them show emotions like pain and misery.
5) There was a lot of virtuoso playing — composers wrote technically difficult music to give performers the chance to show off. It was very exciting to watch and listen to. Rachmaninov and Liszt wrote solo piano music that had to be written on four staves as there were so many notes to play.
6) Lots of Romantic composers were very proud of the countries they came from — they used folk tunes and dance rhythms from their homelands to show their national pride. Tchaikovsky used the French and Russian national anthems in his 1812 Overture.

The Orchestra **Developed** in the **Romantic Period**

1) Orchestras got much bigger as extra instruments were added.
2) The piccolo, bass clarinet and contrabassoon (which plays an octave lower than the bassoon) were added to the woodwind section.
3) Percussion sections grew to include xylophones, glockenspiels, drums, cymbals, bells and triangles as standard. Celestes (keyboard instruments that sound like glockenspiels) and harps were used too.
4) Brass instruments now had valves so were able to play more notes. Trombones and tubas were added.
5) The changes allowed composers to write music with a larger range of texture, timbre and dynamics.
6) The development of the piano (see next page) meant that it became a much more popular and important instrument. Lots of piano music was written in the Romantic period.

REVISION TIP

If music be the food of love — play on...

Make sure you know all the key features of Romantic music — you might need to spot them in the exam. Listen out for dynamic contrasts, variations in tempo and interesting harmonies.

The Romantic Period

The piano was definitely one of the most important instruments in the Romantic period.

The Piano Developed in the Romantic Period

The piano has been around since the 18th century, but the developments in the 19th century made it really popular with Romantic composers.

SIZE: the piano changed shape a bit and got bigger (and louder). This meant it had a bigger dynamic range.

KEYS: the number of keys (and notes) increased to just over 7 octaves. Composers now had a larger range in pitch to compose for.

PEDALS: both pedals (the sustain pedal that holds notes on and the soft pedal) became more effective. Some modern pianos have three pedals — the third pedal allows some notes to be held on while others are not.

STRINGS: the strings inside were both thicker and longer, making a fuller tone. They were also pulled tighter, so they were more tense.

FRAME: the frame used to be made of wood, but was now made of metal (to cope with the new strings). This made it easier to transport them.

HAMMERS: the hammers were given a felt covering (instead of a leather one). This made the tone softer and more rounded.

Melodies Were the Focus of Piano Pieces

1) In Romantic piano pieces, the melody was the most important part. Melodies were often marked *cantabile* — to be played in a singing style.

2) There were lots of virtuosic sections and cadenzas (see p.57) to give the pianist chance to show off.

3) The music had a large range of dynamics, articulation and tone. Pianists had to use the pedals a lot to get the right sounds.

4) The accompaniment was often broken chords (see p.39), but unlike many Classical pieces, the broken chords would be spread across several octaves.

Concertos, Sonatas and Preludes Were Written for the Piano

1) The piano was popular as the solo instrument in concertos — the pianist was able to really show off in the cadenza. Rachmaninov wrote famous piano concertos — there's more about him, and Romantic concertos in general, on p.99-100.

2) Lots of sonatas (see p.93) were written for the piano — Chopin, Liszt, Mendelssohn and Schumann all composed piano sonatas.

3) Preludes were originally the bit of music that came before the main piece. During the Romantic period, they had become popular as stand-alone pieces. Debussy, Liszt and Rachmaninov all wrote preludes for the piano, and Chopin wrote a prelude for each of the 24 keys.

I'll have soup as a prelude to my dinner...

Pianos were popular because they were so versatile — with a range of over seven octaves, composers had fewer limitations when they were composing. The newly-developed piano could play a range of dynamics, and the pedals could be used to change the tone of the instrument too. Perfect for Romantics.

The Romantic Concerto

In the Romantic period, composers wrote concertos to be performed to large audiences in concert halls. They entertained their audiences by creating dramatic contrast between the soloist and orchestra.

Romantic Concertos were for the Piano, Violin or Cello

1) Romantic concertos incorporated all the expressive qualities that were common in Romantic music — such as the emotional style, a wide range of dynamics and tempo, and chromatic harmonies. Composers would increase the dramatic effect by modulating between a number of unusual keys.

2) Composers made use of the large orchestras now available to them. Despite this, they composed for a limited range of solo instruments — the majority of Romantic concertos are for the piano or violin, and some were composed for the cello too.

> • Composers of Romantic piano concertos include Chopin, Liszt, Grieg, Brahms, Tchaikovsky and Rachmaninov.
> • Brahms, Mendelssohn and Tchaikovsky all composed violin concertos.
> • Dvořák, Schumann, Elgar and Saint-Saëns wrote famous cello concertos.

Romantic Composers Experimented with the Concerto

1) Romantic concertos tended to be much longer than Classical ones. The structure developed from Classical concertos — composers became more experimental with the overall structure and the form of the movements.

2) Most concertos still had three movements, but the breaks between them were less obvious. Some composers tried different numbers of movements. Liszt's Piano Concerto No. 1 and Brahms' Piano Concerto No. 2 both have four movements — in each, the additional movement includes elements of a scherzo (like in a symphony — see p.93). Liszt went in the opposite direction for his Piano Concerto No. 2 — that only has one movement.

3) Many composers altered the structure of the first movement. Although some Romantic concertos used the double exposition of the Classical period (see p.95), composers such as Mendelssohn moved away from this. They used a single exposition instead — the soloist would play right from the start, and introduce the themes together with the orchestra. These themes would appear throughout the concerto, linking together the different movements.

The Soloist Became Even More Important

1) Romantic concertos gave the soloist more chance to show off than ever before. The soloist's part was often extremely difficult — passages in Tchaikovsky's Violin Concerto were so quick that they were initially considered to be impossible to play.

2) Solo parts had to be particularly impressive in order stand out from the large orchestra — there was often a lot of contrast between the soloist's part and the rest of the orchestra, which added to the drama of the compositions.

3) The cadenza became a more prominent feature in the first movement — it usually came before the recapitulation (unlike in the Classical period where it came after). Cadenzas were usually written out by the composer — they were no longer improvised.

4) The virtuoso performances given by soloists gained them huge respect — they were the celebrities of their time.

EXAM TIP

Liszt the features of Romantic and Classical concertos...

In the exam you might be asked when a concerto was composed, or to suggest a suitable composer. Knowing the key features of concertos from the different periods will help a lot.

The Romantic Concerto

This page will focus on a couple of Romantic concertos that didn't follow the standard Classical structures.

Mendelssohn's Violin Concerto in E Minor Used New Ideas

1) This concerto was completed in 1844 — it took Mendelssohn six years to write it.

2) The concerto has three movements, with the standard quick-slow-quick tempo structure.

3) The first movement begins with a single exposition — there's no orchestral introduction and the first theme is played by the soloist who enters in the second bar. The tonic key is E minor, and Mendelssohn combines this with chromatic notes to make the opening section very dramatic.

4) The cadenza comes before the recapitulation (at bar 299). It's 36 bars long and is written out in full.

- The cadenza covers a huge range of notes — extremely quick arpeggio-style patterns show off the violinist's skill.
- It also includes semi-quaver runs that reach both extremes of the violin's range.
- There are slower passages too, with dramatic trills and multiple-stopped chords.

5) The soloist is required to use complex techniques throughout the concerto. These include double-stopping, glissando (sliding from note to note on one string) and harmonics (see p.65). The third movement contains tricky phrases where the soloist has to switch from playing with the bow to pizzicato (plucking) and back again very quickly.

6) Sometimes it's the soloist that accompanies the orchestra, rather than the other way round. E.g. at bar 131 of the first movement, the solo violin holds a low G pedal note (see p.39) while the clarinets play the melody, with a harmony on the flutes. The violin then repeats the same melody.

7) There are no breaks between the movements — this was to stop people applauding between them. A bassoon note is held between the first two movements, and second moves swiftly into the third.

Rachmaninov's Piano Concerto No. 2 is Very Dramatic

1) This concerto was composed towards the end of the Romantic period, in 1900-1901. Rachmaninov gave the first performance of the concerto himself.

2) Like Mendelssohn, Rachmaninov didn't stick to the traditional structure — the first movement begins with a single exposition involving both soloist and orchestra. The piano opens the movement, and is unaccompanied until the orchestra enters in bar 11.

3) There is no cadenza in the first movement, but the slow second movement includes virtuosic passages. These have minimal orchestral accompaniment and introduce brand new material.

4) The music is very expressive — Rachmaninov uses lots of different techniques to achieve this:

- The tonic key of the piece is C minor. The first movement opens with big, minor chords on the piano — you need large hands to play all the notes at once.
- There's lots of variation in dynamics throughout the piece. During the first 9 bars the dynamics go from *pp* to *ff*.
- There are lots of changes in tempo.
- The opening and closing sections of the second movement contain frequent changes of metre (between $\frac{4}{4}$ and $\frac{3}{2}$) — this adds to the relaxed mood of these sections.

Sadly you don't have six years to compose your pieces...

Listen to the two concertos described above and see if you can spot the Romantic features.

Warm-up and Exam Questions

Use the warm-up questions to jog your memory, then have a go at the exam question.

Warm-up Questions

1) Name an instrument that was included in the Classical orchestra but was not used in orchestras of the Baroque period.

2) How many movements does a standard Classical concerto have?

3) What are the three main sections of a piece in sonata form?

4) Name two Classical composers.

5) When did the Romantic period start (approximately)?

6) Name two sources of inspiration used by Romantic composers.

7) Describe how Romantic composers used dynamics.

8) Which three instruments were the majority of Romantic concertos composed for?

Exam Question

Give this exam-style question a try.

Track 33 is an extract from the first movement of a concerto.
Play the extract **three** times, leaving a short pause for writing time between each playing.

Track 33

a) What instrument is playing at the start of the extract?

....
[1 mark]

b) i) What is the name given to the part of the concerto heard at the start of the extract?

....
[1 mark]

ii) Give **two** reasons for your answer to i).

....

....
[2 marks]

Exam Question

c) Which of the following musical devices are used in the first part of the extract?
Tick the **two** correct answers.

Trill ☐

Arpeggios ☐

Ostinato ☐

Sequence ☐

Pedal point ☐

[2 marks]

d) What musical term describes the final section of the extract
where the full orchestra is playing? Tick the correct answer.

Exposition ☐

Development ☐

Coda ☐

[1 mark]

e) Name two instruments that you can hear in the final part of the extract.

....

....
[2 marks]

f) Suggest a suitable time signature for the orchestral part of the extract.

....
[1 mark]

g) i) Which musical period is this concerto from?

....
[1 mark]

ii) Write down a suitable composer for this concerto.

....
[1 mark]

Revision Summary for Section Six

You need to be really clued up on concertos in Baroque, Classical and Romantic music — it's really important that you know the key features of each, and the similarities and differences between them. Make sure you know all the background facts about the three musical periods too — you'll need to be able to spot and describe the musical devices that composers used in each era.

1) Give the approximate dates of the Baroque period.
2) What is a basso continuo and what instruments would normally play it?
3) Describe the general structure of a fugue.
4) Which Baroque structure can be described as ABA?
5) What was the function of a prelude in the Baroque period?
6) In theme and variation form, what is the theme?
7) What is the main difference between theme and variation form and ground bass form?
8) Explain what each of these terms means:
   a) melodic inversion   b) retrograde   c) ostinato
9) Name three different ornaments used by Baroque composers and explain what they are.
10) What is a sequence?
11) What is a solo concerto?
12) Name a Baroque solo concerto.
13) What is a concerto grosso?
14) Name a Baroque concerto grosso.
15) Give the approximate dates of the Classical period.
16) Why did the piano become increasingly popular in the Classical period?
17) What was the most important section in a Classical orchestra?
18) Classical music usually has a homophonic texture. What does this mean?
19) In a Classical concerto with three movements, what tempo does each movement have?
20) What form does each movement of a Classical concerto usually take?
21) What is a symphony?
22) How many instruments are sonatas usually composed for?
23) What is rondo form?
24) Name one Classical concerto.
25) In a Classical concerto, what is a double exposition?
26) a) What is a cadenza?
    b) At what point in the first movement of a Classical concerto does the cadenza usually come?
27) Write down the names of two Romantic composers.
28) Give three techniques used by Romantic composers to add drama to their music.
29) What does the tempo marking *rubato* mean? Explain the effect it has.
30) Name two instruments that were added to the orchestra in the Romantic period.
31) Write down three ways in which the piano was developed in the 19th century.
32) How did the role of the soloist in a concerto develop from the Classical to Romantic eras?
33) What change did some Romantic composers make to the structure of the first movement of a concerto?
34) Where did the cadenza usually come in the first movement of a Romantic concerto?
35) Give another way in which Romantic composers broke the rules of the Classical concerto.
36) Name three techniques that the soloist is required to use in Mendelssohn's Violin Concerto in E Minor.

Indian Classical Music — Raga

You'll come across lots of new words for instruments and other musical features in this section. Don't be put off if you see these words spelt differently elsewhere — there are often a few ways to spell them.

Indian Classical Music is Based on Ragas and Talas

1) A raga is a scale that usually has between 5 and 8 notes. There are hundreds of different ragas — each one represents a different time of day or season and creates a mood associated with that time.

2) Raga scales are very different from Western scales. By using microtones (intervals between notes that are smaller than a semitone), they often include notes that aren't heard in Western music.

3) A tala is a pattern of beats that sets the rhythm for a piece — there are hundreds of different talas.

4) The word raga is used as a general term for performances combining the raga and the tala — these performances involve a lot of improvisation, based on the notes of the raga and the rhythm of the tala.

5) Ragas and talas were never written down — they were passed on from generation to generation aurally (i.e. by listening and learning to play from memory), and they're still taught in this way today.

6) In Northern India, raga and tala students join a school of players called a gharana. Each gharana is run by a teacher or 'master', and each gharana has its own traditions and theories about how to play.

7) Spirituality is an important part of almost all Indian classical music. In Southern India, there is a long tradition of the Carnatic kriti. Here, words are set to a raga in praise of a particular Hindu deity.

The Traditional Instruments are Sitar, Tambura and Tabla

Sitar

1) A sitar is a large, long-necked string instrument.

2) On a seven-stringed sitar, five of the strings are plucked for the melody and the other two create drone notes.

3) Sitars also have 'sympathetic' strings underneath the main strings. The sympathetic strings vibrate when the main strings are played, creating a thick, shimmery sound.

4) The frets on a sitar can be moved — they're adjusted to different positions for different pieces.

5) Sitar players can pull strings to make pitch bends. This produces a sound called meend.

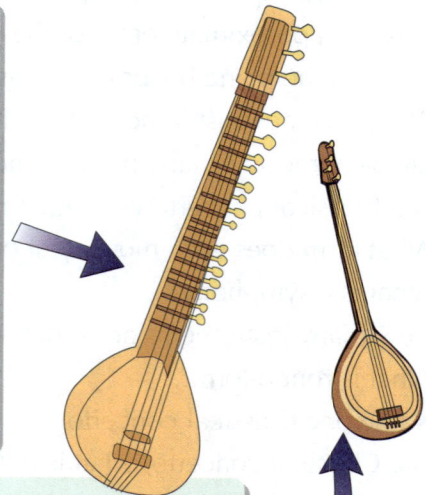

Tambura

The tambura is a similar shape to the sitar. It usually has four metal strings, but can have up to six. It's used as more of a backing instrument.

Tabla

Tabla is a pair of drums. The smaller, higher drum is called the tabla or dayan. The larger, lower-sounding drum is called the baya.

Other instruments include...

• Other string instruments — the surbahar (a bass sitar), the sarod (a fretless mini-sitar) and the sarangi (fretless and played with a bow).

• Wind instruments — the bansuri is a flute made of bamboo and the shehnai is an instrument with a double reed, like an oboe.

• The harmonium — a keyboard instrument powered with air pumped by hand bellows.

• Singers sometimes perform with the instruments as well.

Indian Classical Music — Raga

The sitar, tabla and tambura each have <u>different</u> roles to play in a raga <u>performance</u>.

The **Melody** is **Improvised** on the **Sitar**

1) In a classical Indian group, the sitar player <u>improvises</u> the melody. He or she chooses a <u>raga</u>, and <u>makes up</u> the <u>melody</u> using notes from that <u>scale</u>. (The melody can sometimes be <u>sung</u> instead).

2) The notes of a raga scale are called <u>sa</u>, <u>re</u>, <u>ga</u>, <u>ma</u>, <u>pa</u>, <u>dha</u> and <u>ni</u> (an individual scale doesn't have to contain all of these). Each note is either <u>shuddh</u> (natural), <u>tivra</u> (sharp) or <u>komal</u> (flat) — but only <u>certain notes</u> can be tivra (<u>ma</u>) or komal (<u>re</u>, <u>ga</u>, <u>dha</u> and <u>ni</u>). The notes on the <u>way up</u> the scale can be <u>different</u> from the ones on the <u>way down</u>.

3) Some ragas have <u>rules</u> for individual notes in the scale. There could be notes that are always played <u>quickly</u>, notes that have to be <u>decorated</u>, or made slightly sharper or flatter using <u>microtones</u> (see previous page).

On the way down, the ni is flattened and there are more notes.

RAG DESH — RAINY SEASON RAGA
(see next page)

SA RE MA PA NI SA <u>NI</u> DHA PA MA GA RE SA

The **Tabla** Sets the **Rhythm**

1) The <u>tabla</u> is the <u>percussion</u> section. Tabla players <u>vary</u> the sound they create by striking <u>different points</u> on the drums and by using different parts of their <u>hands</u>. The different sounds are represented by <u>syllables</u> known as '<u>bols</u>', such as <u>dha</u> and <u>tin</u>. Players sometimes <u>speak</u> the <u>bols</u> too.

2) The <u>rhythm</u> of a raga performance is based on a <u>tala</u> — a basic <u>rhythm cycle</u>. A <u>tala</u> has a <u>set number</u> of beats (called <u>matras</u>). There are <u>accents</u> on certain beats, and <u>bols</u> specify how each beat should be played on the tabla. The <u>number</u> of beats in a tala ranges <u>from 3 to over 100</u>.

3) The <u>tala</u> is <u>repeated</u> throughout the piece. The <u>first beat</u> of a tala is called the <u>sam</u>. <u>All</u> the musicians <u>play together</u> on each sam and the whole piece always <u>ends</u> on a sam.

4) Each tala is split into <u>groups</u> called <u>vibhags</u>. A vibhag is a bit like a <u>bar</u> in Western music, except that you can have <u>different</u> numbers of <u>beats</u> in each vibhag.

5) The <u>structure</u> of the tala is indicated by different <u>claps</u>. If the <u>first beat</u> of a <u>vibhag</u> is heavily <u>stressed</u>, a <u>normal</u> clap is used. If the first beat is <u>weaker</u>, this is shown by a '<u>wave</u>' or '<u>khali</u>'— a <u>quieter</u> clap made by tapping the back of the right hand into the left. The <u>musicians</u> or <u>audience</u> might make these claps <u>in time</u> with the tala. A <u>vibhag</u> that starts with a <u>khali</u> beat is only played on the <u>dayan</u> drum.

6) The <u>tabla</u> player doesn't just play the <u>tala</u> rhythm itself — they also <u>improvise</u> more complicated rhythms around it, creating <u>cross-rhythm</u>, <u>polyrhythm</u> and <u>syncopation</u>.

The <u>tintal</u> tala has <u>4 vibhags</u> with <u>4 beats</u> each:

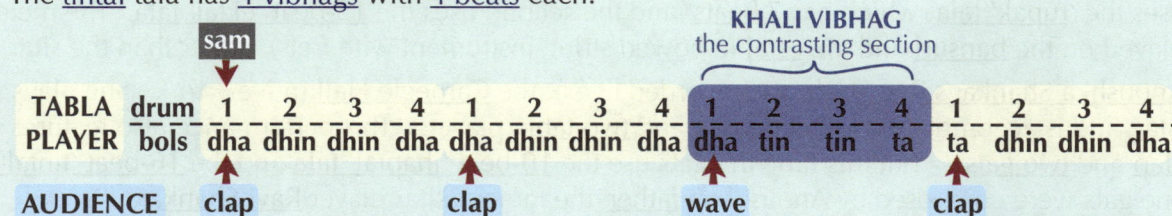

sam

KHALI VIBHAG
the contrasting section

TABLA drum	1	2	3	4	1	2	3	4	1	2	3	4	1	2	3	4
PLAYER bols	dha	dhin	dhin	dha	dha	dhin	dhin	dha	dha	tin	tin	ta	ta	dhin	dhin	dha
AUDIENCE	clap				clap				wave				clap			

The **Tambura** Creates the **Harmony**

1) The <u>tambura's</u> part is often described as a <u>drone</u>. It's not quite as boring as the name suggests, but it is quite <u>repetitive</u>. The tambura player plays a <u>simple rhythmic pattern</u> based on just <u>two notes</u> from the raga (usually <u>pa</u> and <u>sa</u>) all the way through the performance.

2) The <u>sitar</u> player works his or her improvisations <u>around</u> the tambura part — and it's the <u>combination</u> of the two that gives the raga <u>harmony</u>.

REVISION TIP

Just take it one vibhag at a time...

Listen to a recording of any instruments you haven't heard before so you can identify them.

Indian Classical Music — Raga

A performance usually <u>begins</u> with <u>free improvisation</u> on the sitar — the <u>tala rhythm</u> is introduced <u>later</u>.

A Typical Raga has **Four Sections**

The tradition is for a raga performance to have <u>four phases</u> (though some modern performances don't include all the phases). There are usually <u>no gaps</u> between the phases — each one flows into the next.

> 1) **THE ALAP** — the <u>sitar</u> player introduces the notes of the chosen <u>raga scale</u>, improvising freely. There's <u>no beat</u> or pulse to the melody at this point — it just flows along. The only accompaniment at this point is the <u>tambura drone</u>.
>
> 2) **THE JHOR** — in this second section, the music <u>speeds up</u> a bit. It's still just the tambura player and sitar player, but the music gets more rhythmic, and the melody improvised by the sitar player takes on a <u>steady beat</u>.
>
> 3) **THE JHALA** — this section is <u>loads faster</u> than the alap and jhor, and feels a lot more exciting than the bits that came before. The players <u>improvise</u> around the melody.
>
> 4) **THE GAT OR BANDISH** — in the gat, the raga really takes off:
>   * The <u>tabla player</u> comes in (at last).
>   * The group plays a <u>pre-composed</u> piece. It's called a 'gat' if it's for <u>instruments</u> only, and a '<u>bandish</u>' if there's a <u>song</u>.
>   * The players also add <u>improvisations</u> to the gat or bandish, and pass their musical ideas around in a <u>question and answer</u> style.
>   * There are sometimes <u>two</u> gats — a <u>slow</u> one and a <u>fast</u> one.

Performances with the **Same Name** Can **Sound Very Different**

1) Performances are often named after the <u>raga scale</u> they use — but an <u>infinite</u> number of <u>different</u> pieces can be created using the <u>same raga</u>. The use of <u>improvisation</u>, the <u>instrumentation</u> and the choice of <u>tala</u> and <u>melody</u> for the gat or bandish all contribute to create a <u>unique</u> piece.

2) The '<u>Rag Desh</u>' is the raga that is associated with <u>night-time</u> during the <u>rainy season</u> — it's meant to give the feeling of <u>romance</u> and <u>devotion</u>. Below are just two <u>examples</u> of recordings which use this raga but have a lot of <u>differences</u>:

> * <u>Steve Gorn</u> and <u>Benjy Wertheimer's</u> version of <u>Rag Desh</u> (on the album <u>Priyagitah: The Nightingale</u>) has 3 sections — the <u>alap</u> and <u>two gats</u>. Each gat uses a different <u>tala</u> — the first uses the '<u>rupak</u>' tala, which has <u>7 beats</u>, and the second uses the <u>12-beat 'ektal' tala</u>. The melody is played on the <u>bansuri</u> and the <u>esraj</u> (a bowed string instrument with frets), rather than the sitar.
> * <u>Anoushka Shankar's Rag Desh</u> was recorded live at the <u>Carnegie Hall</u> in New York. She plays the <u>sitar</u>, and is accompanied by a <u>tambura</u> and <u>two tabla</u> players. This performance also features an <u>alap</u> and <u>two gats</u> — but this time the gats use the <u>10-beat 'jhaptal' tala</u> and the <u>16-beat 'tintal' tala</u>. The gats were composed by Anoushka's <u>father</u>, the famous sitar player <u>Ravi Shankar</u>.

Raga Influenced **Rock** and **Pop Music**

1) Many <u>rock</u> and <u>pop</u> performers have been <u>influenced</u> by <u>raga</u> music since the <u>1960s</u>.
2) <u>George Harrison</u> of <u>The Beatles</u> had <u>sitar</u> lessons from <u>Ravi Shankar</u> (see above) and the band incorporated Indian <u>instruments</u> and <u>raga</u> sounds and rhythms into some of their songs.
3) '<u>Within You Without You</u>' on The Beatles' album '<u>Sgt. Pepper's Lonely Hearts Club Band</u>' was heavily influenced by <u>raga</u> and features the <u>sitar</u>, <u>tambura</u>, <u>tabla</u>, and <u>dilruba</u> (a bowed string instrument).

Every raga performance is unique...

That's it for raga — it's quite different from Western music, so make sure you've got it well and truly sussed.

Bhangra

Traditional Punjabi bhangra has been <u>fused</u> with modern Western music to create a popular <u>new style</u>.

Bhangra was Originally a **Folk Dance**

1) Traditional bhangra is <u>fast-paced folk music</u> from the <u>Punjab</u> region of <u>northern India</u> and <u>Pakistan</u>.

2) It was originally played at <u>harvest time</u>, when people would dance and sing to <u>celebrate</u> the harvest. It became popular at other <u>celebrations</u>, such as <u>weddings</u> and <u>New Year</u> parties.

3) The key instrument is the <u>dhol</u>, a <u>double-headed</u>, <u>barrel-shaped drum</u>. The two <u>drumheads</u> have <u>different</u> sounds — the larger one is much <u>lower</u> than the other. You hit the larger head with a <u>heavy</u> stick, and the smaller one with a <u>lighter</u> stick. <u>Polyrhythm</u>, <u>cross-rhythm</u> and <u>syncopation</u> can be created by <u>combining</u> rhythms from the two drumheads.

4) The <u>basic rhythm</u> of a bhangra piece is played on the <u>dhol</u>.
The most popular rhythm for traditional and modern bhangra is the <u>chaal</u>:

> **THE CHAAL**
> - It's an <u>eight-note</u> repeated pattern.
> - The quavers are <u>swung</u> like in the blues (see p.136).
> - As in raga music (see p.105), words called <u>bols</u> tell you how to strike the drum — <u>NA</u> means play the <u>small</u> drumhead, <u>GE</u> means play the <u>large</u> one, and <u>DHA</u> means play <u>both</u>.
>
> DHA NA NA NA NA DHA DHA NA

5) The <u>dholak</u> is another popular bhangra percussion instrument. It's similar to the dhol, but <u>smaller</u>. It's played with the <u>hands</u> rather than sticks, which allows <u>more complex</u> rhythms to be created.

6) <u>Singing</u> has an important role in bhangra music. The melodies tend to use a <u>small range</u> of notes, and the lyrics are <u>light-hearted</u>. Backing singers often shout '<u>Hoi</u>' at certain points in the songs.

7) Other instruments used in bhangra music include the <u>alghoza</u> (a double flute), the <u>tumbi</u> (an instrument with a single plucked string), the <u>sarangi</u> and the <u>tabla</u> (see p.104).

Modern Bhangra Developed in the **UK**

1) The <u>modern bhangra</u> style developed in the <u>UK</u> in the <u>1970s and 1980s</u>.

2) Asian musicians <u>fused</u> the <u>chaal</u> rhythm with Western styles like <u>hip-hop</u>, <u>disco</u>, <u>drum'n'bass</u>, <u>rap</u> and <u>reggae</u>. This created a whole <u>new</u> sound and made bhangra popular with <u>mainstream</u> audiences.

3) They also used <u>Western instruments</u> like the <u>electric guitar</u> and <u>synthesizers</u>.

4) <u>Alaap</u> was one of the first successful bhangra bands — their 1982 song <u>Bhabiye Ni Bhabiye</u> was very popular. Other well-known bhangra performers are <u>Malkit Singh</u>, <u>Sahotas</u>, <u>Sangeeta</u> and <u>Panjabi MC</u>.

5) Bhangra is often used in the soundtracks of <u>Bollywood</u> films.

Modern Bhangra Uses Lots of **Music Technology**

<u>Music technology</u> plays a big part in modern bhangra. Listen out for...

1) <u>Remixes</u> — tracks with lots of different <u>layers</u> mixed together in <u>new ways</u>. A remix normally sounds very <u>different</u> from a live performance because so much has been changed in the <u>studio</u>.

2) <u>Samples</u> from other music (see p.74) — e.g. <u>bass lines</u>, <u>drum parts</u>, <u>words</u> or <u>other sounds</u> mixed in with the new track.

3) <u>Drum machines</u> instead of the dhol.

4) <u>DJ sound effects</u> — such as <u>scratching</u>, where you move a <u>vinyl record</u> back and forth with your <u>hand</u>.

SUGGESTED LISTENING

If you see a cross-rhythm, try to cheer it up...

Have a listen to the <u>Bhangra Beatz</u> album, and try to pick out the different influences. Hoi!

Greek Music

Greece's geographical location means that its music has influences from Europe, Asia and the Middle East.

The Bouzouki, Outi and Toubeleki are Traditional Instruments

1) Greek folk music is usually based on modes (see p.27), rather than major or minor scales.

2) The lyrics of folk songs cover a wide range of topics — there are celebratory songs for weddings, sorrowful laments, and songs telling stories of war and heroism. In 'rebetiko' music, the lyrics focus on social and political issues — this form of folk music started out as the music of working people in the cities.

3) Greek folk music uses traditional string, wind and percussion instruments, as well as Western instruments like the clarinet, violin, guitar and brass instruments. Some of the traditional instruments are described below.

STRING INSTRUMENTS include:
- Bouzouki — has a long neck, with three or four pairs of strings, and is played with a plectrum.
- Outi (or oud) — pear-shaped, with a short neck.
- Laouto (or lute) — looks like an oud but with a longer neck. It has frets and is played with a plectrum.
- Lyra — this has three strings and is played with a bow. There are two types — the lyra of Pontos and the Cretan lyra.

WIND INSTRUMENTS include the floyera (a wooden flute), the karamoudza (a wooden instrument with a double reed) and bagpipes.

There are different types of bagpipe, e.g the gaida from northern Greece.

PERCUSSION INSTRUMENTS include:
- Daouli — a drum with two heads, tuned to different pitches.
- Toubeleki — a goblet-shaped drum. Different tones can be created by striking the centre of the drumhead with the whole hand, or by hitting the edge with the finger tips.
- Defi — similar to a tambourine.

This can also be spelt 'toumbeleki'.

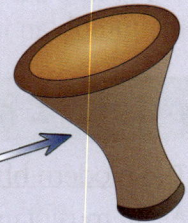

Most Greek Folk Music is for Dancing

There are lots of different folk dances, each with their own rhythms. The rhythm is often played on the toubeleki (goblet drum). Here are some examples:

1) **SYRTOS** — this dance is popular at weddings and festivals. It is in 4/4 time, where the 8 quavers are divided into a 3-3-2 pattern, e.g.

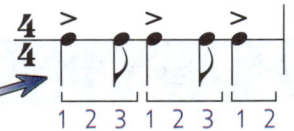

2) **KALAMATIANOS** — this is one of the best-known Greek dances. It is in 7/8 time, and the beats follow a 3-2-2 pattern, e.g.

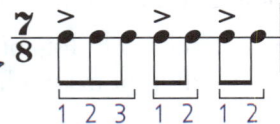

3) **ZEIBEKIKO** — this is an improvised dance for one person. It is in 9/8 time with the beats divided as 2-2-2-3, e.g.

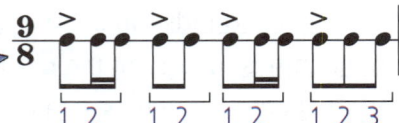

Music from Grease is a very different kettle of fish...

Many of the instruments on this page are used in other Eastern European and Middle Eastern countries too.

Palestinian Music

Palestinian music has similar characteristics to music from other Arab regions, such as Jordan and Syria.

Arabic Music Uses Set Rhythm Patterns

1) Arabic music is based on <u>modes</u> called <u>maqamat</u> — these are ← Maqamat is the plural. different from Western scales as they use <u>microtones</u> (see p.104).

   Maqamat is the plural. A single mode is called a <u>maqam</u>.

2) The <u>melody</u> is dominant — the music is usually <u>monophonic</u>, so it has <u>no harmony</u>. If there are a number of instruments or voices then they will <u>vary</u> their parts with small <u>improvisations</u>, such as adding <u>ornaments</u> — this makes the music <u>heterophonic</u> (see p.45).

3) The <u>percussion</u> rhythms <u>stand out</u> because of the lack of harmony. Arabic music uses <u>rhythmic modes</u> known as <u>iqa'</u>. These are <u>set rhythm patterns</u>, a bit like the <u>tala</u> in Indian music. There are many <u>different</u> iqa', with the patterns ranging from just a few beats to over a hundred. The <u>metres</u> of these rhythms are often <u>different</u> from standard Western <u>time signatures</u> (e.g. $\frac{7}{4}$, $\frac{7}{8}$ etc.).

4) Vocal parts often use <u>melisma</u> (more than one note per <u>syllable</u>) and <u>ululations</u> (high-pitched <u>trills</u>).

5) Traditional Arabic instruments are mainly <u>string</u>, <u>wind</u> and <u>percussion</u> instruments. These are the ones used most commonly in <u>Palestinian</u> folk music:

STRING INSTRUMENTS
- <u>Zither</u> — flat-bodied, with many strings but no neck. It's plucked or strummed.
- <u>Kanun</u> — a large zither
- <u>Oud</u> (see p.108)
- <u>Rababah</u> — a bowed instrument, usually with one or two strings.

WIND INSTRUMENTS
- <u>Mijwiz</u> — made from <u>two pipes</u>, each with a single <u>reed</u> (sounds a bit like a clarinet)
- <u>Arghul</u> — a bit like the mijwiz, with one pipe playing a <u>drone</u>.
- <u>Shababa</u> — a wooden <u>flute</u>.

There are alternative spellings for most of these instruments.

PERCUSSION INSTRUMENTS
- The <u>doumbek</u> (also called <u>darbuka</u> or <u>tablah</u>) is a <u>goblet-shaped</u> drum, like the Greek <u>toubeleki</u> (see p.108).
- Other percussion instruments include the <u>riq</u> (a <u>tambourine</u>), the <u>deff</u> (like a tambourine, but with <u>no bells</u>) and <u>zills</u> (tiny <u>finger cymbals</u>).

The Rhythm is Played on the Doumbek

The <u>doumbek</u> usually plays the <u>main rhythm</u>. There are words for the different drum strokes — <u>dum</u> means strike the drum in the <u>centre</u> with your fingers and palm, and <u>tek</u> and <u>ka</u> mean strike the <u>edge</u> with your finger tips. You <u>alternate</u> the <u>tek</u> and <u>ka</u> strokes between your hands. <u>Dum</u> is played on <u>strong</u> beats, and <u>tek</u> and <u>ka</u> on weaker beats. Dum, tek and ka are often denoted by <u>D</u>, <u>T</u> and <u>K</u>.

- Here's an example of a common rhythm — it's known as the <u>samai thaqil</u> and has a $\frac{10}{8}$ metre.

  Samai thaqil rhythm

  D   T   D D   T

- Palestinian folk music is often <u>dance</u> music — the <u>doumbek</u> provides the rhythm for the dancers. A popular type of Palestinian folk dance is the <u>dabke</u>, where the dancers link arms and dance in a <u>line</u> or a <u>circle</u>. The dance is often performed at special occasions such as <u>weddings</u>.

  Example of a dabke rhythm

  D   T D   T

So many instruments, so little time...

SUGGESTED LISTENING

Have a listen to *Zaghareed* by El-Funoun (a collection of Palestinian folk music for weddings).

Israeli Music

Israel officially became a state in 1948. Its population is made up of people with many different ethnic backgrounds, so folk music has been important in creating the national identity of the country.

Israeli Folk Music Has Lots of Different Influences

1) Jewish people from across the world emigrated to Israel during the 20th century. They brought with them the musical traditions from the communities they came from. Influences from across Europe, North and South America, Africa, Asia and the Middle East can all be heard in Israeli folk music.

2) The wide range of influences means that a great variety of instruments is used in Israeli music. Western string, woodwind, brass and percussion instruments are used, along with Middle Eastern instruments such as the kanun, oud, doumbek and tambourine.

- New folk music (known as Shirei Eretz Yisrael or Land of Israel music) was written from the 1920s to 1960s, to create a common musical identity in Israel. As well as their own cultural background, composers often drew from the local influences of Arabic music (see p.109).
- Composers used minor keys or modal scales, and syncopated rhythms. Some songs celebrated events such as the harvest, or occasions such as weddings. Others were based on religious texts, or explored suffering in war.
- New folk dances were created too. The music and dance steps drew inspiration from the rhythms of Russian and European dances (e.g. the polka and mazurka), as well as local dances such as the dabke (see previous page).

The Horah is a Famous Israeli Folk Dance

1) The Horah was originally from Romania. It's a circle dance, used for celebrations such as bar mitzvahs and weddings. The people at the centre of the celebration (e.g. the bride and groom) are lifted up on chairs during the dance.

2) 'Hava Nagila' is an example of a folk song used to accompany the Horah. It has syncopation in the melody, and most performances have a strong, driving beat in the accompaniment, with an oom-pah pattern. Lots of Israeli folk dance music has this type of rhythm.

3) The Temani dance comes from Yemen — it is also known as Yemenite step. The music often has irregular time signatures and syncopated rhythms.

4) Sara Levi-Tanai was a famous Israeli composer and choreographer, whose parents came from Yemen. Her work was influenced by Yemeni dances, and includes the popular song and dance 'El Ginat Egoz' (which means 'To the Nut Grove').

Klezmer Music Comes From Eastern Europe

1) Klezmer is a popular form of folk music in Israel today. It has its roots in Jewish communities from eastern Europe (particularly Romania).

2) Klezmer instruments include the clarinet, violin, double bass, guitar, accordion, cimbalom (a horizontal string instrument, played with hammers), and percussion.

3) The music usually uses modal scales. Melodies include lots of ornamentation, with trills and glissandi on the clarinet or violin. These often imitate vocal sounds such as crying or laughter.

4) Klezmer usually has a homophonic texture, with melody and accompaniment.

5) It has strong, syncopated rhythms, and is often used for dancing.

It's all very well learning the facts...

... but you really need to listen to some Israeli music. Try 'Ve'Shuv Itchem' from 'Israeli Folk Dances Vol. 1' and see if you can pick out the instruments, rhythms and melodic features.

African Music

The next few pages will focus on the traditional music of sub-Saharan Africa. There are many common musical features seen across this massive region, such as the emphasis on rhythm and the types of instruments that are played. North African music has a different feel, with influences from the Mediterranean and Middle East — see p.108-110.

Drums Play a Big Part in **African Culture**

1) Drums are probably the most widely played instrument in Africa — drummers are highly respected.

2) Drums are played at important events such as births, weddings and funerals. They're used to call people together for these events too — a bit like church bells in Europe. There are different drumbeats for different events, so people from neighbouring villages can tell what's going on just by listening.

3) Drums are used to play an accompaniment for singing and dancing too. They can also be used to accompany manual labour, such as sowing or harvesting crops.

4) Most African drum music is passed on through aural tradition — it's not written down.

These Are the **Main Types of Drum...**

There are a huge number of different African drums — but don't worry, you don't have to know them all. The drums below are some of the most widely used ones — the names for these drums vary from area to area, along with the style in which they're played, and the materials they're made from. The ones on this page all originate from West Africa.

1) The DJEMBE has a single head and is shaped a bit like a goblet. It's played with the hands. The overall size of the drum affects its pitch — smaller drums are higher pitched.

2) DUNDUNS are a cylindrical drums played with sticks. There's a drum skin at each end, so they're played horizontally. There are three types:
   - kenkeni — a high-pitched drum that keeps the pulse going,
   - sangban — a mid-pitched drum,
   - dundunba — a large, low-pitched drum.

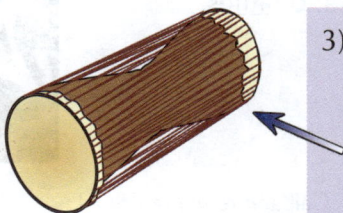

3) The DONNO is also known as the hourglass or talking drum. The player holds it under one arm, and with the other arm hits the drumhead with a thin curved stick.

   The strings round the sides attach to the drumhead. The player can squeeze and release the strings as they play to change the pitch of the drum.

4) The KAGAN, KIDI and SOGO are all barrel-shaped drums — they're held between the drummer's knees and played with wooden sticks.

5) The SABAR drum is usually played with one bare hand and one flexible stick. They come in various different sizes, and are often played together in an ensemble. Sabars were traditionally used to communicate between villages — they could be heard 15 km away.

Drums are very important in African music...

All this drumming's starting to give me a headache — I'm off to have a lie down. Whilst I'm doing that, please can you learn all the stuff on the next few pages? That would be great thanks — you're the best.

African Music

So you've seen a few different types of drum now, but it's not just about learning their names — read on and find out what they're <u>used for</u> and how you <u>play them</u>.

Talking Drums are Used to Send Messages

1) Skilled drummers can make drums '<u>talk</u>'. They <u>change the pitch</u> to imitate changing pitch levels in ordinary <u>speech</u>. The drum sounds carry over long distances, so they can be used to <u>send messages</u>.

2) There are literally <u>thousands</u> of different <u>languages</u> and <u>dialects</u> in Africa. Each drummer imitates his own language to send messages. Drummers like to play on instruments made with <u>local materials</u>. Some believe that this <u>helps</u> the instrument 'speak' the local language.

3) The variety of local languages and materials means you get very <u>different instruments</u> and <u>different playing styles</u> from area to area.

There's a Big Variety of Playing Techniques

There's a bit more to African drumming than hitting a drum with a stick or a brush — there are several different <u>playing techniques</u>.

1) There are no prizes for guessing that one technique is hitting the drum with a <u>stick</u>.

2) A lot of African drummers also play using their <u>hands</u>. There are three basic strokes:

- <u>slap</u> — hit the edge of the drum with the fingers splayed open
- <u>tone</u> — hit the edge of the drum with the fingers held together
- <u>bass</u> — hit the centre of the main drum skin with a flat hand.

3) <u>Dampening</u> is <u>resting</u> one <u>hand</u> or <u>stick</u> on the drum skin whilst playing with the other.

4) On some styles of drum you can <u>change pitch</u> as you're playing, by tightening the skin.

5) To get a <u>contrasting</u> sound you can <u>strike the wood</u> instead of the skin.

The Master Drummer Leads the Group

1) In most African <u>drum ensembles</u> there's a <u>master drummer</u>. He's accompanied by any number of <u>drums</u>, and other percussion such as <u>bells</u> and <u>rattles</u>.

2) A system of <u>call and response</u> is used to <u>structure</u> the music:

The master drummer plays a <u>rhythmic signal</u> which sets the <u>tempo</u> and <u>rhythm</u> for the other players. After this <u>call</u>, the other players join in with the <u>response</u>. This call and response pattern is usually repeated <u>many times</u> during a performance.

Call and response is used in singing too, especially for church music.

3) The master drummer also <u>controls</u> the build-up and release of <u>tension</u>. He leads the other players in changes of <u>dynamics</u>, <u>tempo</u>, <u>pitch</u> and <u>rhythm</u>. In general the drum beats are quite <u>repetitive</u> — these <u>changes</u> are what keep the audience hooked.

4) Performances can last for <u>several hours</u> and involve an <u>audience response</u> — <u>shouting</u>, <u>cheering</u>, and <u>clapping</u> along with the rhythms are an integral part of the performance.

EXAM TIP

Keep going till you've learnt it all...

Make sure you've learnt all these elements of African drumming. Call and response is a key feature of African music — you might need to spot it or describe it in your listening exam.

African Music

African drumming is based on <u>repeated rhythm patterns</u> or cycles called <u>ostinatos</u> (see p.84).

The Rhythms are **Complex**

1) African music is based on <u>rhythmic cycles</u> of varying lengths, with <u>accents</u> on particular beats.

2) Rhythmic cycles with <u>accents</u> in <u>different places</u> are often played at the <u>same time</u> — this creates <u>polyrhythm</u> and <u>cross-rhythm</u> (see p.14), and adds <u>tension</u> to the music.

3) Notes that don't fall on a strong beat can be emphasised, giving a <u>syncopated</u> effect.

4) Although the music is based on repeated cycles, individual players introduce <u>small variations</u>. These gradually <u>develop</u> the basic patterns throughout the performance.

This means 'repeat the previous bar'.

DJEMBE — slap, tone, bass — Starting signal and 1st djembe — 2nd djembe

DUNDUN — closed note, open note — 1st dundun — 2nd dundun

Closed means dampened.

The **Thumb Piano**, **Balafon** and **Kora** are Popular Instruments

Some of the most popular <u>non-percussion instruments</u> are shown below.
The <u>melodies</u> and <u>harmonies</u> in African music are usually based on <u>note systems</u> that are <u>pentatonic</u> (5 notes), <u>hexatonic</u> (6 notes) or <u>heptatonic</u> (7 notes).

A <u>balafon</u> is a wooden xylophone. The lumpy things hanging under the keys are dried <u>gourds</u>. They create a <u>warm</u>, <u>mellow</u> sound.

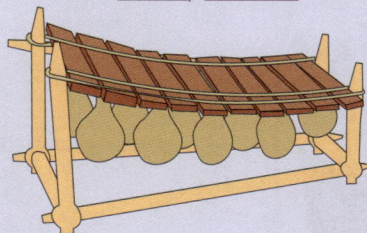

The <u>kora</u> is made and played by the Mandingo people. It's got <u>21 strings</u> and you play it by <u>plucking</u> — a bit like a harp.

The <u>mbira</u> or <u>thumb piano</u> is really popular — partly because it's pocket-sized. It makes a <u>liquid</u>, <u>twangy</u> sound.

These two are mostly played in <u>West Africa</u>.

The thumb piano is played <u>all over</u> Africa.

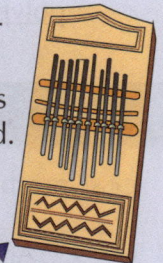

Wind instruments such <u>wooden flutes</u> and <u>whistles</u> are also widely used.

<u>Singing</u> is also very important, both alongside other <u>instruments</u> or <u>a cappella</u>. <u>South African</u> all-male choirs (such as <u>Ladysmith Black Mambazo</u>) sing a cappella. There are two main types of African a cappella singing — <u>mbube</u> (<u>loud</u> and <u>powerful</u> singing, with <u>high-pitched lead vocals</u> over a <u>four-part harmony bass line</u>) and <u>isicathamiya</u> (<u>softer</u> and <u>gentler</u>, with <u>four-part harmonies</u> singing <u>call and response</u>). Isicathamiya has <u>dance moves</u> such as <u>stamps</u> and <u>tip-toeing</u>.

Polyrhythms — learn them parrot fashion...

In the 20th century, Western instruments such as <u>guitars</u> and <u>saxophones</u> became popular in Africa — the 'highlife' music genre combined these Western influences with <u>traditional</u> African drum music.

Calypso

Calypso is a style of music from the Caribbean. It has been influenced by many different cultures.

Calypso Comes from Trinidad

1) The island of Trinidad is the most southern island in the Caribbean.
   It lies off the coast of Venezuela in South America.

2) Calypso music has its origins with African slaves who were brought to Trinidad to work on sugar and cotton plantations. They used the music to communicate with each other about their terrible situation, with clever lyrics that the plantation owners couldn't understand.

3) Over the centuries, the island came under the rule of Spain, France and Britain.
   Calypso music was influenced by the cultures of those countries, in addition to its African roots.

4) The French brought the tradition of carnival to the island — a carnival is still held each year, on the two days before the start of Lent (the period before Easter). Calypso music is an important part of the carnival — steel drum bands (see next page) and singers compete for prizes.

5) The lyrics had a major role in traditional calypso songs. They told stories about important topics such as social issues or relationships, using funny or mocking lyrics. They were often improvised.

6) As calypso developed, improvisation was used less, but today there is a sub-genre of calypso called extempo, where performers are given a topic and improvise lyrics to a well-known tune.

Calypso Uses Syncopated Rhythms

- Calypso music is usually in $\frac{2}{2}$ or $\frac{4}{4}$ time.
- The rhythms are syncopated (see p.136), and mostly follow a 3-3-2 pattern. This gives each bar three beats, but with the final beat shorter than the others. Two examples are shown here, with square brackets marking the beats.
- The songs can have a verse-chorus or a strophic structure.
- The texture can be homophonic, with a main melody and accompaniment, or polyphonic with melodies and countermelodies (see p.45).

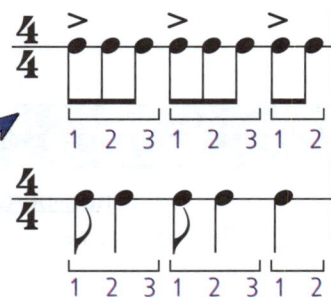

Calypso Bands Use a Variety of Instruments

A calypso band can include a wide range of different instruments:

- Acoustic, electric and bass guitars.
- Brass — such as trumpets and trombones.
- Woodwind — such as clarinets and saxophones.
- Bongos — a pair of small drums.
- Conga drums — these are tall, narrow, barrel-shaped drums.
- Claves — a pair of wooden sticks that produce a ringing sound when one hits the other.
- Other percussion such as bamboo sticks, wood blocks and maracas.
- A modern drum kit might be used too.
- Steel pans are also important in calypso music — see next page.

These instruments are called Latin percussion.

Calypso is all about syncopation...

Make sure you know the facts about the rhythm, structure and texture of calypso music. Oh, and don't forget about that long list of instruments — cover it up and check you can write them down from memory.

Calypso

Calypso music is often played on steel pans — this page explains how they work and how they're played.

Steel Pans Can Play Lots of Different Notes

1) Steel pans are tuned percussion instruments. Each pan can produce a number of different notes. Pans were originally made from large oil drums, but they are now made from sheet metal.

2) Steel pan players are called pannists, and they play together in a steel band. Steel bands also include Latin percussion and a drum kit, and a bass guitar is sometimes added too.

3) Steel pans have a concave surface with a dented appearance — each dent is shaped to produce a particular note when struck.

4) The drums come in different sizes — the deeper the pan, the lower the notes it produces. They have names according to their pitch, e.g. soprano (highest), alto, baritone and bass (lowest).

5) A soprano pan can be tuned to create all the chromatic notes within its range. This is not possible for the other pans — a set of pans is needed to cover the full range of notes. A single bass pan can only produce a small number of notes, so a bass pannist needs between four and six pans to cover the full range.

6) Sets of pans have special names and are used for different purposes. E.g. a set of two baritone drums is called the 'double guitar' — it gets its name because it's used for strumming (playing chords) and can also provide harmony and countermelody.

Dents tuned to different notes.

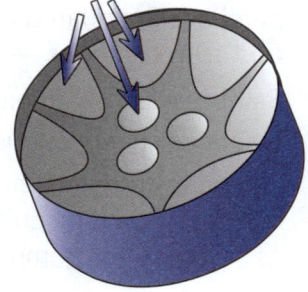

Soprano pans are sometimes called tenors or ping-pongs.

Rolling Creates a Sustained Note

- Steel pans are played with special mallets with rubber heads. They produce a warm, echoing, metallic timbre (see p.75) from the pans. This varies slightly depending on the size of the pan.
- Pannists sometimes hold two mallets in each hand, so they can play chords with up to four notes.
- They can play sustained notes using tremolo or rolling (alternating the hands quickly on a single note). They can also play trills by alternating between different notes.
- They can create dynamic contrast, with crescendos and diminuendos, depending on how hard they hit the pans.
- Steel bands produce music with complex melodies, harmonies and rhythms. They're very versatile — they usually play syncopated calypso rhythms, but can play music of many other genres too, such as folk and jazz.

Calypso Has Evolved Into New Styles

Calypso is still played with traditional instruments, but modern technology has also been incorporated into calypso music, creating new styles.

1) **RAPSO** first appeared in the 1960s — this sub-genre of calypso focuses on the lyrics, which are often about political and social issues. The style developed to use synthesized instruments and modern production techniques.

2) **SOCA** has a faster beat than traditional calypso, making it popular as dance music, particularly at carnivals. It developed in the 1970s, when calypso artists began using electronic drums, synthesizers and studio effects in their recordings.

Cooking with steel pans is not recommended...

SUGGESTED LISTENING

Have a listen to 'Steel Drums of the Caribbean: Calypso Classics', by Jamaican Steel Band.

Samba

Samba is one of the most popular forms of dance music in South America (and around the world).

Samba Comes from **Brazil**

1) Samba is Brazilian dance music. Its origins lie with African slaves, brought to Brazil between the 16th and 19th centuries — many of its influences and traditional instruments can be traced to West Africa.

2) Samba is usually in either $\frac{2}{4}$ or $\frac{4}{4}$, with the emphasis on the second beat of the bar. It sounds cheery and is played at a fast tempo in a major key.

3) Samba instruments include a big variety of percussion (see below), the Portuguese guitar (a bright-sounding guitar with 12 strings), keyboards and whistles. Brass instruments such as saxophones, trumpets and trombones are also sometimes used.

4) Samba bands vary a lot in size — smaller bands are used to play samba music for dança de salão (ballroom dance), or to accompany samba-canção (samba songs).

5) Samba schools are much larger groups of samba musicians and dancers. They tend to be dominated by the percussion section — this is called the bateria and can involve hundreds of players. The music the percussion play is known as batucada — these pages will concentrate on this type of samba.

6) Samba is a major feature of Brazilian carnivals, such as the famous Rio Carnival. Samba schools compete for prizes (just like calypso bands in the carnivals of Trinidad and Tobago, see p.114). They're judged on their percussion performance, and also on a song that's composed and performed by the school. These songs have catchy melodies, and build up with different parts getting added on top.

There Are Lots of **Samba Percussion Instruments**

Many different percussion instruments are played in the bateria.

1) The **SURDO** is a large, loud, resonant bass drum, played with one stick and one hand. Surdos come in different sizes — a bateria will often use three sizes of surdo (see next page). Surdos set the basic beat for the rest of the bateria.

2) The **CAIXA** is a snare drum played with sticks — it can be used to create polyrhythm (see p.14).

3) The **REPINIQUE** is a bit like a tom-tom. It has a high pitch that can be heard above the other drums. The leader of the bateria plays the repinique.

4) The **CUICA** is held horizontally and has a large pitch range. There is a wooden stick inside the drum, with one end attached to the drumskin. The drummer rubs the stick with a wet cloth to produce the sound. They vary the pitch by applying pressure on the outside of the drumskin with their other hand.

stick

5) The **TAMBORIM** is a very small drum — it looks a bit like a tambourine, but without any bells. It has a high pitch and is played with a single beater.

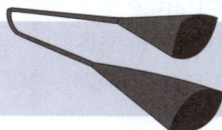

6) The **AGOGO** is a double cow-bell, played with a stick — it's formed from two bells with different pitches.

7) Other percussion instruments include shakers (the ganzá, caxixi, xequerê and afoxé), scrapers (the reco-reco) and tambourines (the pandeiro).

Samba

The various percussion instruments all contribute different rhythms to a samba performance — we'll look at some examples below. The rhythms combine to create music with a complex texture.

The **Surdo de Primeira** Sets the **Beat**

1) The surdo de primeira (first surdo) has the lowest pitch. It's struck with the stick on the second beat of the bar, and then dampened with the hand on the following beat — the pattern is repeated over and over again. This creates emphasis on second beat of each bar.

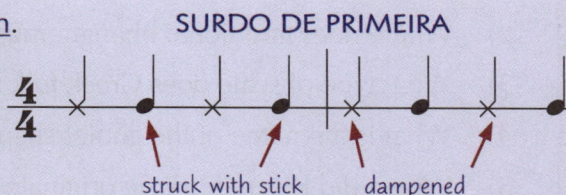

SURDO DE PRIMEIRA

struck with stick   dampened

2) The surdo de segunda (second surdo) is slightly smaller and so has a higher pitch than the surdo de primeira. It's struck on the beats where the surdo de primeira is dampened, so it follows the opposite pattern.

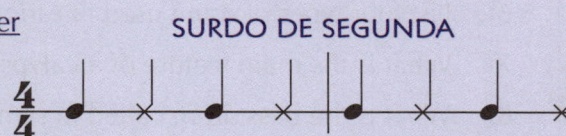

SURDO DE SEGUNDA

3) The surdo de terceira (third surdo) is smaller and at a higher pitch than both the other surdos. It plays more complex, syncopated rhythms, adding a swing to the rhythm produced by the surdos.

Example of a SURDO DE TERCEIRA rhythm

4) The caixa plays faster rhythms — variation is created by playing accents on different notes.

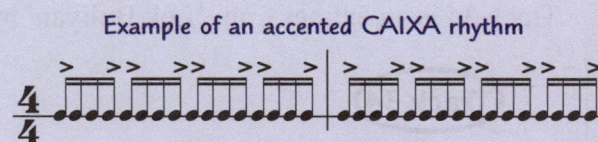

Example of an accented CAIXA rhythm

5) The other instruments add in additional contrasting rhythms and syncopation.

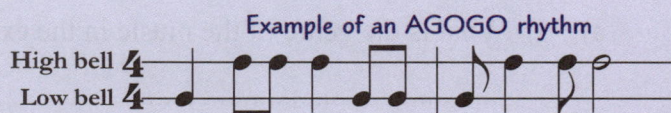

Example of an AGOGO rhythm

High bell
Low bell

The **Repinique** Leads **Call and Response**

1) Some sections of a samba performance involve call and response — these sections contrast with the bits where everyone plays repeated rhythms.

2) The leader of the bateria plays solo rhythms on the repinique, and is answered by the rest of the bateria — they might play the same rhythm, or a contrasting rhythm.

call
response

The **Leader** Plays a **Whistle** Too

1) The leader uses a two-toned whistle called an apito de samba to control the bateria.

2) The whistle sets the tempo and indicates the start of call and response sections. It also signals breaks, where the band stops and then starts again, playing a different rhythm from before.

Put 2nd December in your diary — it's Brazil's National Samba Day...

As with many traditional styles of music, technology has had an impact on samba. It has been fused with styles such as funk, rock and disco, creating sub-genres that feature electronic instruments and effects.

Warm-up and Exam Questions

Feeling jet-lagged? After that whistle-stop tour through world music, it's time for some questions.

Warm-up Questions

1) What is a raga?

2) Where does traditional bhangra music come from?

3) What type of scale does Greek folk music usually use?

4) What is the name of the goblet-shaped drum used in Palestinian music?

5) Where did Klezmer music originate from?

6) List four types of drum used in African music.

7) What is the main feature of a calypso rhythm?

8) What is the bass drum called in samba music?

Exam Questions

Have a go at these exam-style questions.

Track 34 is an extract from 'Lok Boliyan' by Anakhi.

(Track 34)

a)   i) What is the genre of the music in the extract?

....

[1 mark]

ii) Give two reasons for your answer.

....

....

[2 marks]

b)   Suggest a suitable time signature for this extract.

....

[1 mark]

c)   Name two different percussion instruments you can hear in this extract.

....

....

[2 marks]

Exam Questions

d)   Both Western and non-Western instruments are played in this extract.

i) Name one non-Western string instrument that you can hear.

....
[1 mark]

ii) Name one Western string instrument that you can hear.

....
[1 mark]

e)   Part of the extract features singing. Describe the vocal parts that you hear in that section.

....

....

....

....

....
[3 marks]

f)   The feel of the music changes after the vocal section.
Tick the phrase that best describes the change that takes place.

The music changes from **major to minor**. ☐

The music changes from **minor to major**. ☐

The music changes from **tonal to atonal**. ☐
[1 mark]

g)   Which of these examples most closely matches the rhythm played at the during the
instrumental section at the end of the extract? Tick the box next to the correct answer.

[1 mark]

Exam Questions

Track 35 is an extract from 'Carnivale', from the album *Steel Appeal*.

(Track 35)

a) From which region of the world does this style of music originate?
Circle the correct answer.

Latin America   **Caribbean**   **Middle East**   **Africa**

[1 mark]

b) Which of these rhythms shows the main beat or pulse in the first half of this extract?
Tick the box next to the correct answer.

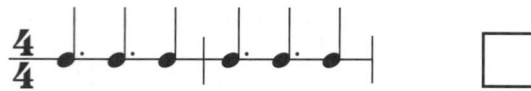

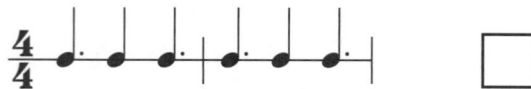

[1 mark]

c) About halfway through the extract, the music changes.
Describe the rhythmic differences between the two sections.

....

....

....

....

[3 marks]

d) The title of this piece is 'Carnivale'. Identify two features of this extract
that make it suitable for a carnival.

....

....

....

[2 marks]

Revision Summary for Section Seven

This section is packed with facts about music from all over the globe. You wouldn't want to confuse your raga with your samba, so use these revision questions to check you've got everything straight.

1) What does a raga represent?
2) What are microtones?
3) Name five non-percussion instruments used in Indian classical music.
4) What do *tivra* and *komal* mean?
5) What instrument plays the rhythm in Indian classical music?
6) What is a tala?
7) What part does the tambura play in a raga performance?
8) Describe the four different sections of a raga.
9) Why can two performances based on the same raga sound very different?
10) What's the name of the most popular rhythm used in bhangra?
11) Which percussion instrument is usually used in bhangra?
12) When did modern bhangra start to develop?
13) Give three different types of music technology used in modern bhangra music.
14) What is the Greek name for a goblet-shaped drum?
15) Name four other instruments used in Greek folk music.
16) What is the rhythm of the Greek syrtos dance?
17) What is the name of a mode in Arabic music?
18) What textures can Arabic music have?
19) Give two features of the vocal parts in Arabic music.
20) Name four non-percussion instruments that are used in Palestinian folk music.
21) How is the doumbek played? What are the names for the different strokes?
22) What is the dabke?
23) Why does Israeli music have lots of different influences?
24) What is Klezmer music?
25) What instruments are used in Klezmer music?
26) When is the Horah usually danced?
27) Where did the Temani dance originate?
28) What are African talking drums used for?
29) Name three different ways that African drums can be played.
30) Describe the master drummer's job.
31) Name three African instruments that aren't drums.
32) Where does calypso music come from and how did it begin?
33) Name three non-percussion instruments used in calypso.
34) Name three Latin percussion instruments.
35) What are steel pans?
36) What is the function of the dents on steel pans?
37) Why do some pannists have to play more than one pan?
38) How do you play a sustained note on a steel pan?
39) Where does samba music come from? What are its origins?
40) Name four samba percussion instruments other than the surdo.
41) What rhythms do the surdo de primeira and the surdo de segunda usually play?
42) What two instruments does the leader of the bateria usually play?

Film Music

SPOILER ALERT: this whole section may contain spoilers. Consider yourself warned.
Composers who write film music have to write music to fit with the action already set by the film makers.

Look Out for **Leitmotifs** in Most Film Music

'Leitmotif' can also be spelt 'leitmotiv'.

1) A leitmotif is a tune that returns throughout the film (there's often more than one).

2) It represents a particular object, idea or character in the story, and often returns in the background or in an altered form.

3) Leitmotifs are used throughout the *Lord of the Rings* films — for example, the one that represents the group of characters who make up the Fellowship of the Ring is heroic, and appears less frequently after the Fellowship falls apart. The leitmotif for the Shire (the home of the hobbits) is a happy melody in a major key. It's light and playful, and reflects the comfort and safety of the Shire.

4) 'Hedwig's Theme' is the main leitmotif in the *Harry Potter* films — it's repeated in all the films and played by different instruments. It's associated with the world of magic and wizards.

5) Sometimes the leitmotifs give you a hint as to what will happen later in the film — if a character turns out to be a bad guy, their theme might have menacing chords being played in the background.

> In the final few bars of 'Anakin's Theme' from *Star Wars®: Episode I — The Phantom Menace™* (1999), you can hear echoes of 'Darth Vader's Theme' from *Episode V* (also by John Williams). This is a subtle hint that Anakin (who's good in this film) will become Darth Vader.

Composers Use Lots of **Repetition** in Film Music

1) Repeated sections of music can be used to link different parts of the film together — it can remind you of something that happened earlier in the film.

2) A leitmotif can be repeated throughout the film, but might be transformed to reflect what's going on. The instrumentation can be changed, or it can be played in a different key. Sometimes just the rhythm of the leitmotif is played in the background — it might be hardly noticeable, but it adds to the drama.

3) Often at the end of a film there's a triumphant modulation of the main theme (as long as the film has a happy ending). It ends in a happy, uplifting key with a drawn-out cadence (see p.42-43), to show that the story of the film has been resolved.

4) Of course, if the film doesn't have a happy ending (or if there's going to be a sequel), the theme may be left unresolved, giving the film a more open or darker ending.

5) Repetition can be used to create tension and suspense — a repeated sequence that's getting louder and louder can really have you on the edge of your seat.

Some Films Use **Pop Songs** to Get **Publicity**

1) Lots of films have pop songs as part of their soundtrack — they're usually released in the charts to generate publicity. They're often performed by famous pop stars — like Pharrell Williams' song 'Happy' for the film *Despicable Me 2* (2013).

2) Some films have pop songs over the opening or closing credits. These songs aren't always in the same style of music as the rest of the film, and often don't appear anywhere else in the film (e.g. Take That's 'Rule The World' is only heard over the closing credits of the 2007 film *Stardust*).

3) A song used as the title track might return in the background later. For example, the song 'My Heart Will Go On' by Celine Dion pops up many times in the film *Titanic* (1997).

A good excuse to watch some films...

COMPOSING TIP

If you decide to compose a piece of film music, think about the atmosphere you want to create. The composition brief might tell you to set a scene, create a mood or describe a character.

Film Music

Film composers use music to <u>set the scene</u> — it helps you believe it's in a <u>different country</u> or <u>time</u>.

Traditional Instruments Give You a Feel for **Time** and **Place**

1) Music can be used to create the mood of a different <u>time</u> or <u>place</u>.

2) <u>Westerns</u> are set in 19th century North America. They generally tell a simple story and they can often be very <u>dramatic</u> and <u>violent</u>.

3) Westerns use music <u>from the time</u> to <u>set the scene</u>. For example, guitarist <u>Ry Cooder</u> composed music for <u>The Long Riders</u> (1980). He used <u>traditional music</u> and <u>instruments</u> like the Spanish guitar, banjo, honky-tonk piano, tin flute, trombone and percussion.

4) Films set in the <u>70s</u> or <u>80s</u> might use <u>pop songs</u> from the time to set the scene. People will <u>recognise</u> the songs and it'll <u>remind</u> them of that decade.

5) <u>John Barry's</u> score for <u>Out of Africa</u> (1985) combines <u>original compositions</u> with <u>traditional African music</u> to help the audience imagine the film's setting. For example, the track 'Karen's Journey' is based on 'Siyawe', a traditional African song.

The Music in **War Films** Creates the **Atmosphere**

1) The music in war films needs to create an <u>atmosphere</u> for the <u>time</u> and <u>place</u> of the war, as well as showing the <u>action</u> and <u>emotion</u> of the plot. For example, the battle scenes of <u>Gladiator</u> (2000) are accompanied by <u>threatening music</u> (by <u>Hans Zimmer</u>) which creates tension.

2) <u>Sound effects</u> (like <u>explosions</u> and <u>gunfire</u>) can be incorporated into the music to suggest <u>war</u>.

3) <u>633 Squadron</u> (1964) is set in the <u>Second World War</u>. The theme music (by <u>Ron Goodwin</u>) is very <u>heroic</u>. It's <u>fast</u> with <u>strong accents</u> — it matches the <u>action</u> of the <u>battle scenes</u>. The <u>soaring brass melodies</u> represent the <u>soaring planes</u>.

Unnatural Sounds Make **Strange Places** Seem Even Stranger

<u>Horror</u>, <u>science fiction</u> or <u>fantasy</u> films are often set in <u>strange places</u> — or other <u>planets</u>. Composers need to <u>transport</u> the audience to a <u>weird reality</u>, where nothing is quite what you'd expect.

1) <u>Unusual harmonies</u> and <u>time signatures</u> are used when things are a bit <u>weird</u> — they're not what you're expecting, so they sound odd.

2) <u>Synthesizers</u> and <u>samples</u> of bizarre <u>sounds</u> often have no relation to what's happening on-screen, but make the audience wonder what's going on and set their imagination racing.

3) <u>Instruments</u> or <u>voices</u> can be <u>distorted</u> using <u>computers</u>.

4) There's often no clear <u>structure</u> so it's hard to predict what's going to happen.

5) <u>Discords</u> and <u>diminished</u> chords make it difficult to listen to.

6) <u>Rapid scalic patterns</u> (going up and down scales) and <u>interrupted cadences</u> (see p.43) can make <u>pulse-raising</u> scenes feel more frantic.

7) In the famous <u>shower scene</u> in <u>Psycho</u> (1960), the <u>stabbing</u> of the <u>knife</u> is accompanied by (and emphasised by) the <u>violins</u> also <u>stabbing</u> out a <u>high-pitched tritone</u> (p.29). Each chord goes right through you, and makes what you're seeing on-screen feel much more <u>real</u>.

8) <u>Planet of the Apes</u> (1968) uses <u>unusual instruments</u> (such as <u>metal bowls</u> as <u>percussion</u>), <u>alternative ways</u> of playing instruments (such as playing horns <u>without mouthpieces</u>), <u>irregular rhythms</u> and <u>dissonance</u> to create a <u>weird</u>, <u>unearthly</u> feeling.

Music revision can be used to put you in a mood...

There are loads of little tricks that composers of film music can use to create an atmosphere and make the viewer more engrossed in a film. Have a stab at writing a mini essay on this page.

Film Music

Sometimes, film music helps you <u>understand</u> what's happening. It's used to help <u>communicate</u> what's going on, instead of just relying on the action and dialogue <u>on-screen</u>.

The **Style** of Music **Changes** With the **Mood** of the Scene

1) The soundtrack for the film *Pirates of the Caribbean: The Curse of the Black Pearl* (2003) was written by Klaus Badelt.
2) There's a simple <u>love theme</u> to accompany the growing romance between Will and Elizabeth, using <u>string</u> and <u>woodwind</u> instruments playing <u>quietly</u>.
3) In the <u>humorous</u> scenes involving Captain Jack Sparrow, the music is <u>playful</u> to create a <u>light-hearted mood</u> and provides a <u>contrast</u> with the <u>fight scenes</u>.
4) During <u>battle scenes</u>, the mood is <u>tense</u> and <u>dramatic</u> — the music is played by <u>low brass</u> instruments.

The Music **Shows** What's **Not On Screen**

It's often the composer's job to create a <u>feeling</u> of something <u>being there</u> that's <u>not seen</u>.

1) <u>Minor</u> and more <u>dissonant chords</u> make you feel <u>uneasy</u>.
2) <u>Low pitches</u> in <u>brass</u> and <u>strings</u> sound <u>dark</u> as if you're <u>underground</u>.
3) <u>Percussive</u>, <u>metallic</u> sounds with <u>reverb effects</u> make you imagine someone <u>lurking</u> about or <u>lying in wait</u>.
4) <u>Suspensions</u> that don't <u>resolve</u> (see p.41) build <u>tension</u> and make you think <u>danger</u> is near.
5) <u>Dynamics swell</u> from <u>quiet</u> to <u>loud</u> and then drop back to <u>quiet</u>, as if someone's coming in and out of the <u>shadows</u>.

Music Has to be **Structured** and **Timed** to **Fit** the Film

1) <u>Film directors</u> need music to be <u>synchronised</u> with the <u>action</u> to the <u>split second</u>.
2) Different <u>sections</u> of a <u>film</u> show different <u>moods</u>. The music can easily be <u>chopped up</u> and <u>moved</u> around using <u>samplers</u> and computer programs such as <u>Cubase</u> and <u>Pro Tools</u>®.
3) Music is used during action scenes to <u>imitate</u> the movements of the actors — like in the <u>chase scene</u> in the 2009 film *Avatar* (which has music by <u>James Horner</u>). <u>Frantic rising trumpet motifs</u> accompany the character as he runs away, and the music <u>stops</u> briefly when he stops moving.

Diegetic Music is Music the Characters Can **Hear**

1) In most films, the music is <u>extra-diegetic</u> — it's <u>not</u> actually <u>part of the story</u>. It's put '<u>over the top</u>' of the action to increase the <u>effect</u> of the film. It's for the <u>audience</u>'s benefit only.
2) Sometimes film-makers want to <u>include</u> music in the story for the <u>characters</u> (as well as the <u>audience</u>) to <u>hear</u> — this is <u>diegetic</u> music.

- In *The Hunger Games: Mockingjay — Part 1* (2014), Katniss <u>sings a song</u> for one of her companions. It is <u>recorded</u> and turned into a <u>propaganda video</u> by the rebels, and used as their <u>battle song</u>.
- In *Inception* (2010), the song 'Non, je ne regrette rien' by <u>Édith Piaf</u> is used diegetically as a <u>plot device</u>. The song helps <u>wake a character up</u> from a <u>dream</u>. Characters in a dream can hear a <u>slowed-down version</u> of the song, while in the real world it's heard at the <u>original tempo</u>. In fact, much of the soundtrack to the film is <u>based on</u> an extremely <u>slowed-down</u> version of the original.

Film Music

Composers have lots of different ways of using the music to build tension and make you jump.
These techniques are used a lot in horror, fantasy and sci-fi films, as well as thrillers.

You Are **Lulled** Into a **False Sense of Security**

1) When music's in a calm major key, you don't feel like anything bad's going to happen.
   For example, in *Gladiator*, the music that plays when Maximus thinks of his home is a
   simple, gentle melody composed by Hans Zimmer and Lisa Gerrard.

2) Beware — sometimes the same theme comes back in an altered form
   (like in a minor key) to show that things have started to go wrong.

Composers Can Keep You on the **Edge** of Your Seat

1) Ostinati keep the audience on edge for a long time. For example, in *Halloween* (1978),
   there's an ostinato played in a minor key — it's then played on a different note to keep
   the audience wondering where the scary person is going next.

2) In some sci-fi films there's background music with just drums and bass,
   generated on computers, that's played under the dialogue throughout the film.
   This lets the audience know that the danger is always there.

3) A good example of this is in *Tron: Legacy* (2010), which has music written by Daft Punk.
   They use computer-generated noises to mimic the sound of high-intensity computer games
   from the '80s, which helps create the virtual-reality setting.

4) Sustained notes create suspense (e.g. tremolo strings).

5) Composers know how to build the tension and make you feel like something bad is going to happen:

   - Dynamics get louder.
   - Tempo gets faster — like the two-note motif in *Jaws* (1975),
     which speeds up (and gets louder) as the shark gets closer.
   - Pitch gets higher.
   - A tune played earlier in a scary bit
     sometimes comes back to remind you.
   - Sometimes they use silence before
     a loud bit just to make you jump.

Thrillers Have Lots of **Tension** and **Action**

1) Thrillers and spy movies are often serious and tense — the music has to
   create the right atmosphere. It has to set the scene for conspiracies and
   people dealing with shadowy figures and underground organisations.

2) There are often lots of layers to the story. A composer uses lots of techniques
   to show that there's more than one thing going on. E.g. in *The Usual Suspects* (1995),
   the composer John Ottman creates tension and drama by using:

   - Long notes in the foreground with ostinato patterns in the background.
   - A repeated pattern on the woodblock sounds like someone's on the move while
     percussive bursts and brass motifs played on top suggest someone's trying to catch them.

REVISION TIP

Silence — something bad's about to happen...

Next time you're watching a film, pay attention to the music and try to work out what effect it
has. You could even watch the scene without the sound to see how important the music is.

Classical Music in Films

Sometimes a director might choose to use an existing piece of classical music, instead of having music specially composed for the film.

Famous Pieces Can Be Used Extra-Diegetically...

See p.124 for more on 'diegetic' and 'extra-diegetic'.

1) The last four pages talk about how composers use music to create atmosphere in a film or scene. This can also be done by using classical music.

2) Often, the requirements for the classical music will be the same as for specially composed music. It should fit with the scene well, and also add something to it.

- The opening to 'Toccata and Fugue in D Minor' by J.S. Bach is famous for its dramatic, haunting tune on the organ. It's been used in loads of horror films — for instance when a monster is on screen, or a character has just arrived at a haunted house. It was used in *Dr. Jekyll and Mr. Hyde* (1931), *The Phantom of the Opera* (1962 — not to be confused with the musical) and *Fantasia* (1940) — see next page.

- Cavatina by Stanley Myers is used in the film *The Deer Hunter* (1978), a film set in and around the Vietnam War. It had previously been used in an earlier film (*The Walking Stick* in 1970), but is so closely associated with the later film that it is often known as 'The Deer Hunter theme'. The music is played on a solo guitar, and is gentle and melancholy. This contrasts with the violence seen in the film, and reminds the audience of a gentler way of life.

- The horror film *The Shining* (1980) uses a dark, ominous-sounding section from Berlioz's *Symphonie Fantastique* for the opening sequence. Without the music, the scene would feel quite peaceful (it's just a car driving beside a lake), but the music creates a tense, threatening atmosphere. This is a synthesized version of Berlioz's original piece, arranged by Wendy Carlos — the otherworldly sound of the synthesized instruments suggests that something isn't right.

... Or Diegetically

Some films use classical pieces as a plot device — the characters are aware of the music, and are often affected by it. Classical music is also used diegetically if characters are playing music themselves.

- In *The Shawshank Redemption* (1994), a prisoner plays a duet from Mozart's opera *The Marriage of Figaro* over the loudspeakers to the other inmates in the prison. All the prisoners stop what they are doing and listen to the music, creating a moment of peace, happiness and hope in an otherwise bleak situation.

- Although it's been used in many films, 'Ride of the Valkyries' by Wagner is probably most famously associated with *Apocalypse Now* (1979), a war film. It is blasted out of speakers as helicopters attack an enemy base. The music was originally written for an opera, and is the leitmotif (see p.122) for the Valkyries, who choose the soldiers who will die in battle — so it is very appropriate for a fight scene. The Valkyries also fly together in a troop — this is mimicked by the helicopters in the film.

Occasionally, a film will use the same piece of classical music both extra-diegetically and digetically.

Rachmaninov's Piano Concerto No.2 is used throughout *Brief Encounter* (1945). Extra-diegetically, it represents the main character's changing emotions as she is tempted to have an affair. At one point in the film, she turns on the radio, and Rachmaninov's Piano Concerto No.2 is playing. The music has become diegetic. Her husband later asks her to turn the music down — this could be seen as him suppressing his wife's emotional needs.

This piece was also used in *September Affair* (1950), *The Seven Year Itch* (1955) and over the end credits of *Hereafter* (2010).

I should have used Bach's Toccata as the soundtrack to my revision...

Some pieces have become so famous for representing a particular mood that they are now used in parody. E.g. the love theme from Tchaikovsky's *Romeo and Juliet* is often used to make fun of romantic moments.

Classical Music in Films

Films use classical music in different ways — some even use it as the inspiration for the whole film.

Some Soundtracks Are Made Up Entirely of Classical Music

For some films, directors have chosen to use only classical music for the whole soundtrack — they have found existing music that exactly matches what they are portraying on screen. An excellent example of this is the 1968 film *2001: A Space Odyssey* (directed by Stanley Kubrick). This film actually has very little dialogue, so relies on classical music and sound effects to convey emotions and stories.

1) Richard Strauss' 'Also sprach Zarathustra' is heard during the opening credits as a sun rises over a planet. This piece is also used as a leitmotif (see p.122) — it's heard each time there is a leap in evolution.

   You might not recognise this piece from the title, but you'll probably recognise the music — it's been used in lots of space films and spoofs.

2) 'The Blue Danube' waltz by Johann Strauss (no relation) is used to accompany spacecraft moving in space and turning like dancers in a waltz.

3) A piece from the ballet *Gayane* by Aram Khachaturian is also used — it's in a minor key, with sparse instrumentation which highlights the isolation and loneliness of space.

4) György Ligeti was a twentieth century avant-garde composer — three of his pieces are used in the film. 'Kyrie' from his *Requiem* (a choral piece) is used as another leitmotif — this one is heard whenever the monolith appears. The film also uses 'Lux Aeterna' (another choral piece) and 'Atmosphères' (an orchestral piece). Ligeti's music is very dissonant (he uses a lot of chromaticism), so it sounds eerie and unearthly.

Another film that uses mainly classical music (and a couple of traditional folk songs) is *Gallipoli* (1981).

Fantasia is a Series of Animations Set to Classical Music

1) Instead of choosing classical music to accompany the action on screen, Walt Disney's *Fantasia* (1940) started with the classical music and produced animations to match. One sequence was abstract, some were dances and others told stories:

- 'Toccata and Fugue in D Minor' (J.S. Bach) accompanies silhouettes of the orchestra playing and abstract images that represent the notes being played.
- 'The Nutcracker Suite' (Tchaikovsky) from the ballet *The Nutcracker* appropriately accompanies a series of animated dances — first fairies, then dancing mushrooms, then flowers, fish, thistles, leaves, a return of the fairies and snowflakes. The sections show the changing seasons.
- 'The Sorcerer's Apprentice' by Dukas is possibly the most famous sequence of *Fantasia*. It tells the story of a disobedient sorcerer's apprentice, played by Mickey Mouse.
- Stravinsky's 'Rite of Spring' accompanies the age of the dinosaurs, ending with their extinction.
- Beethoven's *Pastoral Symphony* is used to accompany a set of mythological characters, including fauns, centaurs, Pan, Pegasus and Greek/Roman gods.
- 'Dance of the Hours' by Ponchielli is another ballet sequence, this time a funnier one featuring animals such as ostriches, hippos, elephants and alligators.
- The final section is set to Mussorgsky's 'A Night on Bald Mountain'. The animation shows a devil and evil spirits and is creepy and atmospheric. At the end of the sequence, the evil spirits are banished by a church bell and 'Ave Maria' by Schubert is heard as monks appear.

2) A later version (*Fantasia 2000*) includes the original section for 'The Sorcerer's Apprentice', along with a number of new animated sequences. The pieces include 'Rhapsody in Blue' by George Gershwin, Elgar's 'Pomp and Circumstance Marches' and Stravinsky's 'Firebird Suite' (as well as many others).

The tutu-wearing hippos are my favourites...

SUGGESTED LISTENING

Listen to 'Also sprach Zarathustra' and try to explain why it's suitable for the scene described.

Game Music

Video games use music to support the action on screen — the music often develops as you get further through the game. Today's video games have much more complex music than early ones.

Early Video Game Music Was Very Simple

1) Due to limited technology, the music for early video games was very simple — it could only have a couple of different instruments or parts, so was often monophonic (or very basic polyphony). It tended to be based on short melodies or motifs that were played on a loop.

2) The music wasn't usually played throughout the game — it would sometimes just be used as a theme tune at the start, or played in response to something happening in the game (e.g. completing a level).

> Two early examples of video game music are Space Invaders (1978) and PAC-MAN (1980). Space Invaders (created by Tomohiro Nishikado) was one of the first games to have music playing continuously throughout the game — it was based on a loop of four descending notes in the bass part, which changed speed to match the movements on screen. The music for PAC-MAN was composed by Toshio Kai and was more melodic — but it was only played at the start (i.e. not during play).

Video Game Music Developed as Technology Developed

1) Early video game music would typically use synthesizers (see p.73) to create and manipulate synthetic sounds (rather than using recordings of real instruments). Synthesizers could also be integrated into the video game hardware.

2) MIDI (Musical Instrument Digital Interface) allowed video game composers to write for a range of instruments that played back consistently on different pieces of equipment (so could be used on different types of computer).

3) Video games in the 1990s were able to use higher quality music with more realistic instrumental timbres because of the technological advances in sound processors of consoles and computers.

4) Nowadays, soundtracks can be created very effectively using DAW (digital audio workstation) software like Logic Pro or Cubase.

Recent Game Music is More Like a Film Score

1) In modern video games, better technology has led to games with a more intricate plot or complicated mission for the player to complete.

2) Similarly, developments in audio technology have allowed the music for video games to become more like a film score. As well as synthesizers, game music frequently uses orchestral and choral elements to set the scene.

3) As there are often different settings within a game, composers will create music to go with each place or time — using similar methods to film composers (see p.123). *Assassin's Creed*® does this particularly well — there's more about this on the next page.

4) Like films, there are different genres of game — e.g. sci-fi, fantasy, war or racing. The techniques that film composers use for these types of film can be used in game music too (see p.123).

5) Some well-known film composers have also written music for games — e.g. Hans Zimmer (who composed the main theme for *Call of Duty*®: *Modern Warfare 2*, as well as music for films such as *Gladiator* and *Batman Begins*) and Harry Gregson-Williams (who composed some of the music for the *Metal Gear Solid*® series of games, the *Shrek* films and *The Martian*).

Learning to locate ancient relics is a vital part of my revision...

Please note — this doesn't give you an excuse to play video games all day and claim you're doing revision. Make sure you don't get distracted — you don't want to fail your mission (by which I mean your exam).

Game Music

The music in video games can make the whole experience more intense for the player.

Game Music Uses **Motifs**

1) Games often use motifs (short melodic ideas) which can be developed to reflect the changing actions. Some ways of altering motifs include sequencing, playing inversions or retrograde versions (see p.84), augmentation and diminution (lengthening or shortening all note values — see p.18). These changes have different effects — e.g. diminution of the note values makes it sound more urgent.

2) Many games use leitmotifs (see p.122) to represent particular places, characters or events. These leitmotifs can be developed using the same techniques mentioned above.

3) A lot of games have some element of danger or jeopardy, so composers need to be able to create a sense of drama and tension. Altering rhythms or texture can help to do this.

4) Polyrhythm, cross-rhythm and syncopation can be used to create a sense of urgency or uncertainty. They can represent chases or tense scenes and often make the player feel unsettled.

5) Texture can show how the story is progressing in a game — e.g. the music might start off sparse and slow-moving, then the texture builds and becomes richer as the situation builds to a climax.

Some Games Have **Full Soundtracks**

ASSASSIN'S CREED®

- In the *Assassin's Creed*® games, the player has to travel to different historical settings (e.g. the Crusades in the Holy Land) to carry out assassinations and avoid the evil Knights Templar.

- Jesper Kyd composed the music for the original game and some of the later games in the series.

- The music effectively sets the scenes for the different cities the assassin visits. For example, to reflect the Eastern and Western influences in the cities in the Holy Land during the Crusades, Kyd uses elements of Eastern and Western music, including Latin and Arabic chanting.

- The main theme of *Assassin's Creed*®: *Revelations* consists of a female voice singing above low, ominous-sounding strings and brass. There are no words in the singer's part — she sings 'ah' in a fairly high register and in a minor key, giving the theme a mournful, mysterious sound. The music builds up toward the end, adding percussion and a full choir, which creates drama and tension.

HALO®

- In *Halo*®, the player takes on the role of the supersoldier Master Chief in a fight against an alien religious group called the Covenant. It is set on a range of planets in the 26th century.

- There have been a number of different composers for the games in the series, including Martin O'Donnell (the lead composer), Michael Salvatori, Stephen Rippy and Neil Davidge.

- The main theme opens with male voices singing (like monks chanting — this represents the Covenant), which sounds eerie and mysterious. A driving syncopated drum rhythm (playing an ostinato) builds up the intensity and creates a sense of excitement. Low strings enter playing the melody, which is based on the same rhythmic pattern over increasing intervals (the first time, it's a perfect octave, then a major ninth and so on) — it sounds a bit like a fanfare. Other string parts are introduced, creating a complex layering of orchestral parts and giving the music energy.

ADVENT RISING

- In *Advent Rising*, the player has to battle an alien race called the Seekers who want to destroy humanity. It is set in space — both on spaceships and alien planets.

- Emmanuel Fratianni, Michael Plowman, Laurie Robinson and Tommy Tallarico wrote the music.

- The main theme opens with female vocalisation (open vowel sounds, with no words) over strings. It also features a male voice choir, piano, brass and percussion. It sounds creepy, sad and alien.

Warm-up and Exam Questions

Here are some nice straightforward questions to test you on film music.

Warm-up Questions

1) What is a leitmotif?
2) How is repetition used in film music?
3) Name one pop song that has been used in a film.
4) Why are instruments from a particular time or place sometimes used in film music?
5) What do the brass melodies represent in the music for *633 Squadron*?
6) What's the difference between diegetic and extra-diegetic music?
7) Name two pieces of classical music that have been used in films.
8) Describe how classical music is used in Disney's *Fantasia*.
9) Name two film composers who have also written game music.
10) How can composers create tension in game music?

Exam Questions

Here are a couple of exam-style questions to test you on film music.

Track 36 is an extract from 'Main Title/Rebel Blockade Runner'
from *Star Wars® Episode IV — A New Hope™* by John Williams.
Play the extract **three** times. Leave a short pause between each playing.

(Track 36)

a) What is the main rhythmic feature throughout this music?
   Circle the correct answer.

   dotted rhythms   **syncopation**   **triplets**   **cross-rhythms**

   [1 mark]

b) i) Which instrument plays the main theme the first time it is heard?

   ....
   [1 mark]

   ii) Why do you think John Williams has chosen that instrument?
       Give one reason.

   ....
   [1 mark]

Exam Questions

c)   Circle two words that describe the string melody when they have the tune.

staccato   legato   conjunct   disjunct   sforzando

[2 marks]

d)   Describe two similarities and two differences between the opening fanfare and the main theme.

....

....

....

....

....

....

[4 marks]

Track 37 is an extract from 'Dies Irae' from Verdi's *Requiem*.
Play the extract **four** times. Leave a short pause between each playing.

(**Track 37**)

'Dies Irae' means 'Day of Wrath'. This piece of music is used to accompany a chase and battle scene in a post-apocalyptic action film. Explain how the music is suitable to accompany this scene. You might want to comment on musical features such as instrumentation, dynamics, harmony and original purpose of the piece.
You must write in full sentences.

You may use this space to plan your answer.

Exam Questions

....

...ght — Film Music

....

....

....

....

....

....

....

....

....

....

....

....

....

....

....

....

....

....

....

....

....

....

....

....

[12 marks]

Revision Summary for Section Eight

Well, that's the end of what I personally think is the most interesting section of the book — I mean, where else are you going to get away with watching a load of films in the name of revision? Anyway, to make sure everything has really sunk in, have a go at these questions. You should be able to answer them without looking back — if there are any you're not sure of, look over that page again.

1) Why do some films use pop songs?
2) Name three traditional instruments used in film music for Westerns.
3) How does John Barry create the African setting of *Out of Africa*?
4) Describe how Ron Goodwin's music in *633 Squadron* represents the battle scenes.
5) What type of films would use unusual harmonies or weird time signatures?
6) Describe how the music in *The Pirates of the Caribbean* films illustrates the different places and characters.
7) Give three techniques that composers use to create a feeling of something that isn't on screen.
8) Name two computer programs that are used to synchronise the music to the action.
9) What is diegetic music?
10) Describe how *Inception* uses 'Non, je ne regrette rien' diegetically.
11) How can a composer show that things have started to go wrong?
12) How do composers create suspense?
13) Give three ways composers build tension.
14) Describe two ways John Ottman creates tension and drama in *The Usual Suspects*.
15) Name one film that uses classical music extra-diegetically.
16) Explain how *Symphonie Fantastique* is used to set the scene in *The Shining*.
17) Describe how Rachmaninov's Piano Concerto No.2 is used both extra-diegetically and diegetically in the film *Brief Encounter*.
18) Name one other film that uses classical music diegetically.
19) Explain how *2001: A Space Odyssey* uses classical music.
20) Name three pieces of classical music that are used in Disney's *Fantasia*.
21) Who wrote the *Pastoral Symphony*?
22) Name two early video games that used music.
23) Give three ways that game music composers can alter motifs.
24) Who composed the music for Assassin's Creed®?

Voices in Pop

Before we get going on the specific types of pop music you need to know about, it's worth spending a bit of time looking at some general things that are relevant to most pop music — starting with vocals.

The **Lead Singer** Sings the **Main Tune**

The lead singer (or vocalist) sings the main tune of a song. They're the soloist, and if they're part of a band, they're often the most famous member (e.g. Freddie Mercury in Queen, Jon Bon Jovi in Bon Jovi and Axl Rose in Guns N' Roses). If you get a pop song in the Listening Exam, say something about the lead vocalist's style. It's even worth mentioning obvious stuff like whether the singer's male or female.

Backing Singers Sing the **Harmonies**

The backing vocalists are the ones who sing the harmonies. These are the main ways backing singers do their thing:

Listen out for the backing vocals in 'Surfin' USA' by The Beach Boys.

IN HARMONY	IN UNISON	DESCANT	CALL AND RESPONSE
all singing different notes	all singing the same notes	singing a higher part in time with the main tune	repeating whatever the lead vocalist sings or answering the lead with another tune

Singers Can Do All Sorts of **Fancy Stuff**

There's more than one way to sing a song.
Make sure you can describe exactly what you're hearing. Listen out for...

Vocal parts can be syllabic (one note per syllable) or melismatic (multiple notes per syllable).

1) **A CAPPELLA** — singing with no instrumental backing.
2) **VIBRATO** — when singers quiver up and down slightly in pitch. It makes the voice sound warmer and more expressive.
3) **FALSETTO** — when men (or occasionally women) make their voices go really high. Sam Smith, The Bee Gees and Michael Jackson are all famous for their falsetto voices.
4) **PORTAMENTO** — when a singer slides from one note to another.
5) **SCAT** — improvising using syllables like 'doo' and 'dat'. Scat comes from jazz music.
6) **RIFFING** — when singers decorate and add bits to the tune. They often go up and down a scale before coming to rest on one note. Riffing usually comes at the end of a phrase, between sections or to finish the song. Whitney Houston, Mariah Carey and Celine Dion are famous for riffing.

Electronic Effects Can Be Added to Vocal Parts

There's more on these effects on p.74 and p.76.

Another way to make the vocals on a pop song sound interesting is to add electronic effects.

1) **REVERB** (short for reverberation) adds an echo to a sound.
2) **MULTI-TRACKING** (or layering) is when each part is recorded on its own track, and all the tracks are played back together. It means one singer can record all the parts in a song — for example, in some Queen songs, Freddie Mercury sings the solo part and the backing vocals at the same time.
3) **SAMPLING** is when you use a short recording (a sample) of someone else's voice in your song.
4) A **VOCODER** (a type of synthesizer) electronically alters a voice recording and lets you create weird effects. Similar technology has been used to auto-tune some singers.

I'm singing in the shower, just singing in the shower...

This Area of Study takes you through pop music decade by decade, from the 1950s up until today. There are a few more pages of background stuff before we travel back to the 1950s for rock 'n' roll...

Instruments of Pop

Pop songs can use any instruments at all — but there are some common instruments that are often used.

Most Pop Songs Use **Electric Guitars**

The **Lead Guitar** Plays **Tunes**, the **Rhythm Guitar** Plays **Chords**

The lead guitar plays the melody, as well as improvised solos in the instrumental sections (Brian May from Queen and Slash from Guns N' Roses are famous for their guitar solos). The lead guitar also adds in fancy bits all the way through to decorate the tune.

The rhythm guitar fills in the harmony all the way through. They either strum the chords or pick out broken (arpeggiated) chords (see p.39) and often play rhythmic riffs (see p.58). Some artists (e.g. Bob Dylan and Ed Sheeran) play rhythms on acoustic guitars instead.

The **Bass Guitar** Plays the **Bass Lines**

See p.66 for more about guitars.

The bass guitar plays the lowest notes. The bass guitarist picks out individual notes (not chords) to form the bass line. As well as picking, bass guitarists sometimes play glissandos by sliding their finger up and down the string (this is easier on a fretless bass).

Electric Guitars Can Play **Effects**

By plugging an electric guitar into an effects box or using different pedals you can get all sorts of effects:
1) **DISTORTION** — a grungy, dirty sound.
2) **FUZZ** — fuzzy-sounding distortion.
3) **CHORUS** — makes it sound like more than one instrument is playing.
4) **FLANGER** and **PHASER** — create a 'whooshing' noise.
5) **WAH WAH** — makes the guitar go, er... "wah wah".
6) **COMPRESSION** — evens out variations in volume.
7) **PANNING** — sends different sounds through different speakers. If you've got two guitarists trading solos, one could be panned left and one right to separate the sounds.

You can also produce reverb (echo) on a guitar as well. There's more about guitar effects on p.76.

The **Drums** Add the **Rhythm**

1) The drummer sets the tempo and plays rhythms to fit the style of the song (like the rhythm guitar).
2) The main instruments of a drum kit are snare drum, bass drum, hi-hat, tom-toms and cymbals.
3) Drum pads and drum machines can replace acoustic drums, or sometimes play alongside them.

The **Piano** or **Keyboard** Provides **Melody** and **Harmony**

The piano or keyboard can play the melody (and instrumental solos) or chords to fill out the harmony. Not all pop songs will have a piano, but some only have a piano accompaniment (e.g. Bob Dylan's 'Make You Feel My Love' and Adele's 'Someone Like You'). These songs tend to be gentler than other pop songs.

Synthesizers Can Do Lots of Jobs

There's more about synthesizers on p.73.

Synthesizers (synths) can play any part — they can make the sound of virtually any instrument you want, e.g. a full string section or brass section (although some bands have live strings or brass). They can play rhythmic chords, solos or hooks (short, catchy, memorable bits).

Influences on Pop

The blues style has been around for years and <u>still</u> has a big influence on pop music today.

African Slaves in America Started the Blues

1) In the <u>1600s</u> and <u>1700s</u>, millions of Africans were captured and taken to <u>North America</u> to be sold as <u>slaves</u>. Many were made to work on <u>plantations</u>.

2) To pass the time and take their minds off their brutally hard work, they sang <u>work songs</u>, using their tools to give the music a <u>beat</u>. The lyrics were often about the <u>hardship</u> and <u>misery</u> of life as a slave.

3) Over the years, <u>African musical styles</u> like <u>call and response</u> singing (p.113) blended with features of <u>European music</u>, especially <u>chords</u>. This combination was the beginning of the <u>blues</u>.

4) Even after slavery was finally <u>abolished</u> in the <u>1860s</u>, ex-slaves living in the <u>southern states</u> were poor and powerless. The <u>lyrics</u> and <u>tone</u> of their songs carried on being <u>sad</u> and '<u>blue</u>'.

5) The traditional blues instruments are <u>harmonica</u>, <u>guitar</u>, <u>banjo</u>, <u>violin</u>, <u>piano</u>, <u>double bass</u> and the <u>voice</u>. They're all <u>acoustic</u> — electric instruments hadn't been invented when blues began.

6) In the <u>early 20th century</u> black Americans started playing the blues in bars and clubs <u>beyond</u> the southern states. By the <u>1920s</u> blues was popular all over America with white <u>and</u> black audiences.

7) In the <u>1940s</u> and <u>1950s</u> a style called <u>rhythm 'n' blues</u> (R&B) was developed. It's a <u>speeded-up</u> version of blues played on <u>electric guitar</u> and <u>bass</u>.

Blues has its Own Scale and Swung Rhythms

1) You get a blues scale by <u>flattening</u> the <u>3rd</u>, <u>5th</u> and <u>7th</u> of any major scale by a <u>semitone</u> (or sometimes just by a <u>microtone</u> — see p.104). The <u>unflattened</u> 5th is played as well. The <u>2nd</u> and <u>6th</u> notes are often left out.

2) The flattened notes are called <u>blue notes</u>.

3) Lots of <u>pop songs</u> use a blues scale and blue notes, as well as other key blues features — <u>swung</u> and <u>syncopated rhythms</u>:

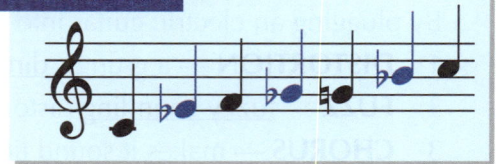

Blues scale on C

- In normal '<u>straight</u>' rhythm the beats split up into <u>equal halves</u>.

- In the blues, the first bit of the beat <u>steals</u> some time from the second bit. The first bit ends up <u>longer</u> and with more <u>oomph</u>. This gives the music a <u>swinging</u> feel.

- The blues uses lots of <u>syncopation</u>. You get a <u>lively offbeat sound</u> by avoiding the <u>strong beats</u> — it puts the <u>oomph</u> in <u>unexpected places</u>.

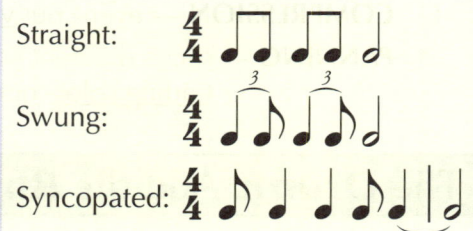

Straight:

Swung:

Syncopated:

Twelve-Bar Blues has a Repeated 12-Bar Structure

12-bar blues uses a set <u>chord pattern</u>, <u>12 bars long</u>:

Bar 1	Bar 2	Bar 3	Bar 4
Chord I	Chord I	Chord I	Chord I

Bar 5	Bar 6	Bar 7	Bar 8
Chord IV	Chord IV	Chord I	Chord I

Bar 9	Bar 10	Bar 11	Bar 12
Chord V	Chord IV	Chord I	Chord I

1) The only chords are <u>I</u>, <u>IV</u> and <u>V</u>.

2) The 12-bar pattern is <u>repeated</u> right through the song.

3) You can make the chords more <u>bluesy</u> by adding <u>minor 7ths</u> (see p.29).

4) When the 12-bar structure is going to be repeated, <u>chord V</u> is played in <u>bar 12</u> instead of chord I. This leads back smoothly to Bar 1.

12-bar blues has had a huge influence on other musical styles including <u>jazz</u>, <u>rock 'n' roll</u> and <u>R&B</u>. Loads of <u>pop songs</u> today still use the standard 12-bar structure.

Influences on Pop

As well as the blues, jazz and folk music have also had an influence on a lot of pop music.

Bluesy Bass Lines Turn Up in Lots of Pop Songs

There are a few bass lines that started life in blues music — they're now often used in pop songs. Learn these two so you can spot them:

1) A **WALKING BASS** moves in steady crotchets up and down the notes of the chords. In a 12-bar blues, the only chords used are I, IV and V, so the walking bass looks something like this:

2) A **BOOGIE-WOOGIE BASS** uses the same notes as a walking bass, but plays them with a boogie-woogie rhythm:

boo-gie woo-gie

Jazz Also Influences Pop Music

Jazz started off as Dixieland jazz in New Orleans in the early 1900s. Dixieland jazz is a mix of brass band marches, ragtime (music with lots of syncopated melodies often played on the piano) and blues.

1) A typical jazz band would have a trumpet, a trombone and a clarinet on the front row. Later, saxophones were included too. The front row instruments play improvised solos. There'd be a rhythm section with piano, guitar, drums and a double bass.

2) Big bands are made up of saxophones, trumpets, trombones and a rhythm section (and sometimes a singer). The sax section has alto, tenor and baritone saxophones and sometimes clarinets.

3) Early jazz music was based on a 12-bar blues. The chords were played by the rhythm section and the front row instruments would improvise over them.

4) Jazz musicians use call and response and blue notes as well as syncopated and swung rhythms.

5) Jazz uses chromatic harmonies (using notes that aren't in the key signature) and jazz chords (ones with extra 2nds, 7ths, 9ths, 11ths and 13ths to create dissonance).

6) Improvisation (soloists making up music on the spot based on the chords being played) is another important feature of jazz. Improvisations are different every time.

All of these features have influenced pop music from the 1950s to today.

Some Pop Songs Have Folk Influences

1) Traditionally, folk music was the music of the ordinary (working) people that they played themselves (there were no radios or record players). It wasn't written down — it was passed down aurally.

2) Folk music often used a pentatonic scale (see p.27) — either major or minor.

3) Traditional British folk instruments included tin whistles, drums (e.g. the Irish bodhrán), fiddles, bagpipes, the hurdy-gurdy, accordions and concertinas. They were usually small and easy to carry.

4) The main types of folk song were work songs (sung by people like farmers, sailors and miners to help them work as a team), ballads (which told stories), short songs and music to dance to.

REVISION TIP

Put your bass on a lead and take it for a walk...

Listen out for these influences on pop — other influences include gospel and country music.

Rock 'n' Roll

Rock 'n' roll is sometimes used to mean rock music in general — but for these two pages, it means the particular style of music that was popular in the USA in the 1950s and '60s.

Rock 'n' Roll Came from the United States in the 1950s

1) Rock 'n' roll developed in the southern states of America in the late 1940s and early 1950s. African Americans moved to urban areas, which meant that black and white people were living closer together than ever before. Their styles of music mixed and evolved, creating new genres of music.

2) Rock 'n' roll was a mix of rhythm 'n' blues (which itself came from blues — see p.136) and country and western music, but also had influences of gospel, folk, and jazz. Typical songs were a faster version of the 12-bar blues with the distinctive twang of country and western singing.

3) It might seem pretty tame today, but rock 'n' roll caused a massive uproar in the 1950s. Teenagers loved it, but their parents' generation hated it — they thought it was tasteless and immoral, and some even went as far as to say it was evil. Teenagers could afford to buy their own records though, so rock 'n' roll was extremely successful, and made superstars out of its biggest artists (e.g. Elvis Presley). It was used in films and TV programmes, which made it even more popular.

4) Rock 'n' roll continued to develop throughout the '50s and '60s, leading to rock music itself from the mid 1960s (see p.140-141).

Cleveland DJ Alan Freed made the term 'rock 'n' roll' popular.

Rock 'n' Roll Songs Were Lively With a Strong Beat

1) Rock 'n' roll songs were generally up-tempo, with a clear beat (most of them were in $\frac{4}{4}$). This made them ideal for dancing — dances in high school gyms were popular (like in *Grease*), and popular TV shows featured teenagers dancing to current hits.

2) The general line-up for a rock 'n' roll band was a lead singer, electric guitars, a bass guitar, a drum kit and sometimes a piano. In earlier bands, the piano played more of a lead role and some had a saxophone as well. A double bass was used before the bass guitar became more common.

3) The lyrics appealed to teenagers because they were about teenage issues, such as love, school, cars and summer holidays. Key lines were repeated throughout the song, which made them memorable.

4) The structure of the songs was fairly simple — most were either strophic (all verses had the same tune — see p.56) or had a verse-chorus structure (see p.58). Some had an AABA structure (four sections, three with the same melody and one that contrasts). A lot of hits featured at least one instrumental section, where a soloist (usually the lead guitarist) would improvise.

5) The verses and choruses themselves were often based on a 12-bar blues. There was a lot of call and response between the lead singer and the band, and most songs had a catchy hook.

Early Rock 'n' Roll Stars Included Bill Haley and Elvis Presley

- One of the first rock 'n' roll hits was 'Rock Around the Clock' by Bill Haley & His Comets.
- Elvis Presley was a huge star — his early hits included 'Hound Dog', 'Heartbreak Hotel' and 'Jailhouse Rock'. Elvis also acted and sang in films, which made him even more popular. He was adored by teenage girls — at his concerts, his gyrating hips caused a commotion.
- Bill Haley, Elvis Presley, Jerry Lee Lewis (who sang 'Great Balls of Fire') and Buddy Holly ('That'll Be The Day') were all rockabilly singers (a sub-genre of rock 'n' roll).
- Other famous singers from the start of the rock 'n' roll era included Chuck Berry ('Johnny B. Goode') and Little Richard ('Tutti Frutti').

You ain't nothin' but a revision dog...

In a nutshell, rock 'n' roll took the African American rhythm 'n' blues and made it accessible to young people of all backgrounds. Rock 'n' roll was more than just a type of music — it was an entire culture.

Rock 'n' Roll

By the early 1960s, the original rock 'n' roll style was becoming less popular —
but it developed into sub-genres that were very successful in their own right.

Surf Music is a Sub-Genre of Rock 'n' Roll

Surf music came about in the early 1960s in California (it's sometimes referred to as 'California Sound').
Some surf music was just instrumental, but it was surf songs (such as those by The Beach Boys)
that made it really popular.

THE BEACH BOYS

- The Beach Boys are an American band from California,
  famous for their songs about surfing and their vocal harmonies.

- The original band was made up of Brian, Dennis and Carl Wilson
  (who were brothers), Mike Love (their cousin) and Al Jardine.

- Their '60s hits included 'Surfin' USA', 'Wouldn't It Be Nice',
  'God Only Knows', 'I Get Around' and 'Good Vibrations'.

- Although The Beach Boys used similar instruments and structures to standard rock 'n' roll,
  it was their complex backing vocals that really made them stand out. A lot of their songs
  have a lead singer accompanied by close four-part harmony in the backing vocals.

Have a listen to some of their songs and pay attention to the backing vocals.

The Beatles Were Part of the British Invasion

1) Although there were some successful British rock 'n' roll artists in the late 1950s,
   it wasn't until the 1960s that British artists really took over.

2) Bands like The Beatles brought their own unique style to rock 'n' roll and helped revive its popularity in
   the USA. This was known as the British Invasion — it also included The Rolling Stones and The Who.

3) The Beatles' huge popularity and the excitement they inspired became known as Beatlemania.

THE BEATLES

- The members of the band were John Lennon, Paul McCartney,
  George Harrison and Ringo Starr. They were all from Liverpool.

- Their standard line-up was Lennon on rhythm guitar, McCartney on bass guitar,
  Harrison on lead guitar and Starr on drums, although there was some variation.
  All four members provided vocals, and Lennon and McCartney were the main songwriters.
  In later songs, they used a variety of other instruments, including the piano and sitar.

- Their early songs (such as 'I Saw Her Standing There' and 'She Loves You')
  were influenced by Elvis Presley, Chuck Berry and other rock 'n' roll stars.

- However, their style changed so much over the years that it's almost impossible
  to put them into one category. As well as rock 'n' roll, they used musical ideas from
  rhythm 'n' blues, folk, classical music and non-Western cultures (such as Indian music).
  They also used pioneering recording techniques such as sampling.

- They had loads of hits — some of their most famous songs include 'Yesterday', 'Hey Jude',
  'All You Need is Love', 'A Hard Day's Night' and 'I Want to Hold Your Hand'.

- The Beatles have had a huge influence on many genres
  of pop music and musicians since the 1960s.

SUGGESTED LISTENING

Yesterday — wish my music exam was yesterday...

Have a listen to The Beach Boys' 'Wouldn't It Be Nice', but be warned — it's really catchy.
Unfortunately, I only know one line, so I get the same 17 words stuck in my head ALL DAY.

Rock Anthems

For all you wannabe rock stars out there, these are the pages for you.

Rock Music Started Out As Rock 'n' Roll

1) During the 1960s, rock 'n' roll evolved into more guitar-dominated music known simply as rock.
2) Like the 12-bar blues (see p.136), rock songs tend to be based around the chords I, IV and V (and sometimes VI). Songs are often in 4/4 with a steady drum rhythm and follow a verse-chorus structure.
3) A rock band was originally made up of a lead electric guitar, a rhythm electric guitar, a lead singer, a bass guitar and a drummer.
4) As rock developed, more instruments were added. In some songs, bands might use a string section (with violins and cellos), a brass section (trumpets and trombones) or a wind section (flutes, clarinets, saxophones and oboes). They also brought in pianos or keyboards and synthesizers.
5) Musicians used the effects on electric guitars to produce new sounds — like distortion, feedback (the noise you get when you stand too close to a speaker with a guitar or microphone) and reverberation (echo).
6) Rock bands use lots of other techniques to get unusual sounds — the band Led Zeppelin used a pounding beat turned up really loud as their main rhythm. They sometimes used violin bows on their guitar strings to get a sustained note.

Developments in technology have played an important part in rock music.

In the 1970s, Rock Songs Started to Develop

Bands in the 1970s started to develop the basic rock formula to make their songs last longer. Their songs had themes and some even told stories.

- Queen's 'Bohemian Rhapsody' lasts for a whopping 6 minutes. It doesn't have a chorus — it's made up of unrelated sections, including a slow ballad, a guitar solo, an operatic section and a heavy rock section.
- Pink Floyd's 1973 album 'The Dark Side of the Moon' is a concept album — there's a theme that links all the tracks.

'Bohemian Rhapsody' is through-composed (see p.56).

There Are Lots of Types of Rock

Over time, rock has branched out into lots of different sub-genres. Here are some of the most popular:

HARD ROCK
- Loud and aggressive, dominated by a distorted electric guitar — solos and power chords (made up of the tonic and the fifth) were key features.
- Bands include Led Zeppelin and The Who.

GLAM ROCK
- Theatrical and glitzy.
- Easier to listen to than hard rock, with a more rock 'n' roll feel and catchy hooks.
- Performers dressed up in spangly catsuits and wore lots of make-up.
- Artists include David Bowie and Kiss. Some of Queen's songs are glam rock.

HEAVY METAL
- Harder and more distorted than hard rock, with even longer guitar solos.
- Bands include Black Sabbath and Iron Maiden.

PROGRESSIVE (PROG) ROCK
- Songs were experimental and complicated, and albums often had a theme (see above).
- Features long instrumentals, electronic effects and mythological or nonsensical lyrics.
- Bands include Yes and Pink Floyd.

PUNK ROCK
- Harsh and angry — it's all about anarchy and rebellion. Lyrics were often shouted.
- Bands include The Sex Pistols and Blondie.

Rock Anthems

Don't worry, you don't need to know masses of detail about the different types of rock music.
Make sure you're happy with their common features though, such as the importance of the guitar.

Rock Songs Became a Way of **Expressing Yourself**

1) Lots of rock bands write their own lyrics to songs (as well as the music).
They use things like religious themes, political causes and personal experiences of love.

2) Led Zeppelin, David Bowie and Bob Dylan all use the influences of folk music
— they've written whole albums in a folky style.

3) Bob Dylan is also famous for his protest songs — his folky 'Blowin' In The Wind'
(see next page) is used as an anti-war song.

4) The more rock developed, the fewer rules it followed. Songs could be any length,
and follow any chord pattern (or none at all). Bands could have any instruments,
and the lyrics could be about whatever the band wanted.

5) Costumes were used to help the music along — David Bowie's jumpsuits and make-up
(such as his famous lightning bolt make-up) really helped to set the scene for the characters
that appeared in Bowie's songs (e.g. Major Tom and Ziggy Stardust).

Arena Rock Started in the **Mid-70s**

Arena rock is also known as stadium rock.

1) By the middle of the 1970s, developments in technology meant that rock bands could be amplified
more. This allowed them to perform in larger spaces, such as arenas and stadiums (hence the name).

2) Technology also meant that special effects (such as pyrotechnics and light shows) could be used.
Arena performances were about the effects and experience as much as the music.

3) Arena rock was mainly performed by hard rock and heavy metal bands
(and glam metal bands — another sub-genre that included bands like Bon Jovi).

4) However, their music was often more mainstream and radio-friendly — bands sang
rock anthems (see below) and power ballads (see next page for more on ballads).

Classic Rock Songs are Known as **Anthems**

Because of the powerful nature of the music and lyrics, a lot of rock songs can be described as anthems.
They usually have memorable, singable (or shoutable) choruses. There are lots of famous rock anthems,
especially from the 1970s and '80s — here are a few examples:

- 'We Will Rock You' by Queen was released in 1977. The only accompaniment
to the vocals is the instantly recognizable 'stamp stamp clap' rhythm
that continues throughout the song (go on, you know you want to).
'We Will Rock You' is often played at sporting events.
The chorus is just one repeated line, almost like a chant.
An electric guitar comes in right at the end and plays a solo.

- Bon Jovi's 'Livin' On A Prayer' is a rock anthem from 1986. Electronic effects can be heard in
some of the vocal parts, as well as in the prominent guitar part (which also has a solo). The
powerful chorus ('whoaa') is perfect for audiences to sing along with at the top of their voices.

- Another '80s anthem is 'Sweet Child O' Mine' by Guns N' Roses (released in 1988).
The opening guitar riff is one of the most popular riffs ever, and the song also features
an epic guitar solo. The chorus line is simple and memorable, and the repeated line
at the end ('where do we go') gives the audience another opportunity to join in.

Do some revision and we'll make it — I swear...

'We Will Rock You' features in the 2001 film *A Knight's Tale*, where it's played at a jousting tournament.
Perhaps not the most historically-accurate choice of song, but you can't beat a classic rock anthem.

Pop Ballads

Time for a bit of a change of mood — we're onto pop ballads of the '70s, '80s and '90s.

Pop Ballads Tell Stories

1) Ballads have been around since at least the fifteenth century. Back then a ballad was a long song with lots of verses that told a story. It's the type of thing that was sung by wandering minstrels.

2) Modern pop and rock ballads still tell stories. Often they're slow and sad and tell some kind of love story. Songwriters like to put a romantic or spooky twist near the end to keep people listening.

3) Ballads follow a variety of different structures. In some, each verse has the same rhythm and tune but different lyrics (a strophic structure — most traditional ballads are strophic). Some have repeated choruses (so a verse-chorus structure) and some are through-composed. They're usually in $\frac{4}{4}$.

4) You'll hear ballads sung in many different styles — a rock ballad accompanied by heavy drums and amplified guitars sounds pretty different to a folk ballad played on an acoustic guitar.

5) Emotional, slow ballads sung by boy and girl bands such as Take That and The Spice Girls were huge in 1990s pop — ballads were the perfect song type to get teenage fans to fall in love with the band.

Singer-Songwriters Write Lots of Ballads

Singer-songwriters are artists who write and sing their own stuff. They tend to accompany themselves on either the guitar or piano and write a fair few ballads. The style of the music depends on the singer's own personal style. Here are a few performers who write their own songs — they all sound very different:

Bob Dylan

- Bob Dylan's most famous ballad, released in 1963, is an anti-war song called 'Blowin' in the Wind'. He sings a simple tune in a major key and accompanies himself on an acoustic guitar with simple strummed chords giving the song a folky feel. All the verses have the same music and the same last line — 'The answer my friend is blowin' in the wind, the answer is blowin' in the wind'. The repeated line works like a mini-chorus.
- A later song (released in 1997) is a love ballad called 'Make You Feel My Love'. It's in a major key and has a piano accompaniment. All four verses have the same music, and the same last line ('To make you feel my love'), and there are two bridge sections.

Sting

- Sting just about always writes his own songs.
- He accompanies himself on bass guitar, but he's also backed by his band.
- Sting's music takes a lot from soul and jazz. 'Seven Days' is a particularly jazzy ballad — it's in $\frac{5}{4}$ and uses major seventh chords, as well as notes from the blues scale.

Kate Bush

- Kate Bush bases the story of her ballad 'Wuthering Heights' on the book with the same name.
- No one else in pop sounds quite like Kate Bush — she sings in a wailing, ghostly manner.

Elton John

- Elton John has written many famous ballads. He accompanies most of his songs on the piano.
- His accompaniments combine rhythmic chords and snippets of the tune.
- Elton's 'Your Song' was his first pop success. In this piece he blends soul, folk and jazz styles and mixes vocals with piano, acoustic guitar and string accompaniment.
- He also wrote 'Candle in the Wind' which was originally a love ballad about Marilyn Monroe. For Princess Diana's funeral he changed the words to 'Goodbye England's Rose...'
- Elton has influenced a lot of singer-songwriters and helped to make pop ballads popular.

There's nothing that I wouldn't do — to make you do some revision...

If you're wondering when I'm going to run out of song lyrics about revision, the answer is NOT YET.

Pop Ballads

Pop ballads tend to be quite sentimental — get your hankies at the ready.

Some Ballads Have Been **Covered** By **Other Artists**

1) Sometimes, the person who makes a ballad <u>famous</u> isn't the person who <u>originally performed</u> or <u>wrote</u> it. It's not unusual for a <u>cover version</u> to be more <u>popular</u> than the <u>original</u> version.

2) The cover version my be performed in exactly the <u>same way</u> as the original, or the new artist might change the <u>accompaniment</u>, <u>tempo</u> or <u>style</u> of the song.

- <u>'Wind Beneath My Wings'</u> was written in <u>1982</u>, and recorded by a <u>few different artists</u> (including a <u>country</u> version, which was released in <u>1983</u>). It only became really popular when <u>Bette Midler</u> recorded it for the <u>1988</u> film *Beaches*, which she also starred in.
- Midler's version is accompanied by a <u>keyboard/synthesizer</u>, and a <u>drum kit</u> comes in half way through (the main accompaniment for the country version was a <u>guitar</u> and <u>drum kit</u>).
- It <u>isn't</u> a typical love song — the lyrics express <u>gratitude</u> to someone who has always <u>supported</u> you and allowed you to achieve your <u>potential</u> (sometimes at their own expense).
- It has also been covered by many other singers, including <u>Celine Dion</u> and <u>Shirley Bassey</u>.

- <u>Bob Dylan's</u> <u>'Make You Feel My Love'</u> (see previous page) has also been covered by other artists. <u>Billy Joel</u> covered the song in <u>1997</u> (his version was actually released <u>before</u> Dylan's).
- Whereas Dylan's version just has a <u>piano accompaniment</u>, Joel's has a <u>piano</u>, <u>drum kit</u> and <u>guitars</u>, with a <u>harmonica</u> and <u>electronic organ solo</u> in the middle.
- <u>Garth Brooks</u> (an American <u>country</u> singer) covered it in <u>1998</u> in a country style, accompanying himself on the <u>guitar</u> (there's also a <u>piano</u> and some <u>backing vocals</u>).
- <u>Adele</u> covered the song in <u>2008</u> — the <u>piano</u> provides the main accompaniment, but there is an <u>instrumental solo</u> on a <u>violin</u> in the middle. <u>Both</u> instruments accompany the next verse.

The **Accompaniment** Complements the **Voice**

VOICE The <u>story</u> is the most <u>important part</u> of a ballad — e.g. Bonnie Tyler's <u>'Total Eclipse of the Heart'</u>. Vocals are <u>clear</u> and <u>unhidden</u> by the <u>accompaniment</u>. Singers often hold on <u>long notes</u>, and use <u>rubato</u> to add <u>emotion</u>.

ACCOMPANIMENT The <u>accompaniment</u> generally <u>reflects</u> the themes of the vocals. There's usually a lot of <u>repetition</u> or <u>inversion</u> of <u>motifs</u> that are sung in the main melody. The <u>texture</u> of the accompaniment often varies to make the <u>dynamics</u> (crescendos and diminuendos) more dramatic. Sometimes there's an <u>instrumental</u> section where an instrument (e.g. saxophone or electric guitar) does a <u>variation</u> on the tune.

1) As you can see from the examples given on these two pages, the <u>instruments</u> that make up the accompaniment <u>vary</u> — they depend on the <u>performer</u>, and the <u>mood</u> they want to create.

2) Some ballads are accompanied by a <u>standard rock band</u> (see p.138), some have a simple <u>piano</u> or <u>guitar</u> accompaniment, and some have more <u>orchestral</u> instruments, such as a <u>string section</u>.

3) The accompaniment can change the <u>feel</u> of the ballad (like in the <u>cover versions</u> above) — an emphasis on <u>guitar</u> and <u>drums</u> can make the ballad feel <u>powerful</u> (<u>power ballads</u> were popular in the '80s), whereas a <u>quiet piano</u> or <u>sweeping string section</u> can make it feel <u>heartfelt</u>. It all depends on what <u>story</u> the ballad is telling.

4) Often, the accompaniment <u>changes</u> throughout the song to reflect the <u>developing story</u> — like a big, dramatic <u>crescendo</u> and build-up of <u>instrumentation</u> to accompany the <u>emotional climax</u> of the song.

COMPOSING TIP

You are the revision beneath my exam success...

OK, that one was pretty terrible — I'm struggling a bit now. You could write a pop ballad for one of your compositions — make sure you think about the accompaniment as well as the voice.

Solo Artists

Although there have been solo artists in every decade, the next two pages are just going to look at those from 1990 onward. Today's charts are dominated by solo artists.

Solo Artists Reflect the Styles of the Time

1) There are solo artists in just about all genres of music — their styles usually reflect the type of music that is popular at the time.

2) A solo artist whose career lasts for many years will often adapt their style to follow current trends. For example, artists like Michael Jackson and Madonna have reinvented themselves several times, experimenting with genres as styles and tastes changed.

3) Solo artists often make use of developments in technology — there's more on this on the next page.

4) There are a number of solo artists who started their careers in bands before leaving to go solo. Sometimes they continue to perform songs in the same genre as their old band, but sometimes they choose to branch out and find their own sound. Examples include Beyoncé (who was in Destiny's Child), Justin Timberlake (*NSYNC) and Robbie Williams (Take That).

The Singer's Voice is a Key Feature

Many solo artists have distinctive vocal features that make their songs instantly recognisable.

- Michael Jackson was well known for his high (sometimes falsetto) singing voice. He also used 'vocal hiccups' (a short intake of breath) and vowel sounds (such as "ah" and "hee hee").
- Whitney Houston had an impressive vocal range and was capable of producing big sounds. She was famous for her use of melisma and riffing (see p.134).
- Adele's rich, soulful voice is capable of producing a range of timbres, from a gentle, raspy sound (like at the start of 'Turning Tables') to a big, powerful sound (like the chorus of 'Skyfall').
- Lana Del Rey has a sultry, dreamy voice.
- George Ezra, Amy Winehouse, Robbie Williams and Paloma Faith all have voices that are easy to recognise.

The Artist's Personality is Important

1) Although image is important to all pop musicians, solo artists in particular need their personalities to come across — both in their music and in their media coverage.

2) Personality can help sell a song — charismatic solo artists can engage with an audience on a more personal level than a band. Performing alone gives them the opportunity to show their emotions — wavering or cracking voices show vulnerability. This can be particularly effective in live performances.

Adele's emotional live performance of 'Someone Like You' at the 2011 Brit Awards made both her and her music really popular. The song was about a break-up, and the personal experience evident in the song resonated with the audience. Her personality and emotions are clear in many of her songs (most of which she writes herself), which makes it easy for the audience to relate to her.

3) Lady Gaga's image and personality are a key part of her performances — she is known for her elaborate costumes, which allow her to reinvent herself as she experiments with new styles of music.

4) Today, artists can control their image through social media accounts — they can share aspects of their personalities and 'private' lives with their fans, and use it as a platform to promote their music. Taylor Swift, Katy Perry and Rihanna all use social media to engage with their fans.

The revisers gonna revise, revise, revise, revise, revise...

It's unlikely that the examiners will actually get the solo artist to perform live for you in the exam, but listen out for vocal features, techniques and emotions coming across in their recordings. Be prepared to weep.

Solo Artists

The different decades have had different styles of music — this page covers a few examples.

The **Accompaniment** and **Structure** Varies

Solo artists use different <u>accompaniments</u> and <u>structures</u> depending on the <u>style</u> and <u>purpose</u> of the song.

1990s

- '<u>Black or White</u>' by <u>Michael Jackson</u> (released in 1991) has a <u>typical rock band</u> accompaniment (electric guitars and a drum kit — see p.138). The song has a number of different <u>sections</u>, starting with an <u>intro</u> that features <u>electric guitars</u>, <u>percussion</u> and Jackson's distinctive <u>falsetto</u> '<u>ow</u>'s. The <u>verses</u> end with a <u>mini chorus</u> ('it don't matter if you're black or white'). There's also a <u>half-chanted</u> section, a <u>rap</u> section (performed by the rapper L.T.B.) and an <u>outro</u>, with <u>guitar interludes</u> between each section. The main <u>message</u> of the song is that <u>race doesn't matter</u>.
- <u>Bryan Adams</u>' '<u>(Everything I Do) I Do It For You</u>' (also released in 1991) starts with a <u>simple piano accompaniment</u>, before the <u>rest</u> of the <u>rock band</u> comes in, building up the <u>texture</u>. This song also has a <u>guitar solo</u> in the middle.

2000s

- '<u>Can't Get You Out Of My Head</u>' by <u>Kylie Minogue</u> (released in 2001) has two memorable <u>hooks</u> — the repeated '<u>la la la</u>' and the first line of the <u>chorus</u> ('I just can't get you out of my head'). The song <u>doesn't</u> follow a standard structure — the <u>choruses</u> and sections with <u>long</u>, <u>held-on notes</u> are broken up by the '<u>la la la</u>' sections. The song uses <u>synthesized instruments</u> and has a <u>strong drumbeat</u> which makes it ideal to <u>dance</u> to in a nightclub.
- <u>Britney Spears</u>' hit '<u>Toxic</u>' (2003) also uses <u>synthesized instruments</u>, <u>distorted guitars</u> and <u>wailing strings</u> to create a <u>futuristic</u> sound. It has a <u>strong</u>, <u>driving beat</u>.

2010s

- '<u>Someone Like You</u>' by <u>Adele</u> (released in 2011) has a <u>simple</u> accompaniment of a <u>piano</u> playing <u>broken chords</u> (see p.39). The song has a rough <u>verse-chorus</u> structure, but with some <u>variations</u> — the verses are <u>different lengths</u>, and one <u>repeated</u> verse has a <u>different melody</u>. There is a <u>bridge</u> with <u>backing vocals</u> sung by Adele herself (see below). The verses are quite <u>quiet</u>, whereas the choruses are <u>louder</u> and more <u>emotional</u>. In the second-to-last chorus, the broken chords <u>stop</u>, and the piano just plays <u>block chords</u> underneath the vocal melody.
- For his 2014 single '<u>Sing</u>', <u>Ed Sheeran</u> accompanies himself on the <u>acoustic guitar</u>, but the song also has <u>electric guitars</u>, <u>percussion</u> and <u>backing vocals</u>. There are several <u>different sections</u> to the song — including <u>falsetto</u> sections, repeated '<u>oh</u>'s and a <u>half-sung</u>, <u>half-rap</u> verse.

Artists Use **Technology** to Create **Vocal Effects**

As well as synthesized instruments, many solo artists use different forms of <u>technology</u> and <u>vocal effects</u> to add <u>variety</u>. Here are a few examples:

- 'Can't Get You Out Of My Head' was recorded using <u>MIDI technology</u> (see p.73).
- 'Someone Like You' uses <u>overdubbing</u> in the <u>bridge</u> section. A <u>separate track</u> of Adele singing in <u>harmony</u> with the melody is recorded and then <u>mixed in</u>.
- '<u>Telephone</u>' by <u>Lady Gaga</u> (featuring <u>Beyoncé</u>) uses different vocal effects such as <u>delay</u>, <u>reverb</u> and <u>pitch bends</u>, as well as <u>samples</u> (see p.74) of a <u>telephone ringing</u> and a <u>telephone operator</u> speaking.

EXAM TIP

Keep revising until you can't get it out of your head...

It's hard to make generalisations about solo artists as they're so varied. You might be asked about the soloist, the accompaniment, technology or style — try and pick out the key features.

Warm-up and Exam Questions

Before you get stuck into the exam-style questions, have a go at these warm-up questions first.

Warm-up Questions

1) What does a cappella mean?
2) Name one singer who sings falsetto.
3) What is portamento?
4) Name three effects used by electric guitars.
5) Where did blues music come from?
6) Write out the chord pattern for a 12-bar blues.
7) What instruments were in a typical jazz band?
8) When did rock 'n' roll become popular in the USA?
9) Name the four members of The Beatles.
10) Describe four different sub-genres of rock music.
11) Name three different artists who sing pop ballads.
12) How does personality help a solo artist become popular?
13) Name two songs that were hits for solo artists in the 2010s.
14) Describe one effect used on Lady Gaga's 'Telephone'.

Exam Questions

To make sure you really know your stuff, here are a couple of exam questions.

Track 38 is an extract from 'Can't Get You Out Of My Head' by Kylie Minogue.
Play the extract **three** times. Leave a short pause between each playing.

(Track 38)

a) In which decade was this piece composed?

....
[1 mark]

b) Suggest a suitable time signature for this song.

....
[1 mark]

c) What is the tonality at the start of this extract (the 'la la la' section)?
Circle the correct answer.

     major   **minor**   **pentatonic**   **atonal**

[1 mark]

Exam Questions

d) Name two electronic effects heard in the vocal part of this extract.

....

....

[2 marks]

e) This song features hooks. Identify one of these hooks
and explain what is meant by a hook.

....

....

[2 marks]

f) i) What genre of music does this song belong to?
Circle the correct answer.

house   **pop rock**   **techno**   **dance pop**

[1 mark]

ii) Give one reason for your answer.

....

[1 mark]

g) Describe the similarities and differences between the vocal parts
in the three different sections of this extract.

....

....

....

....

....

....

....

....

[6 marks]

Exam Questions

Track 39 is an extract from 'Killer Queen' by Queen.
Play the extract **three** times. Leave a short pause between each playing.

Track 39

a) What is the texture at the start of the extract? Circle the correct answer.

       monophonic   **heterophonic**   **homophonic**   **polyphonic**

[1 mark]

b) Name two ways in which Queen used technology in this song.

....

....

[2 marks]

c) What vocal effect is heard on the word 'Queen' in the chorus?
Circle the correct answer.

       vibrato   **riffing**   **improvisation**   **portamento**

[1 mark]

d) Describe the accompaniment during the verse and chorus.

....

....

....

....

....

....

[4 marks]

e) What instrument is playing the solo?

....

[1 mark]

Revision Summary for Section Nine

That section was a bit of a whizz through 20th century pop music — with a bit of the 21st century too. Just have a go at these revision questions, then you can stop to catch your breath and work out which decade you're in. You know the drill — try and answer them without looking back at the section, then go back over any bits you're not sure about.

1) Describe four different ways backing vocals can be sung.
2) Describe: a) scat
              b) riffing
3) Name two electronic effects that can be added to vocal parts.
4) Describe typical lead guitar, rhythm guitar and bass guitar parts in pop music.
5) Write out the blues scale starting on a C.
6) What are blue notes?
7) Describe the difference between straight, swung and syncopated rhythms.
8) Describe two different bass lines that come from blues music.
9) What's improvisation?
10) What scale is traditional folk music usually based on?
11) Name three different folk instruments.
12) What were the two main influences on rock 'n' roll music?
13) Who made the term 'rock 'n' roll' popular?
14) Write down three things that rock 'n' roll songs were often about.
15) Name three early rock 'n' roll stars.
16) What sub-genre of rock 'n' roll did The Beach Boys' music belong to?
17) Name three bands who were part of the British Invasion.
18) Name three songs by The Beatles.
19) Describe the line-up of a typical rock band.
20) What is meant by a concept album?
21) Describe punk rock.
22) What is arena rock?
23) Name two rock anthems.
24) What is a pop ballad?
25) What was the structure of a traditional ballad?
26) Who first made the song 'Wind Beneath My Wings' popular?
27) Write down three different artists who have performed 'Make You Feel My Love'.
28) Name three solo artists who have distinctive voices.
29) How do some solo artists use social media to increase their popularity?
30) Describe two different solo artists from the 1990s.
31) Describe the accompaniment of Adele's 'Someone Like You'.
32) What technology was used to record Kylie Minogue's 'Can't Get You Out Of My Head'?

General Certificate of Secondary Education

GCSE
Music

Listening and
Appraising Exam

Surname
Other names

Time allowed: 1 hour 30 minutes

Instructions
- Write in black ink or ballpoint pen.
- Answer **all** questions in the spaces provided.
- Give all the information you are asked for, and write neatly.
- Do all rough work in this book. Cross through any work you do not want marked.

Information
- The marks are shown by each question.
- The maximum mark for this paper is 80.
- For each question you will need to play one or more tracks from the CD.
  You will be told how many times to play each track.
- Read through the question before you play the track(s).
- Leave a gap between each playing to give yourself time to write.
- You will be assessed on the quality of your writing in questions marked *.

Instructions for playing the CD:
- There are 8 questions, covered on the CD by tracks 40-48.

Question No.	1	2	3	4	5	6	7	8
CD Track No.	40	41	42	43	44, 45	46	47	48

- Leave 2 minutes at the start to read through the exam.
- Play the CD, one track at a time, stopping the CD after each track.
- Each question will tell you how many times the track should be repeated.
- Allow a short pause between each playing for writing time.
  After the final playing of each track, allow some time for writing.

Answer ALL questions

1   This question is based on Area of Study 3: Rhythms of the World
    Play the track **four** times.

(Track 40)

a) From which country does this music originate? Circle the correct answer.

Egypt   **India**   **Greece**   **Syria**

(1 mark)

b) i)   Name the string instrument that plays the melody in this extract.

....

(1 mark)

ii)   Name the percussion instrument heard in this extract.

....

(1 mark)

c) Tick one box for each statement below to indicate whether it is true or false.

	True	False
The solo vocalist's melody is mainly conjunct.	☐	☐
One singer is male, the other is female.	☐	☐
The two voices sing in parallel harmony.	☐	☐
The two voices sing in imitation.	☐	☐

(4 marks)

d) Describe how the timbre changes throughout the extract.

....

....

....

....

(3 marks)

2   This question is based on Area of Study 5: Conventions of Pop
Play the track **three** times.

(Track 41)

a) In which decade was this song first released? Circle the correct answer.

        1950s   **1970s**   **1990s**   **2010s**

(1 mark)

b) i)   What instrument is playing the melody at the start of this extract?

....

(1 mark)

    ii)   Circle the word that best describes the part this instrument is playing.

              call and response   **riff**   **rubato**   **improvisation**

(1 mark)

c) Suggest a suitable tempo for this extract.

....

(1 mark)

d) Identify one difference between the first verse and
the bridge section (which starts 'these four walls').

....

....

(1 mark)

e) This piece can be described as a 'rock anthem'.
Identify **three** features of this extract that fit this description.

....

....

....

....

(3 marks)

3   This question is based on Area of Study 4: Film Music
Play the track **three** times.

(Track 42)

a) What rhythmic feature can you hear in the first part of this extract?
Circle the correct answer.

     augmentation   **triplets**   **bi-rhythms**   **syncopation**

(1 mark)

b) Tick one box for each statement below to indicate whether it is true or false.

	True	False
There is a brass fanfare at the start of the extract.	☐	☐
The strings play in unison when they first come in.	☐	☐
The woodwind section can be heard in this extract.	☐	☐
Percussion is only heard during the opening section of the extract.	☐	☐

(4 marks)

c) Describe how the texture changes in the two different parts of this extract.

....

....

(2 marks)

d) Circle the word that best describes the string melody.

     pizzicato   **legato**   **marcato**   **tremolo**   **con sordino**

(1 mark)

e) This music is for a game in which the player has to carry out a heroic quest to save
the world. Describe **two** features of this extract that make it suitable for this purpose.

....

....

(2 marks)

Turn over

154

4   This question is based on Area of Study 2: The Concerto Through Time
     Play the track **four** times.

     This extract begins in bar 11 of the piece.
     The solo instrument's part for bars 11-20 is given on the opposite page.

     (Track 43)

     a) Fill in the missing notes in bar 17. The rhythm is given above the stave.

                                                                                    (6 marks)

     b) What instrument is playing the solo part?

        ....
                                                                                    (1 mark)

     c) i)   In which period of Western musical history was this piece composed?

             ....
                                                                                    (1 mark)

        ii)   Suggest a suitable composer for this concerto.

             ....
                                                                                    (1 mark)

     d) What is the key signature at the beginning of this extract? Use the score to help you.

        ....
                                                                                    (1 mark)

     e) What is the name of the ornament in bar 14? Circle the correct answer.

            mordent   **turn**   **appoggiatura**   **acciaccatura**

                                                                                    (1 mark)

     f) Which movement of the concerto do you think this extract comes from?
        Give a reason for your answer.

        ....

        ....
                                                                                    (2 marks)

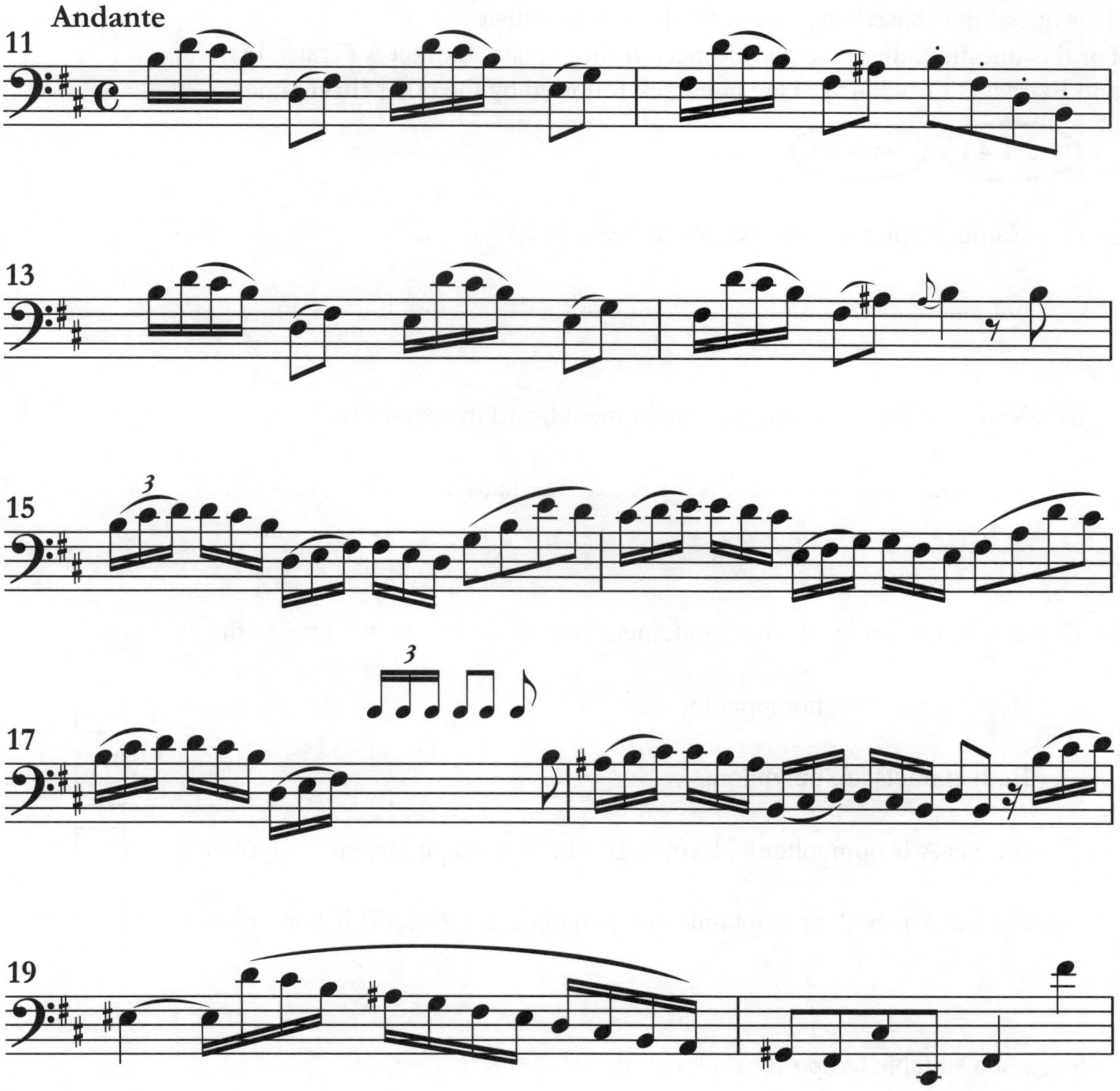

Turn over

5   This question is based on Area of Study 4: Film Music
For this question, there are two extracts of film music, Extract A (Track 44)
and Extract B (Track 45). Play one track followed by the other **three** times.

Track 44   Track 45

a) i)   Name the percussion instrument heard in Extract A.

....

(1 mark)

ii)   Name a different percussion instrument heard in Extract B.

....

(1 mark)

b) Tick one box to indicate which statement best describes the textures of the extracts.

Both extracts are homophonic. ☐

Both extracts are polyphonic. ☐

Extract A is homophonic, Extract B is both homophonic and polyphonic. ☐

Extract A is both homophonic and polyphonic, Extract B is homophonic. ☐

(1 mark)

c) Suggest a suitable tempo for each extract.

Extract A: ....

Extract B: ....

(2 marks)

d) Both extracts have the same tonality.
Circle the word that best describes the tonality of these extracts.

major   **minor**   **modal**   **pentatonic**   **atonal**

(1 mark)

e) Extract A is the opening to a film which features an epic journey through space.
Extract B accompanies a film about the survivors of a war in space.
Describe the similarities and differences in the two extracts and how they match the
similarities and differences of the two films. You should think about instrumentation,
rhythm and dynamics.

....

....

....

....

....

....

....

(6 marks)

6* This question is based on Area of Study 2: The Concerto Through Time
Play the track **four** times.

(Track 46)

This extract is from Brahms' Violin Concerto, which was written in the Romantic period.
Write a paragraph describing how this extract is typical of music of this period.
You should think about musical elements such as the instrumentation, texture,
harmony, dynamics and any other relevant features.

....

....

....

....

....

....

....

....

....

....

....

....

....

....

....

(9 marks)

7 This question is based on Area of Study 5: Conventions of Pop
Play the track **three** times.

(Track 47)

a) i) What genre of music does this song belong to? Circle the correct answer.

  jazz   **rock**   **blues**   **rock 'n' roll**

(1 mark)

ii) Identify **three** features of this extract that are typical of this genre.

....

....

....

(3 marks)

b) Tick **two** boxes to indicate which statements best describe the rhythms in this extract.

The rhythms are straight.   ☐

The rhythms are swung.   ☐

The rhythms are on the beat.   ☐

The rhythms are syncopated.   ☐

(2 marks)

c) What instrument plays a solo in the second half of this extract?

....

(1 mark)

d) Suggest a suitable time signature for this extract.

....

(1 mark)

Turn over

160

8   This question is based on Area of Study 3: Rhythms of the World
Play the track **four** times.

(Track 48)

a) Describe the order in which the percussion instruments enter at the start of the extract.

....

....

....

....

(4 marks)

b) Tick the rhythm played by the first drum you hear at the start of the extract.

(1 mark)

c) Some of the percussion rhythms don't fit perfectly into the $\frac{4}{4}$ bars.
What is the technical term for such a combination of rhythms?

....

(1 mark)

d) Circle **two** phrases below which correctly describe the devices used in the vocal section.

four-part harmony   singing in unison   polyphony

parallel motion   repeated phrases

(2 marks)

e) Describe how the rhythms of the vocal parts interact with the percussion rhythms.

....

....

....

....

(2 marks)

END OF TEST

Answers

Section Two — Reading and Writing Music

Page 15 (Warm-up Questions)

1)

2) A sharp sign raises the pitch of the note (and other notes of the same pitch later in the bar) by one semitone.
A flat sign lowers the pitch of the note (and other notes of the same pitch later in the bar) by one semitone.
A natural sign cancels out a flat or sharp sign in the key signature or earlier on in the bar.

3)

4) Three beats

5) In simple time, the main beats are divided into 2, 4, 8, etc. but in compound time the beats are divided into 3, 6, 9, etc.

6) Regular, irregular and free

Page 15 (Exam Question)

Track 1

a)

(1 mark for each correct note or correct interval between two adjacent notes, up to 8 marks)

b) *(1 mark)*

c) *(1 mark)*

d)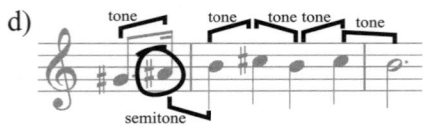

(up to 3 marks, one for each different feature identified)

Page 21 (Warm-up Questions)

1) 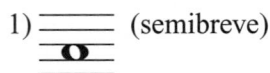 (semibreve)

2)

3) Dotted crotchet, one and a half beats
Quaver, half a beat
Dotted minim, three beats

4) A tie joins two or more notes of the same pitch together. A slur joins two or more notes of different pitch together.

5) Presto, allegro, moderato, andante, largo

Pages 21-22 (Exam Question)

Track 2

a) dotted notes *(1 mark)*

b) allegro *(1 mark)*

c) forte *(1 mark)*

d) energico *(1 mark)*

Section Three — Keys, Scales and Chords

Page 31 (Practice Questions)

Track 10 a) natural minor   b) melodic minor
c) whole tone   d) major

Track 11 Pentatonic (major isn't wrong, but pentatonic is more accurate)

Track 12 a) unison   b) perfect 5th   c) major 3rd
d) minor 3rd   e) major 7th   f) perfect 4th
g) minor 6th   h) augmented 4th/ diminished 5th

Track 13 a) minor 2nd   b) major 3rd   c) perfect 4th
d) octave   e) major 6th   f) perfect 5th
g) minor 7th   h) major 2nd

Page 32 (Warm-up Questions)

1) Eight

2) They tell you what sharps or flats to play.

3) They are relative scales – they have the same notes/same key signature.

4) Natural, harmonic and melodic

5) Major pentatonic

6) It includes every white and black note on a keyboard.

7) A harmonic interval.

8) Diminished 7th

Pages 32-33 (Exam Question)

Track 14

a) i) Four *(1 mark)*

ii) Perfect fourth *(1 mark)*

iii) Minor third/augmented second *(1 mark)*

b) C♯ minor *(1 mark)*

c) Tenuto — played full length or longer *(1 mark)*

Page 40 (Practice Questions)

Track 17 a) major   b) minor   c) major

d) augmented   e) minor   f) diminished

g) diminished   h) minor

Track 18 a) root   b) 2nd   c) root

d) 2nd   e) 1st   f) 2nd

g) root   h) root

Pages 49-50 (Practice Questions)

Track 21 a) perfect   b) plagal   c) interrupted

d) imperfect   e) interrupted   f) perfect

g) imperfect   h) perfect

Track 22 a)

b) first inversion

c) plagal

Track 23 a)

b) homophonic

c) perfect

d) A

Track 24 a)

b) F sharp

c) interrupted

Track 25 a)

b) (see above)

c) Relative minor

Track 26 a)

b) E flat major

c) G minor

d) pivot chord

e) V, III

Page 51 (Warm-up Questions)

1) e.g. piano, guitar

2) I, IV and V or tonic, subdominant, dominant

3) First inversion

4) Block chords, rhythmic chords, broken / arpeggiated chords

5) Diatonic

6) Any three of the following: auxiliary notes, passing notes, appoggiaturas, suspensions, trills or other sensible answer.

7) In the middle of a piece, or at the end of any phrase except the last phrase.

8) Contrapuntal

Pages 51-52 (Exam Question)

Track 27

a) Piano *(1 mark)*

b) Alberti bass / broken chords / arpeggios *(1 mark)*

c) Imperfect *(1 mark)*

d) G major *(1 mark)*

e) Accidental *(1 mark)*

f) Staccato *(1 mark)*

g) Homophonic *(1 mark)*

Section Four — Structure and Form

Page 60 (Warm-up Questions)

1) *Conjunct* — melodies move mainly by step. Notes are a major 2nd (a tone) or a semitone apart.

Disjunct — melodies have a lot of jumps. Notes are more than a major 2nd apart.

Triadic — melodies made up of the three notes in a triad.

Scalic — melody moves up and down the notes of a scale.

2) A form where each verse has different music.

3) A repeated bass part, usually four or eight bars long that is played by the left hand on the piano or harpsichord, or by cello and double bass in an orchestra.

4) e.g. jazz, rock, Indian music.

164

Pages 60-61 (Exam Questions)

Track 28

   a) i) G major *(1 mark)*

      ii) Minor third *(1 mark)*

   b) Call and response/question and answer *(1 mark)*

   c) A *(1 mark)*

Track 29

   a) Baroque period *(1 mark)*

   b) Oboe, bassoon, violin, viola, harpsichord.
      (1 mark for each instrument, up to 2 marks)

   c) i)

(1 mark for each correct note or correct interval between two adjacent notes, up to 7 marks)

      ii) Conjunct *(1 mark)*

   d) Basso continuo *(1 mark)*

   e) Bassoon / Harpsichord *(1 mark)*

Section Five — Instruments

Page 77 (Warm-up Questions)

1) E.g. slide — trombone
Single reed — clarinet or saxophone
Double reed — oboe or bassoon
Pizzicato — violin, viola, cello, double bass
Wooden bars — xylophone

2) *Tremolo* — trembling sound on string instrument (fast, short, light strokes with the bow). Guitars can also produce this type of sound.
Con sordino — 'with mute', mute placed on the bridge of string instruments to make them sound further away. Brass instruments can also be muted.
Tenor — higher male voice.
Falsetto — someone with a lower voice singing much higher than their normal range.

3) Acoustic guitar — e.g. played by strumming or plucking six or twelve strings.
Electric guitar — e.g. needs an amplifier and loudspeaker to be heard.
Bass guitar — e.g. has only four strings, is pitched lower than electric and acoustic guitar, needs amplification.

4) Baroque

5) A military band is a marching wind band, with woodwind, brass and percussion. A brass band has brass and percussion. A jazz band can include woodwind, brass, percussion and any other instruments too, and sounds quite different.

6) Piano trio — piano, violin, cello.
Clarinet quintet — clarinet, first violin, second violin, viola, cello.

7) MIDI — musical instrument digital interface
Sampler — record, process and play back samples of music
Remix — mixing together samples of pop or dance music to a fast drumbeat, often speeded up
Sequencer — computer program that records and replays many tracks of music together

Pages 77-79 (Exam Question)

Tracks 30 and 31

   a) Flute *(1 mark)*

   b) Piano *(1 mark)*

   c) Shape B *(1 mark)*

   d) The left hand of the piano has chords, the right hand melody imitates the flute part. One follows the other around. / The melodies interweave in a two-part texture at a similar pitch. / The parts are contrapuntal.
   (1 mark for each sensible comment up to a maximum of 2 marks)

   e) Flute, clarinet *(1 mark for each)*

   f) Strings *(1 mark)*

   g) Chromatic *(1 mark)*

   h) Shape C *(1 mark)*

   i) Crescendo *(1 mark)*

Section Six — The Concerto Through Time

Page 88 (Warm-up Questions)

1) There were sudden changes in dynamics (no crescendos or diminuendos).

2) a) A small group of solo instruments.
   b) A larger group of accompanying instruments (often a string orchestra).

3) Subject

4) A repeated pattern, often in the bass line.

5) A note that clashes with a chord, but which is followed by a note belonging to the chord (usually a tone or semitone away from the first note).

6) Three movements — fast, slow, fast

7) The Brandenburg Concertos

Answers

Pages 88-89 (Exam Question)

Track 32

a) i) Recorder/flute, violin *(1 mark for each)*

ii) Any one of: cello, double bass, harpsichord *(1 mark)*

b) Perfect fourth *(1 mark)*

c) Contrapuntal *(1 mark)*

d) i) Concerto grosso *(1 mark)*

ii) There's a small group of soloists (concertino) rather than a single soloist. / There's a small group of soloists (the concertino) and a string orchestra (the ripieno) *(1 mark)*.

e) Bach (accept Handel/Corelli/Telemann/any other Baroque composer) *(1 mark)*

f) E.g. *presto/allegro/vivace (1 mark)*

g) - There's not much variation in dynamics, and no crescendos or diminuendos.
- Dynamic contrast is achieved by adding additional instruments — the music is fairly quiet when just the concertino are playing, suddenly louder when ripieno enter.
- This lack of variation is typical of the Baroque period — things were played either loud or soft, mainly due to the lack of variation in dynamics possible on the harpsichord.
- Crescendos and diminuendos were rarely used.
(Award 1 mark for identifying a feature of the dynamics and a further mark for relating this to Baroque music, up to a maximum of 4 marks)

Page 101 (Warm-up Questions)

1) E.g. clarinet

2) Three movements — first movement in sonata form (quick), second movement in ternary or variation form (slow), third movement in rondo, variation or sonata form (quick).

3) Exposition, Development and Recapitulation.

4) E.g. Mozart, Haydn

5) About 1820

6) E.g. contrasting emotions, nature

7) E.g. they used a wide range of dynamics (from *ppp* to *fff*) with sudden changes.

8) Piano, violin, cello

Pages 101-102 (Exam Question)

Track 33

a) Flute *(1 mark)*

b) i) Cadenza *(1 mark)*

ii) Any two of:
- It's a solo section/unaccompanied
- It's virtuosic
- It could be improvised
- It shows the skill of the performer
- It's difficult music (fast notes, large range)
(1 mark for each, up to a maximum of 2 marks)

c) Trill *(1 mark)*, Sequence *(1 mark)*

d) Coda *(1 mark)*

e) Any two of:
violin, viola, cello, double bass, horn, oboe
(1 mark for each, up to a maximum of 2 marks)

f) 4/4 *(1 mark)*

g) i) Classical *(1 mark)*

ii) Mozart (accept Haydn/Beethoven/any other Classical composer) *(1 mark)*

Section Seven — Rhythms of the World

Page 118 (Warm-up Questions)

1) A scale, representing a season or time of day.

2) The Punjab region of northern India and Pakistan.

3) Modal

4) Doumbek (also known as the darbuka or tablah)

5) Eastern Europe (particularly Romania)

6) Any four of: djembe, dundun, donno (also known as the hourglass or talking drum), kagan, kidi, sogo, sabar.

7) Syncopation

8) Surdo

Pages 118-120 (Exam Questions)

Track 34

a) i) Bhangra *(1 mark)*

ii) Any two of:
- Traditional Punjabi instruments are used alongside Western instruments.
- Fusion of Punjabi music (e.g. syncopated rhythm/chaal rhythm) with modern Western music.
- Use of technology (e.g. electronic instruments, samples).
- Strong rhythm.
(1 mark for each, up to a maximum of 2 marks)

b) 2/4 or 4/4 *(1 mark for either answer)*

c) Any two of: drum kit, drum machine/sequencer, dhol, dholak, tabla.
(1 mark for each, up to a maximum of 2 marks)

d) i) Sitar *(1 mark)*

ii) Any of: electric guitar, bass guitar. *(1 mark)*

e) Any three of:
- Male lead singer and male backing singers.
- Strong sound with heavy accents.
- Backing singers repeat words — 'ho ho' / 'hi hi'.
- Interaction between lead and backing singers in a call and response style.
- Backing vocals are initially sparse, but they later sing a repeated phrase that build up to the end of the section.
- Lead singer uses note bends/microtones, and portamento.
- Lead part uses a limited range.
(1 mark for each, up to a maximum of 3 marks)

f) The music changes from minor to major. *(1 mark)*

g) The first option is correct. *(1 mark)*

Track 35

a) Caribbean *(1 mark)*

b) The second option is correct. *(1 mark)*

c) Any three of:
- In the first half, the rhythm follows a 3-3-2 pattern.
- In the second half, it has a steady 4-beat pattern.
- The first half has syncopated rhythms.
- The second half has little syncopation/mainly on-beat rhythms.
- The first half has longer notes (crotchets and dotted crotchets).
- The second half mainly has running quavers.
(1 mark for each, up to a maximum of 3 marks)

d) Any two of:
- It's in a major key which sounds happy — this makes it suitable for a carnival.
- It has a bright, lively tempo so sounds fun.
- It's easy to dance to, which is suitable for a carnival.
(1 mark for each, up to a maximum of 2 marks)

Section Eight — Film Music

Page 130 (Warm-up Questions)

1) A phrase of music that represents a character, place or emotion.
2) E.g. to link parts of the film together.
3) E.g. 'Happy' by Pharrell Williams
4) To create the mood of a specific time or place.
5) Soaring planes
6) Diegetic music is music the characters can hear, extra-diegetic music is for the audience only.
7) E.g. *Symphonie Fantastique* by Berlioz, *The Marriage of Figaro* by Mozart
8) E.g. Animations were produced to match the pieces of classical music being used.
9) Hans Zimmer, Harry Gregson-Williams
10) E.g. altering rhythms or texture, creating polyrhythm, cross-rhythm or syncopation.

Pages 130-132 (Exam Questions)

Track 36

a) Triplets *(1 mark)*

b) i) Trumpet *(1 mark)*

ii) E.g. It sounds heroic. / It sounds like a fanfare. / It sounds ceremonial. / It sounds hopeful.
(1 mark)

c) Legato *(1 mark)*, conjunct *(1 mark)*

d) Similarities:
Any two of:
- Mainly brass and percussion.
- Loud.
- Triplet rhythms.
- Pulse stays the same.
(1 mark for each, up to a maximum of 2 marks)
Differences:
Any two of:
- Main theme accompanied by woodwind and strings as well.
- Fanfare is polyphonic whereas the main theme is homophonic.
- Full orchestra is playing for the main theme.
- It changes from 4/4 to 2/2.
(1 mark for each, up to a maximum of 2 marks)

Track 37

Any six of:

Instrumentation:
- The music uses a full choir, with a lot of singers. This gives it impact, which is suitable for a battle scene.
- The choir is accompanied by a large orchestra, with prominent brass and percussion playing accented notes which match the action of a battle.
- Strings play rapid ascending runs, which make the music sound frantic, like a chase would be.

Dynamics:
- Dynamics are generally loud throughout, with crescendos to increase impact. It sounds angry like a battle.

Pitch:
- There is a range of pitches — the female voices in the choir sing in a very high range, representing the screams of battle. The male voices, brass and lower strings are much lower and represent the fighting.

Harmony:
- There is a lot of dissonance/clashing chord in this piece, representing the clashing weapons and horrors of battle.

Texture:
- The music is often homophonic (playing in chords) or polyphonic — the choir are singing overlapping parts, while the brass play fanfare-like melodies underneath. The rich, thick textures represent the complexities of the battle and all the different things going on.

Tempo:
- The music is quick — it feels frantic and desperate, which matches the chase and battle going on in the film.

Other:
- A requiem is a mass for the dead, so is appropriate to accompany a battle. This section is the 'day of wrath', which again is suitable for a battle in a post-apocalyptic world.

(For each, award 1 mark for a correct feature and a further mark for explaining how this is suitable for the scene, up to a maximum of 12 marks. Deduct up to 2 marks for poor writing style.)

Section Nine — Conventions of Pop

Page 146 (Warm-up Questions)

1) Singing without accompaniment (i.e. no instrumental backing)
2) E.g. Michael Jackson
3) Sliding from one note to another
4) E.g. distortion, fuzz and chorus
5) African slaves in America.
6) I, I, I, I, IV, IV, I, I, V, IV, I, I
7) Trumpets, trombones, clarinets, saxophones, piano, guitar, drums and double bass
8) 1950s
9) John Lennon, Paul McCartney, George Harrison, Ringo Starr
10) E.g. hard rock — loud and aggressive, dominated by distorted electric guitar
    Glam rock — theatrical and glitzy, with costumes and make up. Rock 'n' roll feel with catchy hooks.
    Heavy metal — harder and more distorted than hard rock, with longer guitar solos.
    Progressive rock — experimental and complicated, albums often had a theme.
11) E.g. Bob Dylan, Elton John, Bette Midler
12) E.g. it helps them engage with their fans.
13) E.g. 'Someone Like You' by Adele 'Sing' by Ed Sheeran
14) E.g. it uses samples of a telephone ringing and a telephone operator speaking.

Pages 146-148 (Exam Questions)

Track 38

a) 2000s *(1 mark)*
b) 4/4 *(1 mark)*
c) Minor *(1 mark)*
d) Any two of:
   - over-dubbing/doubling
   - echo
   - vocoder
   (1 mark for each, up to a maximum of 2 marks)
e) Either 'la la la' or 'can't get you out of my head' *(1 mark)*
   A hook is a catchy bit of tune or lyrics that gets stuck in your head *(1 mark)*.
f) i) dance pop *(1 mark)*
   ii) It has a prominent/strong steady beat which makes it easy to dance to *(1 mark)*.

168

g) Any six of:
Similarities:
- Each section has a small vocal range.
- It's mainly syllabic (one syllable per note).
- Mainly on-beat rhythms (except for places identified below).
- Electronic effects (over-dubbing) throughout.
- Voice sounds quite breathy.
Differences:
- First section ('la la la') almost like a chant — all on the same note.
- Mainly crotchets with the occasional quaver to create syncopation for a bar.
- Notes are strongly accented.
- Repeats the same syllable over and over.
- Second section ('can't get you out of my head') has crotchets and pairs of quavers.
- Actual words (not 'la's).
- Notes are strongly accented
- Third section ('there's a dark') has long, held on notes and more legato.
- Notes are in a higher register and sound even more breathy than the other sections
- They're also quieter/fainter.
- Some notes are melismatic.
- Actual words (not 'la's).
(1 mark for each, up to a maximum of 6 marks)

Track 39

a) Homophonic *(1 mark)*

b) Any two of:
- layering
- guitar distortion
- reverb
- flanger effect
- studio effects
(1 mark for each, up to a maximum of 2 marks)

c) Portamento *(1 mark)*

d) Any four of:
- Light instrumental accompaniment.
- Short piano chords, mini guitar fills between lines, drum roll and bell.
- 4-part harmony in the second half of the verse and in the chorus.
- Backing vocals mainly sing 'oooh' and 'aaah' but sometimes echo the soloist.
- Steady, on-beat rhythms / swung rhythms.
- Layering of vocals (as more than one part of the harmony is performed by the same singer).
- Flanger effect on some words (e.g. laser beam).
(1 mark for each, up to a maximum of 4 marks)

e) (Electric) guitar *(1 mark)*

Pages 150-161 — Practice Exam

1 *Track 40*

a) Greece *(1 mark)*

b) i) Bouzouki (accept outi or laouto, but not lyra) *(1 mark)*

ii) Toubeleki (accept alternative spelling) *(1 mark)*

c) The solo vocalist's melody is mainly conjunct — T *(1 mark)*
One singer is male, the other is female — F *(1 mark)*
The two voices sing in parallel harmony — T *(1 mark)*
The two voices sing in imitation — F *(1 mark)*

d) Any three of:
- The timbre alternates between instrumental sections and vocal sections.
- In the instrumental sections there's just bouzoukis and drums, with the main focus on the bouzouki, so the timbre is quite twangy.
- The male solo vocalist sings over plucked string chords, so the timbre is smoother but still linked to the earlier timbre.
- Two male vocalists sing in harmony, which produces an even smoother timbre.
(1 mark for each, up to a maximum of 3 marks)

2 *Track 41*

a) 1970s *(1 mark)*

b) i) (Electric) guitar *(1 mark)*
ii) Riff *(1 mark)*

c) Any of: *moderato, allegro moderato,* moderate/moderate rock, 110-130 bpm *(1 mark)*

d) Any of:
- key change/modulation
- drums stop/guitar stops
- keyboard enters
- higher vocal line
- accompaniment becomes more staccato/less legato
(1 mark)

e) Any three of:
Features of rock:
- Typical rock band line-up (electric & bass guitars, drums, singer, keyboard).
- Guitar is the main instrumental focus.
- Steady drum rhythm.
Features of an anthem:
- Sounds powerful.
- Chorus is memorable and easy to join in with.
- Song is quite loud.
(1 mark for each, up to a maximum of 3 marks)

3 *Track 42*

a) Triplets *(1 mark)*

b) There is a brass fanfare at the start of the extract — T *(1 mark)*
The strings play in unison when they first come in — F *(1 mark)*
The woodwind section does not appear in this extract at all — F *(1 mark)*
Percussion is only heard during the opening section of the extract — T *(1 mark)*

c) The texture is homophonic throughout, but the first part is melody with accompaniment *(1 mark)* whereas the second part is chordal *(1 mark)*.

d) Legato *(1 mark)*

e) Any two of:
- It opens with a fanfare, which sounds heroic.
- It's in a major key, which represents good characters.
- The main theme is smooth but also has leaps, representing the highs and lows of the quest.
(1 mark for each, up to a maximum of 2 marks)

4 *Track 43*

a)

(Award 1 mark for each correct note, up to a maximum of 6 marks. If the starting note is wrong the but the shape of the rest of the melody is correct, award a maximum of 3 marks.)

b) Bassoon *(1 mark)*

c) i) Baroque *(1 mark)*
ii) Vivaldi (accept Bach, Handel or other Baroque composer) *(1 mark)*

d) B minor *(1 mark)*

e) Appoggiatura *(1 mark)*

f) Second movement *(1 mark)* because it's slow *(1 mark)*.

170

5 *Tracks 44 & 45*

  a) i) Timpani (or kettledrum) *(1 mark)*

     ii) Snare drum *(1 mark)*

  b) Extract A is homophonic, Extract B is both homophonic and polyphonic *(1 mark)*.

  c) Extract A: *andante/largo/larghetto/adagio* *(1 mark)*
     Extract B: *moderato/allegro* *(1 mark)*

  d) Major *(1 mark)*

  e) Any six of:
    Instrumentation:
    - Both extracts feature the brass section playing fanfares, which sound heroic.
    - In extract A, the trumpets start the fanfare, then lower brass add harmony and drama.
    - Timpani play in between the phrases.
    - The strings only come in at the end of the extract.
    - Extract B starts with lower brass.
    - The trumpets come in part way through the extract and play a polyphonic fanfare.
    - After the fanfare, the strings play the main tune with a driving snare drum beat, which is reminiscent of a war.
    Rhythm:
    - Both extracts use triplet rhythms to give the music a heroic, adventurous feel.
    - However, extract A has longer notes (and is slightly slower), which makes it feel grander and more epic.
    - Extract B has shorter rhythms (including semiquavers and quavers) and a quicker tempo which makes it dance along and suggest urgency.
    Dynamics:
    - Both extracts use crescendos to add drama.
    - In extract A, the dynamics build from very quiet to very loud (*pp* to *ff*) within a couple of bars.
    - It also uses *fp* to make it even more dramatic and sound more epic.
    - The end of the extract is loud.
    - Extract B starts with a fairly soft (*mp*) melody punctuated by forte chords.
    - The fanfare is loud, then the following melody is a bit softer.
    - Towards the end of the extract, the dynamics drop right down, before building up with a dramatic crescendo.
    (1 mark for each, up to a maximum of 6 marks. Award a maximum of 3 marks if only one piece is discussed.)

6 *Track 46*

  Any nine of:
  - The extract features a solo violin, accompanied by an orchestra of strings, woodwind, brass and timpani. It was common for Romantic concertos to feature a large orchestra.
  - The extract opens with a virtuosic section on the solo violin, featuring fast, scalic phrases covering a very large range of notes. Such complex, virtuosic playing from the soloist is typical of concertos in the Romantic period.
  - During this opening section, the accompaniment from the orchestra is very simple, consisting only of a few pizzicato notes in the string section.
  - This section is followed by an ascending phrase with an accented, dotted rhythm from the soloist. The soloist uses double-stopping here, again showing off their skill.
  - The orchestra have a bigger role at this point — they follow the soloist's phrase with an inversion of the melody, with the same rhythm. The strings are still dominant, and the accompaniment continues with steady chords which sometimes create dissonance (a feature of Romantic music) with the soloist.
  - Tremolo is used in the string accompaniment, making the music more dramatic.
  - After the initial virtuosic solo section, the full orchestra enter loudly, with a rich texture. They repeat the theme that was stated earlier by the violin. This is common in concertos — themes pass between the soloist and the orchestra.
  - During this section the soloist interjects with short phrases, fighting with the orchestra for attention.
  - The orchestral section includes call and response style passages, with short melodic phrases passing between the strings and woodwind, and then between the lower strings and brass.
  - Towards the end of the extract, timpani add a dramatic, driving rhythm.
  - The piece moves between major and minor keys. This adds drama and was common in Romantic concertos. The initial solo section is in a major key, and most of the extract is major, but with the chromatic notes that were common in the Romantic era. Towards the end of the piece the orchestra move to a minor key, but then right at the end of the extract the soloist comes back in with a contrasting major key.

- In both the solo and orchestra parts there are crescendos and diminuendos, along with sudden *sforzando* notes. Such variation in dynamics was common in the Romantic era.
- There's lots of variation in the articulation in both the soloist's and the orchestra's parts — there are both legato and staccato phrases, and sections with heavy accents. Such contrast is a feature of the Romantic period.
(1 mark for each, up to a total of 9 marks. Deduct up to 2 marks for poor writing style.)

7 *Track 47*

a) i) Rock 'n' roll *(1 mark)*

ii) Any three of:
- repeated lyrics
- call and response between band and singer
- catchy lyrics
- fairly bright tempo (easy to dance to)
- steady beat
- typical rock 'n' roll instrumentation (drums, electric guitar, bass guitar, piano, singer, saxophone)
- walking bass line
(1 mark for each, up to a maximum of 3 marks)

b) The rhythms are swung *(1 mark)*.
The rhythms are syncopated *(1 mark)*.

c) Saxophone *(1 mark)*

d) 4/4 or 2/2 *(1 mark)*

8 *Track 48*

a) Any four of:
- Single drum (djembe) at the start, quickly joined by another drum
- Sticks/wood block
- Bell
- Shaker
- Bass drum
(1 mark for each in the above order, up to a maximum of 4 marks. If all the instruments are correct but in the wrong order, award no more than 2 marks.)

b)

(1 mark)

c) Cross-rhythm *(1 mark)*

d) Singing in unison *(1 mark)*
Repeated phrases *(1 mark)*

e) Any two of:
- Initially the percussion provides a rhythm underneath the singing.
- The singing has different rhythms, e.g. the long held note on 'lo'.
- Later in the vocal section the singers have the same rhythm as the percussion, when they repeat 'gin go bam bam go ba'.
- At these points there are also more intricate rhythms in the percussion section.
(1 mark for each, up to a maximum of 2 marks)

Index and Glossary

Index and Glossary

Index and Glossary

Index and Glossary

Greek music 108
Grieg 99
ground bass A way of playing **variations** with a strong repeating bass part as the main **theme**. **57, 83, 84**

H

hammer-on A guitar technique that allows you to play notes quickly and in a *legato* style. **66**
Handel 81, 87
hard rock A type of **rock music**, usually very loud and aggressive. **140, 141**
harmonic A technique on stringed instruments (including guitars) that produces a high, ringing note. **65**
harmonic interval The difference between two notes played at the same time. **28**
harmonic minor scale 8-note scale using notes from the **minor key** except for the seventh note, which is sharpened by one **semitone**. **25**
harmonic progression A series of chords. Another name for a **chord progression**. **36**
harpsichord A keyboard instrument shaped like a small grand piano. It was popular in the **Baroque** period. **57, 67, 81, 87, 91**
Haydn 90-93, 95
heavy metal A type of **rock music** that uses a lot of **distortion**. **140, 141**
hemiola When the music feels like it's in triple time when it's actually written in duple time, or vice versa. **14**
heterophonic In heterophonic music all the parts have different versions of the tune. **45, 109**
home key The key that a piece of music starts and ends in. **44**
homophonic Where the tune is accompanied by chords, keeping to roughly the same rhythm. **45, 47, 90, 92**
hook A catchy tune used in **pop music**. **135, 138**
Horah An Israeli **folk** dance. **110**
hurdy-gurdy A **string instrument** with a keyboard used in **folk music**. **137**

I

imitation A phrase is repeated with little variation. Could be one instrument or voice, or two or more imitating each other. **46, 82, 84**
imperfect cadence A **cadence** that usually moves from chord I, II or IV to chord V. **42, 43**
improvisation Music that's made up on the spot by a performer, often based on a given **chord progression** or set of notes. It's used a lot in **jazz**. **59, 105, 137, 138**
Indian classical music 55, 104-106
interrupted cadence A **cadence** that moves from chord V to any chord except chord I. **42, 43**
interval The gap in pitch between two notes, played one after another or at the same time in a chord. **28, 29**
inversion (chord) Using a chord in a position other than its root position. **37, 38**
iqa' An Arabic rhythmic **mode**. **109**
Israeli music 110

J

jazz Music with lots of **syncopation**, **improvisation** and quirky harmonisation. Influenced many different musical styles, such as hip-hop and salsa. **59, 137, 138**
jazz band A band that plays **jazz** music. **70, 137**

K

kagan A type of African drum. **111**
kanun A Palestinian string instrument. **109, 110**
key signature Sharps or flats just before the **time signature**, to tell you what key the music's in. **11, 24-26, 44**
kidi A type of African drum. **111**
Klezmer A type of Israeli **folk music**. **110**
kora A West African harp-like instrument. **113**

L

laouto Another name for a **lute**. **108**
larghetto 60-66 beats a minute. Broad and slow, but less so than *largo*. **18**
largo 40-60 beats a minute. Broad and slow. **18**
Latin percussion 114
layering Using technology to record several parts separately and layer them one on top of another. **46, 134**
lead guitar 135
ledger lines Extra lines added above or below the stave, to write high or low notes. **16**
legato Play smoothly. **19**
leitmotif A phrase or piece of music that represents a person, place, time or emotion in film music or musicals. **122, 127, 129**
listening exam 2, 7
Liszt 97-99
Logic Pro 128
loop Section of music repeated over and over. **46, 76, 128**
lute A **string instrument**. **108**
lyra A Greek **string instrument**. **108**

M

major key A **key** using notes from a **major scale**. **92**
major scale Series of eight notes (the first and last notes are the same). The **intervals** between them are: **tone**, tone, **semitone**, tone, tone, tone, semitone. **24**
major triad A **triad** with an **interval** of four **semitones** between the bottom and middle notes, and three semitones between the middle and top notes. **35**
male voice choir A **choir** made up of two groups of **tenors** as well as **baritones** and **basses**. **69**
maqam An Arabic **mode**. The plural is 'maqamat'. **109**
maracas Latin American **percussion** instruments. **114**
marcato Play all the notes with **accents**. **20**
mbira Another name for a **thumb piano**. **113**
melismatic A single syllable of text is sung over a succession of notes. The opposite of **syllabic**. **109, 134, 144**

Index and Glossary

tempo The pace or speed of the music. **18**

tenor Voice that sings roughly in the range from the C below middle C to the G above. **69**

tenor clef One octave lower than a **treble clef**. **10**

tenuto Play the note for its full length, or slightly longer. **19**

ternary form Piece in three sections. The first and last are much the same. The second's a bit different and in a different (but related) key. **56, 82, 90**

tessitura The **range** of a singer's voice. **69**

texture The way different parts are woven together. **45-47, 92**

theme Musical idea. The bit you hum. In **theme and variation** and **rondo** forms this is the bit that gets repeated. **56, 83, 94**

theme and variation form First you hear a simple tune. After a short pause you hear a **variation** on the tune. Then there's another pause and another variation, another pause, another variation, etc. **83, 90**

third inversion An **inversion** of a chord with the seventh below a standard **triad**. **37**

through-composed form Type of **structure** where the music is different in every verse. **56, 140, 142**

thumb piano A small African instrument. **113**

tie A curved line that joins two notes of the same pitch, so when they're played they sound like one note. **17**

Tierce de Picardie When a piece in a minor key finishes with a major chord (e.g. a piece in A minor finishes with an A major chord). **43**

timbre The type of sound an instrument makes. Also known as tone colour. **75, 76, 144**

time signature Numbers at the beginning of a piece that tell you how many beats there are in a bar. **12, 13**

timpani A large **percussion instrument** often used in **orchestras**. Also called kettledrums. **91**

tonal Music that's written in a specific key. **81**

tone The gap in pitch between e.g. A and B, E flat and F or G and A. One tone = two semitones. **9, 24, 25, 27 , 75**

tonic key The key a piece starts in. **44**

toubeleki A Greek drum. **108, 109**

treble Boy who sings at **soprano** pitch. **69**

treble clef A clef used for higher-pitched music — it's the upper clef in piano music. **10, 16**

tremolo Play in a trembly, nervous sounding way. **65**

triad 3-note chord which uses a root, a third above and a fifth above. **34-37**

triadic A melody that moves using notes of the triad. **54**

trill Twiddly **ornament**. **85**

trio Second part of a piece in **minuet and trio** form or a piece for three players or three singers. **71**

trionfale Play in a triumphant, confident-sounding way. **18**

triplet Three notes played in the space of two. **17**

tritone Uncomfortable-sounding interval of three tones. **29, 123**

turn Another twiddly **ornament**. **85**

U

unison Everyone plays or sings the same notes at the same time. **45, 134**

upbeat Another name for an **anacrusis**. **12**

ululation A high-pitched **trill**. **109**

V

variation Either a recognisable version of the main **theme** of a piece, or a self-contained piece of music in its own right based on a single theme. **57, 83**

verse-chorus structure Structure used in **pop** songs. Verses have the same melody but the lyrics change each time. Choruses have a different tune to the verse but the words don't change. **58, 138, 140, 142**

vibhag A group of beats in Indian classical music that's a bit like a **bar**. **105**

vibrato When singers make their voices wobble, giving a richer sound. String instruments can produce a similar effect too. **75, 134**

video games 128, 129

virginal A table-top version of a **harpsichord**. **67**

vivace 168-180 beats a minute. Very lively. **18**

Vivaldi 81, 86

vocal hiccups 144

vocoder A type of **synthesizer** used on the voice. **134**

voice 69, 75

W

Wagner 97

wah wah A guitar effect that makes the guitar sound like it's saying 'wah'. **135**

walking bass A bass part that moves in **crotchets**, usually either in step or **arpeggios**. **39, 137**

whistle An instrument often used in samba, usually to lead the band. **116**

whole tone scale 6-note scale with a **tone** between each note and the next. **27**

wind band A fairly large band made up of **woodwind**, **brass** and **percussion**. **70**

wind quintet A group made up of a flute, a clarinet, an oboe, a horn and a bassoon. **71**

woodwind instruments Instruments that make a sound when you blow them (not including **brass instruments**). **64, 72, 75, 81, 91, 97**

Z

zither An Arabic **string instrument**. **109**

Acknowledgements

The publisher would like to thank the following copyright holders for permission to reproduce material:

Track 1	*Caro Nome*, from *Rigoletto*, by Verdi. Performed by the Slovak Philharmonic Orchestra. Licensed courtesy of Naxos Rights US Inc.
Track 2	*Oboe Concerto No. 3 in G minor*, by Handel. Performed by the City of London Sinfonia. Licensed courtesy of Naxos Rights US Inc.
Tracks 3-13	Composed and performed by Sam Norman. © 2010 Coordination Group Publications Ltd.
Track 14	*Prelude in C♯ Minor*, Op. 3, No. 2, by Rachmaninov. Performed by Idil Biret. Licensed courtesy of Naxos Rights US Inc.
Tracks 15-26	Composed and performed by Sam Norman. © 2010 Coordination Group Publications Ltd.
Track 27	*Sonatina 3*, Op. 36, *un poco adagio*, by Clementi. Performed by Sam Norman. © 2010 Coordination Group Publications Ltd.
Track 28	*St Louis Blues #2*, by WC Handy. Performed by Louis Armstrong. Licensed courtesy of Naxos Rights US Inc.
Track 29	*Courante*, from *Suite No. 1 in C major*, BWV 1066, by J.S. Bach. Performed by the Cologne Chamber Orchestra. Licensed courtesy of Naxos Rights US Inc.
Track 30	*Le Merle Noir*, by Messiaen. Performed by Patrick Gallois & Lydia Wong. Licensed courtesy of Naxos Rights US Inc.
Track 31	*Flight of the Bumble Bee*, by Rimsky-Korsakov. Performed by the CSR Symphony Orchestra. Licensed courtesy of Naxos Rights US Inc.
Track 32	*Brandenburg Concerto No. 4*, BWV 1049, 3rd movement: *Presto*, by J.S. Bach. Performed by the Swiss Baroque Soloists. Licensed courtesy of Naxos Rights US Inc.
Track 33	*Flute Concerto No. 2 in D Major*, K. 314, 1st movement: *Allegro aperto*, by Mozart. Performed by Herbert Weissberg and the Capella Istropolitana. Licensed courtesy of Naxos Rights US Inc.
Track 34	*Lok Boliyan*, by Surjit Singh and Pete Ware. Performed by Anakhi. Licensed courtesy of Naxos Rights US Inc.
Track 35	*Carnivale*, performed by the United States Navy Steel Band. Licensed courtesy of Naxos Rights US Inc.
Track 36	*Main Title Theme*, from *Star Wars: Episode IV — A New Hope*, by John Williams. Performed by the Richard Hayman Orchestra. Licensed courtesy of Naxos Rights US Inc.
Track 37	*Dies irae, dies illa*, from *Messa da Requiem*, by Verdi. Performed by the Hungarian State Opera Chorus and the Hungarian State Opera Orchestra. Licensed courtesy of Naxos Rights US Inc.
Track 38	Kylie Minogue *Can't Get You Out Of My Head* (Davis / Dennis) Published by EMI Music Publishing Ltd. / Universal/MCA Music Ltd. (P) 2001 Parlophone Records Ltd. A Warner Music Group Company. GBAYE0100913 Licensed Courtesy of Warner Music UK Ltd.

Acknowledgements

Track 39   *Killer Queen*
                  Written by Freddie Mercury
                  Published by: B. Feldman & Co. Ltd.
                  Bass Guitar: John Deacon
                  Guitars & Backing Vocals: Brian May
                  Lead Vocals, Piano, Jangle Piano & Backing Vocals: Freddie Mercury
                  Drums, Percussion & Backing Vocals: Roger Taylor
                  Produced by Roy Thomas Baker and Queen
                  Engineered by Mike Stone
                  Recorded at Trident, Wessex, Rockfield and Air Studios
                  (P) 1974 Queen Productions Ltd., under exclusive licence to Universal International Music BV
                  ISRC: GB-CEE-93-00004
                  Licensed courtesy of Universal Music Group Limited.

Track 40   *Istoria enos Bouzoukiou* (History of a Bouzouki).
                  Performed by The Athenians.
                  Licensed courtesy of Naxos Rights US Inc.

Track 41   *Since You Been Gone*
                  Written by Russ Ballard
                  Published by: Sony/ATV Tunes LLC
                  Produced by Roger Glover
                  Engineered by Gary Edwards
                  Recorded by Dr. Michael Palmer & Leigh Mantle of Maison Rouge
                  Vocals: Joe Lynn Turner
                  Guitar: Ritchie Blackmore
                  Bass Guitar: Roger Glover
                  Keyboards: David Rosenthal
                  Drums: Chuck Burgh
                  Recorded at Chateau Pelly De Cornfeld, somewhere in France, 1979 with the Maison Rouge Mobile Studio
                  (P) 1979 Universal Records, a Division of UMG Recordings, Inc.
                  ISRC: US-PR3-79-30021
                  Licensed courtesy of Universal Music Group Limited.

Track 42   *Main Theme*, from *Final Fantasy*, by Nobuo Uematsu.
                  Performed by the London Philharmonic Orchestra.
                  Licensed courtesy of X5 Music Group.

Track 43   *Bassoon Concerto in E Minor*, RV 484, 2nd movement: *Andante*, by Vivaldi.
                  Performed by Frantisek Herman and the Capella Istropolitana.
                  Licensed courtesy of Naxos Rights US Inc.

Track 44   *Also sprach Zarathustra*, Op. 30, TrV 176: *Introduction*, by Richard Strauss.
                  Performed by the Richard Hayman Orchestra.
                  Licensed courtesy of Naxos Rights US Inc.

Track 45   *Battlestar Galactica: Main Themes*, by Glen A. Larson and Stu Phillips.
                  Performed by the Richard Hayman Orchestra.
                  Licensed courtesy of Naxos Rights US Inc.

Track 46   *Violin Concerto in D Major*, Op. 77, 3rd movement: *Allegro giocoso,
                  ma non troppo vivace*, by Brahms.
                  Performed by Ilya Kaler and the Bournemouth Symphony Orchestra.
                  Licensed courtesy of Naxos Rights US Inc.

Track 47   *Tutti Frutti*, written by Dorothy LaBostrie, Joe Lubin and Richard Penniman.
                  Performed by Little Richard.
                  Licensed courtesy of Naxos Rights US Inc.

Track 48   *Gin-Go-Lo-Ba*, from *Drums of Passion*, by Olatunji.
                  Licensed courtesy of Sony/ATV Music Publishing.

Every effort has been made to locate copyright holders and obtain permission to reproduce copyright material.

For material where it has been difficult to trace the originator of the work, we would be grateful for information.

If any copyright holder would like us to make an amendment to the acknowledgements, please notify us and we will gladly update the book at the next reprint.

MURS41